PENGUIN BOOKS
THE WORLD OF ZINES

Mike Gunderloy has been reading since before he can remember, and writing since shortly after that. His career includes stints as a Kelly Girl, shipping clerk in a liquor warehouse, archival gofer, and computer repairman. His cars tend to run for roughly one month per hundred dollars of original purchase price, and he has bred a strain of cats who are excessively curious about showers. *The World of Zines* is his first mass-market book, although he has published several million words in the zine world itself.

Cari Goldberg Janice lives in a house in Albany, New York with her husband and many hundreds of books. In addition to co-publishing *Factsheet Five*, her *other* past jobs include waitress, chef, secretary, bookstore clerk, Meals-on-Wheels deliverer, perzine publisher, and typesetter. Her range of talents includes being able to detect celebrity voices and appearances in the movies, radio or television and to cross-reference them better than anyone else. Anyone wishing to exploit this talent or offer her another book deal can reach her in Albany.

The World of Zines

A Guide to the Independent Magazine Revolution

by Mike Gunderloy and Cari Goldberg Janice

Penguin Books

PENGUIN BOOKS
Published by the Penguin Group
Viking Penguin, a division of Penguin Books USA Inc.,
375 Hudson Street, New York, New York 10014, U.S.A.
Penguin Books Ltd, 27 Wrights Lane,
London W8 5TZ, England
Penguin Books Australia Ltd, Ringwood,
Victoria, Australia
Penguin Books Canada Ltd, 10 Alcorn Avenue, Suite 300
Toronto, Ontario, Canada M4V 3B2
Penguin Books (N.Z.) Ltd., 182-190 Wairau Road,
Auckland 10, New Zealand

Penguin Books Ltd, Registered Offices:
Harmondsworth, Middlesex, England

First Published in Penguin Books 1992

ISBN 0 14 01.6720 X

Printed in the United States of America
Set in ITC Avant Garde and Zapf Calligraphic

To Karl, with all my love

To Carolyn, for putting up with me

Contents

Introduction

Zines

Resources

Part 1:
Introduction

A revolution in technology has inspired an amazing surge of free expression and cultural ferment creating the world of zines: thousands of small publications which are produced primarily for love rather than money. Individuals pursuing their passions by publishing and reading zines have created geographically sprawling communities of people networked together by common interests. There are at least ten thousand zines being published in the United States today, and hundreds more will begin publishing while this book is being prepared, as hundreds of others publish their last issue and quietly vanish. Even though most zines reach only a few hundred readers, their total audience is in the millions. What this book will do is help you find the zines you are interested in, and show you how to join the ranks of zine publishers yourself. Self-expression is addictive, and once you've discovered the pleasures of publishing your own words, you'll never go back.

Zine pleasures come in many different flavors. Consider a few of the various publications you'll find in the zine world:

• A newsletter produced by an author between assignments, ruminating on interesting things in his life and inviting publishers to get interested too.

• A zine for people who collect Pez candy dispensers, tying together an otherwise scattered community who once met only through mail auctions.

• A safe place for readers to write about sex of any variety, without worrying whether the boss or the neighbors will learn of the Awful Truth.

• Suggestions and instructions for those brave or foolhardy enough to tamper with the phone system — or, in another zine, with the devil himself.

Why do people spend their time and money producing a zine which, at best, probably fewer than a thousand people will ever see? Lloyd Dunn, a long-time denizen of the experimental small press, once said, "One publishes because one must; which is to say that *I* publish because I don't know what *else* to do to make my voice heard outside of the narrow confines of my home turf." This is a common theme for many zine people: we're somehow driven to publish, and fortunate enough to have something to say.

But there are other reasons for doing zines, perhaps as many as there are zines. Some people do it just to have fun, or to explore an area of the world which the mainstream media doesn't adequately cover. Some are in it to cause trouble, or bring about social change. Some find it more congenial than a soapbox in the park for spreading views, while others just use a zine to keep in touch with family and friends. A few brave souls even try to make a living at zine publishing, though they usually fail.

There are many reasons for publishing various kinds of zines, but there is an overall purpose: people are building networks independent of big business, big government, and big media. The zine world is in fact a network of networks. Some groups, such as music fans or SubGenii, have their own relatively closed network of zines, acting as a sort of social glue between farflung people and groups. Yet gradually these small networks are joining up into what some have called The Network, an overarching collection of mini publications which fill mailboxes around the world, generally unnoticed by most people.

The terminology of the small press world is a confusing tangle. In this book we've chosen to use the generic term "zine" for the publications we write about, but there are lots of other choices. Investigating these will help us define somewhat the boundaries of our subject.

Underground Press was a term of the Sixties, a way to refer to the newspapers of the time which aggressively challenged authority. Though some of the big underground papers grew, changed and survived, many more vanished in waves of police repression and activist burnout. Today's small press is for the most part anything but underground: many publishers go so far as to print their phone numbers inviting readers to call in.

The *Alternative Press* is another question-begging term: alternative to what? For the most part it conjures up images of slick magazines with slightly different slants than the most established major media. *Mother Jones* and *The Nation* are alternative press, but they're too big and respectable themselves to fall within the scope of this book.

Small Press would be an ideal name for our subject, but it's such a perfect term that it's already been appropriated for different purposes at least three times. The literary crowd grabbed it first: if you say "the small press" around most college english departments they will assume that you are talking about the thousands of small literary and poetry magazines. Both the comics fans and the wrestling fans seized the term "the small press" to describe their own networks of publications. And independent book publishers are also "the small press" movement, with *their* own magazine to prove it.

Fanzines hits closer to the mark. It's a contraction of "fan magazines," first applied by science fiction enthusiasts to the publications they were producing (in contrast to the "prozines," which actually paid for work). From there, "fanzines" expanded to apply to several other fields, notably music. Some of the first music fanzines were produced by expatriate SF fans. Independently produced magazines of cartoons and comic art have also been called fanzines for some time. Although the term has been applied widely (mostly through the efforts of *Factsheet Five*) there are those who rail against its "dilution" and insist that it should properly refer only to the SF variant.

And so we come to *Zine*, an all-purpose contraction. It's hard to say what defines a zine, though we think all of the publications described and excerpted in this book fit. Generally they're created by one person, for love rather than money, and focus on a particular subject.

No one knows how many zines there are. We at *Factsheet Five* have seen about five thousand different titles over the past decade, but we're sure we haven't seen them all. One clue lies in the review columns in various zines, which list other zines in their field. For example, there are about 40 different zines for fans of professional wrestling. Yet we only know this because they're all mentioned in the half-dozen or so wrestling zines we actually get on a regular basis. Apply this same ratio to our list of 2,000 or so zines, and it seems likely that there must be tens of thousands of them out there. It's even more difficult to assign a definitive number since the boundaries of the zine field are fluid; by the broadest definition, every church bulletin and college litmag in the country would be a zine.

And how many active zine readers might there be? Some zines have five readers, some have five thousand. If there were an average of fifty per zine, our estimate of 20,000 zines would indicate a million readers, scattered across the country. Maybe the guy in the next cubicle at work reads a zine. Maybe your IRS auditor publishes one in her/his spare time.

The zine field is in the middle of a boom that's been going on at least since the Seventies, and there is no end in sight. Cheap photocopying, cheap computers and cheap postage (at least compared to other industrialized countries), have made it easier than ever to publish a zine. And the Reagan years, with their legacy of a tattered safety net, have encouraged people to depend more on their own talents and abilities for everything from survival to entertainment. In some subcultures, like punk rock or wrestling, everyone knows about zines. They're epidemic there, by now an accepted way to participate in the scene. Other areas may have only one or two pioneer zine publishers — or still are ripe for the picking.

Over the centuries, as we've gone from the hired scribe to the first printing press to the photocopy machine (and now on to the computer networks), the print media have become more democratized. While a few mass media continue to dominate the communication channels, there are plenty of holes between their coverage where the dedicated and passionate small publisher can make a difference. Most zines start out with the realization that one need no longer be merely a passive consumer of media. Everyone can be a producer! That's the underlying message of the zine world, and the greatest thing about zines. Come join us in this untamed new world.

Mike Gunderloy

Cari Goldberg Janice

Since 1982 *Factsheet Five* has reviewed many thousands of zines. The zines we included in this book were chosen because we like them. There are many zines being published today, and all of them have something to say that someone would be glad to hear. Zine publishers have a quality not found universally these days — the best word for it is "gumption." Anyone with the perseverance and vision to produce a zine can hardly avoid doing something that will be interesting to someone. In creating this guide to zines we could not be comprehensive, nor did we try to choose the "best" (a meaningless word in such a broad field) zines. Rather, we want to offer a survey and an overview — including some of the more popular and typical zines and also many of the odder and more unusual fish. If you like what you see here, you can find out about hundreds more by subscribing to *Factsheet Five*.

The best way to use this book is to think of it as a road map rather than a museum. Get involved and experience zinedom and discover its charms firsthand. The zine world is disorderly at best. While we've made the attempt to group like zines together in subject categories, there are many which resist being shoehorned into any orderly arrangement (how many zines about window washing did you expect, anyway?) so we've sprinkled "potpourri pages" throughout.

Contact and ordering information is given for every zine we list. When you spot one that interests you, drop them a line. Cash is always appreciated, though most zine publishers also take checks. (If we list a publisher's name, make the check out to the person rather than to the zine, which probably doesn't have a bank account).

By the time you get to the last page of listings, we hope you'll keep right going into the "how-to" section and join us on the other side of the writing gap. Who knows, maybe *your* zine will make it into the second edition of this book!

Mike Gunderloy founded Factsheet Five in 1982 as the only guide to all facets of the zine world. Cari Goldberg Janice later joined the staff and became co-editor. In 1991, after 44 issues, they passed the zine on to a new publisher in order to pursue other projects (including this book). Every issue of FF reviews over a thousand zines, along with books, records, tapes, t-shirts, computer software and other independent media. You should contact the current publisher for information on sample and subscription rates:

Hudson Luce

PO Box 8615

Prairie Village, KS 66208

Part 2:
Zines

Fringe Culture

Zines are an incredible melange, a hotbed of cultural ferment far removed from traditional mainstream high culture. It's not the "low culture" of bowling and weenie roasts either, but rather a mix that includes pop icons, esoterica, and wishful thinking about the possibilities of breaking out of mainstream molds. To recognize this stuff as interesting is to be admitted to the current councils of hipness; to be fascinated with it is to take chances that your neighbors will forbid their kids to play with yours.

DADATA
SASE from M. Dupinhead, PO Box 33, Stillwater, PA 17878

Dadata is actually more of a project than a zine, a series of collaged posters which appear at irregular intervals and go to a select but mysterious mailing list. The mysterious M. Dupinhead generally selects images from the mass media and adds his own wry comments in the form of blown-up typewriter script, seeking the few apt words to puncture the balloon of progress wherever it rears its antihumanist head. Fascinating and occasionally distressing.

SCRAP
$3 print/$5 audio from Chris Winkler, Plutonium Press, PO Box 61564, Phoenix, AZ 85082

Chris has spent years wallowing in the experimental media underground on several continents and publishing the best he can find — collages, snippets of audio tape, concrete poetry, computer art, and more. Every issue of **Scrap** starts out as an exercise in being perplexed, only gradually unfolding to the persevering reader as she spends time with the individual pieces. Even the format changes with unpredictable frequency; I fondly remember one issue with a sandpaper cover, making it dangerous to store next to other zines.

SENSORIA FROM CENSORIUM
$17 from Mangajin Books, Box 147, Stn. J, Toronto, Ontario, CANADA, M4J 4X8

This one started out zine-like, spawned a bunch of stickers and arm bands and posters, and ended up as a full-size trade paperback book with an inserted record — and the promise of more issues to come. In many ways, the first issue mined some of the same territory as this book, looking into the networks on the fringes: zines, mail art, visual poetry, cassette culture, retrofuturism, and more. The meat of **SfC** is a series of articles from well-known networkers on what they do and why, but it's almost obscured by the trimmings, dozens of pieces of art and prose from the denizens of this farflung cultural conglomeration.

The face of the network changes constantly, but it is always open, always ready for anyone who wishes to use it. As a friend once wrote, outsiders who view the informality of the network, with no organization or hierarchy and its open structure must think of the web as being democratic, but anarchic is more apt a description. We follow no predetermined rules or laws, there are no boundaries we cannot cross. Each member of the network utilizes the network to suit themselves while maintaining control of their activities. Anyone can play.

MALLIFE
$10/3 issues from Mike Miskowski, PO Box 17686, Phoenix, AZ 85011

Weird and wild stabs at creating a new type of culture from a number of the fringe's best (or at least most notorious) artists and writers. Editor Miskowski seems partial to things that shock, either with their subject matter or their lack of relation to normal prose styles (or both). **Mallife** occasionally emits cassette issues and other propaganda, and an SASE will net you a full catalog.

Stop fish back where the corn never grew, came an elder queer. Blintzing a hammer stew. After what seemed like years the boss came running down garbage chutes too lazy to complain about ringworm donut holes moist to the tooth. In a roundabout rendition of a shoping fool, the presidents wife is about to vomit on tv, where's the popcorn?

MODOM
Contact Jake Berry, PO Box 3112, Florence, AL 35630

Jake has succeeded in creating an art zine open to everyone in a completely decentralized fashion. **Modom** started out as a broadsheet for his own intricate doodles and offbeat words. Then he began accepting contributions from others on the margins of the literary world. Finally, Jake issued the poster shown above, announcing phase 2 of the **Modom** project and letting the whole world in on the fun. Since then we've seen **Modom**s from Canada, New York, Texas and elsewhere.

INTRODUCING MODOM:PHASE 2. All sentient beings are encouraged to participate. If you want to do an "issue" of MODOM all you have to do is write the word MODOM in capital letters on an object, publication, building, street, WHATEVER, and assign it a number above 50. This number could be a fraction, decimal point, or any other kind of number. Then send a letter to the address on this page documenting your MODOM, be sure to include a description of your MODOM, and the number you assign it, and your name(if you wish). If you like, keep a log of your MODOMs and send in documentation of many at one time. All documentation will in turn be placed in the megalog of all MODOMs, and at some point in the future, published in stages as the documentation arrives. If your MODOM is a publication or a collection of objects, please send one to the MODOM address and one to Factsheet Five. And Remember, anything can be a MODOM, a thought, other creatures ("real" or imaginary), ANYTHING. Simply record each one & send documentation

MODOM is an idea spawned by the happily dysfunctional intelligences at
9th Street Laboratories
METASEMANTIC LIBERATURE FOR PANDIMENSIONAL REALITIES

no deadline - MODOM never stops
MODOM pobox 3112 florence, al 35630

this ad is MODOM # 932.615¼

MURDER CAN BE FUN
$2 from John Marr, PO Box 640111, San Francisco, CA 94109

John has carved out a distinctive niche for himself in the zine world as a combination historian of the bizarrely dangerous and modern observer of cultural folly. **MCBF** has developed a cult following among people who are fascinated by Karen Carpenter's anorexia, historical cannibals, the attempt to assassinate Andy Warhol, the Tacoma Narrows bridge, Cornell Woolrich's fiction, faith healing, Fatty Arbuckle and the notorious coke bottle, and other subjects not often considered the stuff of uplifting literature. There's a huge reservoir of interest in these subjects and very few places to go to read about them. The audience is what fellow publisher Candi Strecker calls Hip Mutants.

THE EGG CUP

Momentarily distracted by his sister's cries, young Peter looked up from his work to the largest egg cup he had ever seen. Inside the cup, rested an egg the size of a Nerf football.

"Why, where did you ever get *that*?" he asked his sister Jill.

"From Mrs. Klaussman," Jill replied. "She found it in her basement. She said it must have been her husband's."

Filled with glee, the two children spent the rest of that sunny afternoon admiring their egg, their wonderful egg.

Conservatism has ruled the field of plastic surgery for too long. Bored housewives argue over the ideal buttock tuck and twitter over the reshaped chin. Think plastic surgery and right away someone says nose job or breast implant. Routine! Feeling in a rut? Want a new you? Be the hit of the season with Dada Surgery. Remember: **there's no tissue rejection when it's your own body.** One of the most exciting Dada procedures begins with the ear. You only need the hole to hear — the whole outer ear could be put anywhere. A properly placed ear on one of the forehead folds would flap any time you furrowed your brow. A show stopper.

Pointed up on the chin, an ear could be used to collect any spilled soup. And remember, you have two, so you could do a symmetrical thing — say, on the back of each hand. I think something really cute could be done around the navel — particularly if you moved some of the nose down with them.

For sheer strangeness, no disaster has ever topped Boston's Great Molasses Flood. Other disasters have run up higher body counts, caused more damage, inspired books & movies, & are remembered as Important Historical Events. The Molasses Flood was none of these: a mere 21 dead & $1 million damages, it's only been the subject of a handful of obscure magazine articles & newspaper clippings. Historically, it's peanuts, not even worthy of a footnote. But the idea & irony of 2 1/2 million gallons of molasses raging through city streets, knocking over buildings & killing people in the middle of January...unbeatable. The date was January 15, 1919. At the intersection of Foster & Commercial streets in Boston's North End, the Purity Distilling Co. had a large, riveted steel storage tank, 50' high & 90' in diameter. The tank stored shipments of raw molasses received from Cuba & the West Indies. The molasses would then be pumped from the tank into rail cars bound for a distillery in Cambridge which produced industrial-grade alcohol for the munitions industry. On that particular day, the tank was almost full, holding 2.3 million gallons weighing over

27 million pounds. Although cloudy, the weather was unseasonably warm for a Boston winter: 44°F with light winds. At 12:41, it happened. Most people heard nothing; others remember a low rumbling or sharp tearing sound. The two bottom rows of plates on the tank tore open, unleashing a 20' high wave of molasses moving some 35 mph onto the unsuspecting streets of the North End.

GOING GAGA
$4 from Gareth Branwyn, 2630 Robert Walker Pl., Arlington, VA 22207

Gareth is a tireless miner of the more outre creations of the mind: drug stories, art manifestoes, virtual reality, and more. Issues have been published in a variety of media including t-shirt and cassette as well as the more traditional print. Cyberpunk, dada, the Situationists — a dizzying array of modern thought shows up here, gets run through the blender and emerges as new toys for the mind. A happy reckless journey for the brave traveler of new spaces. "Art, Information, Noise" is the enigmatic tagline here.

THRIFT SHOP CONFIDENTIAL — PART II: STILL MORE FUTURE COLLECTIBLES

"HAVE YOU EVER NOTICED THAT 90% OF ALL THRIFT SHOPS HAVE AT LEAST ONE BREAST PUMP?"
—REID OF DICKTOOL, IN CORRESPONDENCE

SOCK MONKEY DOLLS

HAVING ONE SITTING ON YOUR COUCH IS JUST REGRESSIVE NOSTALGIA. BUT 15 OR 20 IS A SERIOUS DESIGN STATEMENT.

WE'RE GOING TO GET YOU UP AND ON RC 89

WHAT DO YOU MEAN: NOONE CARES?

LOOSEN UP

MARCOS LIES IN STATE.

HIS ADMIRERS FLOCK TO SEE HIM AND BEAT THEIR BREASTS

gunning down a couple of crazed thuggee cattle mutilators out in the street.

The rewards of being an altar boy also included monetary gain. I once did three weddings on one Saturday afternoon and was tipped a total of $25. Not a bad day's haul for a ten year old. Then there was the outright stealing of cash. Little old ladies would come up to the altar rail after mass and request that a candle be lit in memory of a loved one. They would fork over a buck, and we were supposed to put the money in this locked, tube-like thing with a slit on top to slide the bill through. Much of the time, the bill went right into our pockets. If you were short of cash, and no one bought a candle to help save someone's soul from purgatory, you could straighten out a coat hanger, slip it through the slot and spear a couple of bills with it. I remember one guy, Paul S., who one Easter served about six masses. I asked him why he did so many. "Big day for buying candles," was his reply.

HEADPUMP
$1 from Rich, PO Box 93, Bronx, NY 10461

A continuing collection of weird collage and cut-up writing, plus other bits of experimentalism. The rare editorial comments are usually given over to promoting free speech on the margins, and identifying cases where it's been suppressed. A curious little zine.

INFOCULT
$2 from Johnny Walsh, PO Box 3124, East Hampton, NY 11937

"The Journal of Strange Information" certainly is. It's full of weird religions, Lee Harvey Oswald, smoking dope, psychedelic enlightenment, hypnotism, mind control, strange prophecies, and puzzling evidence about the way the world works. Reading an issue of this tabloid is like stepping out to pick up the morning paper and discovering the Men In Black

VIRUS 23
$7 from PO Box 46, Red Deer, Alberta, CANADA, T4N 5E7

Wild ideas abound on the margins, and sometimes they coalesce into one heap of weird stuff. One such is **Virus 23**, full of Hilbert Space and Thee Temple Ov Psychick Youth and the New Age and strange drugs and shamanism and more. They cover cyberpunk and Crowley with equal elan, investigate brain machines and reprint the weirder bits of mainstream news they run across. They also discuss the joys of fake news, throwing their own memes into the growing pool of disinformation that surrounds us.

We shot a scene from Nightbreed in a real mortuary which appears in the movie. The crew were very reverential when they came in. They thought I was a sick fuck for wanting to shoot there. I said, "No No, we want to get the flavour of the place.' The pathologist's assistant was this lady who looked like a Charles Addams cartoon. She was standing there with this gray face and gray eyes. So eventually I said, 'I have to ask

lite is just lite for elite

Breakfast Theory: A MORNING METHODOLOGY

More than just a cereal, it's a commentary on the nature of cereal-ness, cerealism, and the theory of cerealativity. Free decoding ring inside.

Post Modern Toasties "Like everything you've had before, all mixed up."

DECONSTRUCTION BREAKFAST FOOD PRODUCT: contents: Pretty dry and flavorless isn't it?

Your question is informed, or should I say misinformed, by the conventionalized bourgeois cereal paradigms that center on such outmoded excretory notions as taste, nutrients and edibility.

Sugar Fat Verbiage

Foucault Flakes: But it's empty But of course

Finally, a breakfast commodity so complex that you need a theoretical apparatus to digest it. You won't want to eat it, you'll just want to read it. A literary tour de force: Breakfast as text!

"It's French, it must be good."

dadata

because you don't look very happy: why do you work in a mortuary?' She said, 'Do you really want to know?' I said "Yes I really want to know,' and she says, 'I'm morbid.' Anyway, we were shooting in this place with coffins and everything. Halfway through the day, a human leg is brought in. You've never seen so many grown technicians run for their lives shouting, 'It's a leg! Oh my God, it's a leg!' One of the actors, playing the pathologist's assistant passed out. It was just a great experience. (from an interview with Clive Barker)

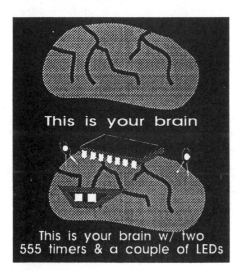

This is your brain

This is your brain w/ two 555 timers & a couple of LEDs

XYY
$2 from John F. Kelly, 82 Kimball Ave., Yonkers, NY 10704

"The New Look in Madness" is a mix between hard-boiled fiction, deranged comics, and rants and raves from social critics who usually lurk far outside of the public prints. John has cultivated a stable of friends and acquaintances who take violence in stride and use it to satirize the world at large — at least, I hope it's satire. Add his own sardonic wit and talent for appropriated art forms and you get a wild mix indeed.

I think what this country really needs is some left-wing radicals packing some heavy firepower and wiping out all the power-broker assholes in power. Earth First!, other ecoterrorists, and the really crazed animal rights groups are a good start, but they're not focussing on social

issues that many would argue are of more immediate import. Like if all the drug dealers in Compton drove down to L.A.'s City Hall in a huge convoy of BMWs, Jeeps, and boom trucks, with their AK-47s and shotguns and Uzis, demanding a complete overhaul of the city's social programs or else, motherfuckers...

OFFICE NUMBER ONE
$2 from Carlos B. Dingus, 1709 San Antonio St. #1, Austin, TX 78701

This one is so weird it may not even belong here, but then again it's hard to say whether it belongs anywhere. It's a zine of news and commentary from alternate dimensions, or parallel earths, or paratime or some damned thing. Whatever it is, **ONO** is consistently puzzling, and surprisingly compelling.

ANTI-TIME ANTI-CHANGE BILL CREATES TRASH PROBLEM

Supporters of the recently passed ATAC bill in parallel universe 6, Earth 6 have encountered an unexpected trash problem. It seems no one can empty the garbage.
"I don't know where it's all coming from," said psychic correspondent Tasmerilla Dingus. "But there are piles and piles of it sticking all over the place in that sphere. No one there can do anything about it."
Experts speculate that other universes are merely dumping their excess garbage into the motionless world of Earth 6. Tasmerilla Dingus confirmed these suspicions. "It's be the easiest thing in the world to do. Once the trash is there, it's gotta stay. Everything will become more and more dense. Even light can't move. Pretty soon we're gonna have a black trash hole on the edge of our reality."
Since the ATAC bill went into effect, no one has been able to determine if it was a good idea. Police and criminals are the only two groups that still move. Yet Police are not allowed to express their opinion because they are a special interest. And criminals' opinions are ignored because they are criminals. The

rest of the world is obeying the law and so can't move. In the meantime, the garbage keeps mounting.

OTISIAN DIRECTORY
$3 from J. Stevens, Intergalactic House of Fruitcakes, PO Box 235, Williamstown, MA 01267-0235

These people run the only Otis worshipping organization on the planet — and despite a heck of a lot of mail, it's hard to say just what that means. They seem to be a joke religion, spitting out new bits of faith at random intervals. But they also publish a directory of fringe groups that is an excellent resource if you want to get in touch with the odd people out there.

OVO
Send SASE for current price list from Trevor Blake, PO Box 23061, Knoxville, TN 37933-1061

Trevor has been involved in all manner of revolutionary projects in the past several years (more artistic than political, though he crosses that imaginary divide with ease) and has grown into something of an archivist of the crazy world. Mass murder, anarchist prisoner support,

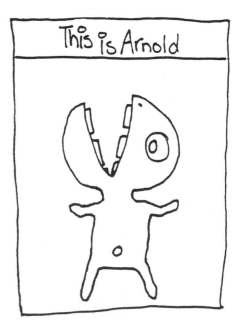

This is Arnold

audio and video networking, psychiatric repression are among his interests. He reviews all sorts of stuff he gets in the mail, reprints communiques, and all in all acts as a clearing point for some of the offbeat notions you'll find in psychospace these days.

Wilhelm Reich was driven half-mad and killed by agents of the Emotional Plague — maybe half his work derived from sheer paranoia (UFO conspiracies, homophobia, even his orgasm theory) — BUT — on one point we agree whole-heartedly — sexpol: sexual repression breeds death obsession, which leads to bad politics. A great deal of avant-garde art is saturated with Deadly Orgone (DOR). Ontological Anarchy aims to build aesthetic cloud-busters (OR-guns) to disperse the miasma of cerebral sado-masochism which now passes for slick, hip, new, fashionable. Self-mutilating "performance" artists strike us as banal and stupid — their art makes everyone more unhappy. What kind of two-bit conniving horseshit...what kind of cockroach-brained art-creeps cooked up this apocalypse stew?

SYZYGY
$2 from Seth Tisue/Plaster Cramp Press, PO Box 5975, Chicago, IL 60680

Seth is in touch with a lot of the madmen on the underground circuit and does a good job of juxtaposing various text, visual and mixed (such as concrete poetry, using letters to make pictures) pieces with one another. The zine hops from interview to collage to story to random assortments of letters, providing a quick cross-section of life on the fringes. A well-done and knowledgeable review section is a welcome addition here, putting current fringe excesses in the context of the main streams of the movement.

bOING bOING
$3.95 from Mark Frauenfelder, PO Box 18432, Boulder, CO 80308

This is one of *the* places to go for info on mind machines, self-metaprogramming, and other fun activities to make use of that hunk of protoplasm between your ears. Mark reviews freaky software and bits of machinery designed to expand your head, talks to people like Robert Anton Wilson and Antero Alli, and tries to give your cortex a kick in the butt. Fully lives up to its self-awarded designation as "The world's greatest neurozine!"

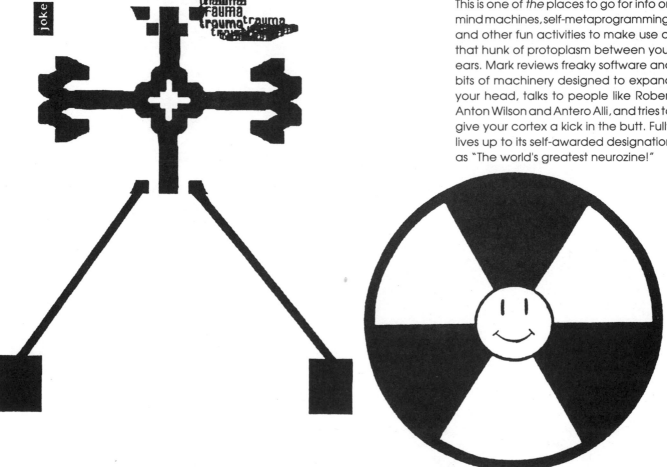

Comics & Assorted Humor

"Humor" is a pretty broad category for zines, and "comics" is a world unto itself. However, because these two categories involve the more lighthearted efforts of the small press, they do belong at least close to each other, though they can be worlds apart. Humor zines are very often political, targeting reknowned politicians or labor unions and any point in between. Comics and "minicomics" (about an eighth of the size of a standard comic -- it can fit into your back pocket) can be anything from amateur doodling to fine art with plots and stories to rival any major comics publisher.

THE REALIST
$2 from PO Box 1230, Venice, CA 90294

There are amateur smartasses, and then there are professional smartasses. This is a watering hole for the latter, and a voice of fierce satirical opposition to the System — and if you haven't heard of this longest-of-running underground periodicals by now, you'd better go back and take another look at contemporary history. Editor Paul Krassner has been needling the Establishment for decades now and he's not about to stop. Cheerfully irreverent, this journal continues to explore and satirize the boundaries of our wacky culture with humor and social commentary — and sometimes it's hard to know where one stops and the other begins. A few terrific examples include reports on the filming of "Michael and Me," a retaliation exercise from GM honcho Roger Smith; investigations of the connections between Walt Disney and UFOs; a serious article on Jack-and-Jill-Off Parties; the role of George Bush in the JFK assassination, rides on the Merry Prankster bus, a comparison between Andrew Dice Clay and Lenny Bruce (Dice comes up way short); Hitler's 100th birthday party (with some surprise guests of honor!); excerpts from Noriega's diary; and a wonderful hypothetical resignation letter from LAPD chief Daryl Gates (written by Harry Shearer) that the **LA Times** refused to print because it was "inappropriate." Sophisticated humor for the intelligent person who thinks things are more than a little strange in this country.

We're No Angels

"Thanksgiving with Jane and Tom" — It was Abbie Hoffman who once said that

"Tom Hayden gives opportunism a bad name." After Hayden's marriage to Jane Fonda broke up, she was courted by Ted Turner. **People** magazine reports that the romantic couple are "sharing each other's interests." "He's been working out some and she's tried fly-fishing and turkey-hunting."
Turner has banned the word "foreign" on CNN, requiring newscasters to say "international" instead. Syndicated columnist Lewis Grizzard asks: "Does Ted Turner have an airplane? I'm sure he does. What does it say in the restroom? **Do not flush any international objects down the toilet?"**

WAGE SLAVE WORLD NEWS
$1 from PO Box 1217, Madison, WI 53701-1217

The official newsletter of the "Sensationalist Workers of the World," and modeled after **The Weekly World News**, this is a satirical independent-anarchist-labor-unionist periodical — very likely the only one of its kind. It's dressed up to look like a supermarket tabloid, and sports the same banner headlines and attention getting techniques while looking at the current struggles between workers and management. Past announcements and such have included such outrageous items as attempts to use Elvis to save the AFL-CIO, how Bart Simpson is actually drawn by underpaid Korean slave labor and how Jimmy Hoffa's body was discovered in Reagan's head. One of our favorites was the story about the plan to summon UFOs to help get anti-scab legislation passed, since they figure this has a better chance than trying to override a Bush veto. They have a deliberately campy format with screaming headlines ("Bigfoot Joins Earth First!"), unbelievable photos (George Bush turns up in a pork chop), and flat-out lies (issue #6 reports that the First Amendment was never ratified) that make it great reading, especially if you recognize the in-jokes (e.g. eating Joe Hill's ashes, George Meany pin-ups, etc). A rather wobbly publication (nyuk, nyuk).

CRY FOR DAWN
$2.50 from Joe Monks, 360 W. Merrick Rd., Suite 350, Valley Stream, NY 11580

An independent comic that should be gaining lots more attention soon. A standard sized comic book, with a glossy exterior, from two young men with an unusual vision of life behind the facade of reality. Beautifully drawn comics, with each page almost a painting in blacks and grays — with the most gruesome of topics covered: child molesting, murder, suicide, mutilation and baldfaced racism for starters. We think they are not so much in love with the material as they are determined to get people to squirm — kind of like horror movies. Deeply disturbed and disturbing work.

REALITY SANDWICH
75¢ from PO Box 2092, Baltimore, MD 21203-2092

Politically-soaked humor, with the layout of a supermarket tabloid, that goes off in some pretty strange directions. Their social barbs are mainly directed at the powers that be with special attention paid to sometimes very touchy subjects. But if you don't get a chuckle out of reading about how golf pros are being sent to clear the landmines of Iraq, or how Bush and Saddam are leading off the "New World Order Die-A-Thon," or the report that war causes yeast infection as well as turning the tides of fashion, then you probably should just keep on reading **Newsweek** and be done with it. These are keen eyes on the world; where else would you hear about "S.C.U.D. AID?" ("Thousands Dead — Let's Rock and Roll!!") Strictly for the confirmed cynic.

BABY SUE
$8 CASH/4 issues from PO Box 1111, Decatur, GA 30031-1111

This little zine of sick humor and comics is a lot more diverse now than it was at first, and the better for it. Besides the obnoxious, sick comics they've always had, they print obnoxious, sick text (the one on veal and the one on recycling compete for political incorrectness honors) and more interviews. The humor is nasty, but you gotta laugh at some of the sickest stuff around. "Recipes for the 90s" includes everything from turd sandwiches to Ted Bundy's favorites.

ROUND HOUSE COMICS
$1 from Victor Gates, 552 Lancelot Drive, N. Salt Lake, UT 84054-2230

Victor publishes mini-comics, the kind that fit neatly into your back pocket. This series took one of Victor's existing characters, "the Geep," married him off to Maxine, and put them in charge of "BWOC — Big Women on Campus," a sorority for large women. This is a fat-admirers' mini, which just might change a few people's preconceptions. All the lead characters here are overweight by contemporary standards, but learning to like themselves and be loved by others. And the series gets you involved with the characters's lives, as young couples fall in love, deal with interracial relationships and even the Mormons come into it too, as Victor explores a number of relationships somewhat out of the ordinary. BBW liberation lives!

ANACHRONISTIC TIME BOMB FUNNIES
$2.50 from Nathan Tolzmann, 1905 Treehouse, Plano, TX 75023

This is as much art as comics, visual poetry passing down the page in some pieces, action/adventure in others. It's a relatively new entry which follows no clear path but for the counterculture feel to it. Nathan and company have strange ways of looking at the world, and keep stories short on words and long on extracted feeling — intentionally and paradoxically, such as "Reverend Zilmo's Sinner's Corner," or "Marmot" and his caravan of 1950s promotional materials. It reminds us just a little of the old underground comics you'd only be able to find at head shops of yore.

SNICKER
$3 from Rich Balducci, 1248 Oak Bark Dr., St. Louis, MO 63146

Thumbs up to this humor tabloid which managed to get itself in trouble almost at the start, being sued by Anheuser-Busch for printing a "Michelob Oily" parody ad on the back of their issue (referring to a nasty spill in the local river). They confront the evil lawyers, lampoon Siskel and Ebert (who review the Zapruder (JFK assassination) film in a stunning display of bad taste), print bizarre comics about "Mentally Disturbed Teachers," and give us lots to laugh and snicker about. Snippy, sophisticated, rude, crude and pretty darned funny.

THWACK!
$3 from Vinnie Bartilucci, 45 Newburgh St., Elmont, NY 11003

An amateur press association (apa) devoted to the discussion of, rather than the drawing of, comics, both mainstream and independent. There are many people out there who love to write and talk about comics, from the classics to the current stuff on the racks and this is

their forum. They also list stuff for sale, draw parodies of the Ninja turtles and sometimes even insert things like the **Marvel** stock prospectus. Looks like a friendly crowd.

KING-CAT COMIX AND STORIES
$1 from John Porcellino, 1954 Brookside Lane, Hoffman Estates, IL 60194

A collection of charming everyday comics and drawings from John; he has a style that looks like it ought to be crude but somehow comes off as economical instead. He has an entire stable of characters, from Racky Raccoon (a kind of blue-collar Everyman) to The Mouse. Many of these are drawn from life (finding a superball, being a jerk at a party, beating up bullies on the beach) but many others deal with dreams (a visit to a train where strangers have sex if they talk to one another). There have been special theme issues — like the all-Spanish, all-animals one or the tribute to **Marvel** comics — but mostly John just follows his muse into Real Life, a shining example of which was "Ranks of the Damned," a tale of adolescent sex and its ramifications for a boy not yet ready. Delightfully strange material with a great sense of story.

LIFE IS A JOKE
$1 from Joe Franke, 2288 Hawk St., Simi Valley, CA 93065

A zine of offbeat humor and bizarre cartoons. Sometimes there's lots of downbeat material — zombies, playing basketball with a dead cat, etc. But it's all very funny, and might turn a few depressions around. There are crazy

comics and survival tips that, tongue-in-cheek, do a lot to make modern life look stupid. (The "ode to coffee" issue was a triumph.) Editor/artist Joe looks at the world sideways; for example, one of his graphic comics is captioned, "Isn't is convenient that we breathe oxygen rather than cat blood?" Atypical stuff.

THE MUNDANE ADVENTURES OF DISHMAN
75 cents from PO Box 671, Guelph, Ontario, CANADA N1H 6L3

Dishman is a superhero with a rather small power: he can clean dirty dishes by teleportation. Meanwhile, as Paul Mahler, he teaches school and tries to figure out how to use this power for teaching. Clean line art make this spoof of superheroes a joy to read — and you find that you really want to know what's going to happen next. This is just like real life — with complications from personal life and the trials of a caped crusader.

MIKE THE POD COMIX
$1 from Matt Anderson, 33 Beech Road, Glen Rock, NJ 07452

Setting aside the fact that Mike the Pod is a cult and not a very clear-cut cult, this is a fine comic with some pretty talented people on its side. It's mostly made up of collegiate escapades, but the kind you remember and wish you had written down when they happened (like the bruiser down the dorm hall whom you accidentally woke up when you thought it was your friend's room). There're also consumer follies, self-deprecation and the mystic power of Elvis. One panel that stands out was "I Was A Middle-Aged Cabbage Patch Kid," which was a real toot. The attitude of this zine is amply captured by one of the panels: "Mr. Potato Head Goes Bad!"

HEY, NEETERS!
$1.50 from PO Box 1378, Belmont, CA 94002

Funny animal adventure comics that

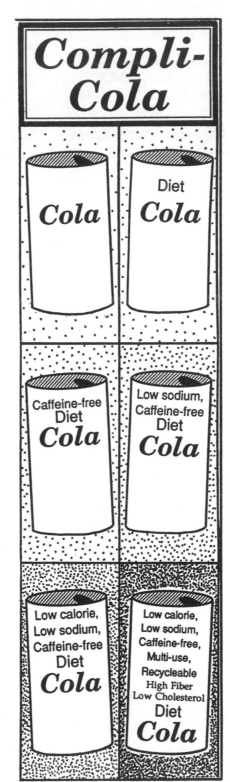

are more cute than sexy, even though they're about young folks in love and have strong relationships as the base of the story. There's lovelorn Turbo and his fiancee Lori; Terrence (Class of '77) who finds his yearbook and looks back on some lost opportunities; the pals cruising around town trying to get over a broken heart, and more Real Life in this charming comic.

TWISTED IMAGE NEWSLETTER
$1 from Ace Backwords, 1630 University Avenue #26, Berkeley, CA 94703

The demand for the **Twisted Image** comic strip was so high that Ace began making them available in this handy forum to anyone with a buck. If you've been paying attention, you've seen Ace's ubiquitous comic strip in countless numbers of zines by now. If not, then pay attention now. You may be amused by his ruthless fun-poking at relationships, politics, music and the terribly ironic world we live in. Ace knows how to push buttons and has a terrific grasp of society's fickle finger. Funny and many times politically incorrect (proudly so, we would venture to guess), but designed to make you think about hypocrisy, social ills, and any number of human adversities. He also indulges in longer, written rants about many topics — how he was black-balled from a semi-major music rag, pornography, revisionism and other perversions. He also publishes "crank" mail from heavy hitters like Paul Krassner (**The Realist**) and Joe Bob Briggs (**We Are The Weird**). Bravely politically incorrect for any side you care to try.

THE SNOPESES GO CAMPING
$1 from Stephanie du Plessis, PO Box 191206, San Francisco, CA 94119

Hilarious **National Lampoon**esque white trash humor in a serialized novel form, this stuff is unequaled even by those supermarket tabloids from whence comes its inspiration. The story revolves around the Snopes family, whose main characteristics include unwed pregnancies, souped-up cars that don't run, a

family tree that "does not fork," and big hair. Between adventures at the trailer home that Marty Sr. built for his horde of hare-lipped children, the mall where Gram dies in an attempt at stealing a glimpse at June Allyson, and possible blood ties to Elvis, the family is trying to fulfill their dream of going camping. Some of the best humor out there is in here.

YOU KNOW YOU'RE A SNOPES IF:
* *Your richest relative buys a new house and you have to help take the wheels off.*
* *There is a stuffed possum mounted in your home.*
* *You consider a six pack and a bug zapper quality entertainment.*
* *Less than half the cars you own run.*
* *Your mother doesn't remove the Marlboro from her lips before telling the state patrolman to "kiss her ass."*
* *Your family tree does not fork.*
* *Your wife's hairdo has ever been ruined by a ceiling fan.*
* *The neighbors started a petition over your Christmas lights.*
* *The diploma hanging in your den includes the words "Trucking Institute."*
* *You have a rag for a gas cap.*
* *Directions to your house include "turn off the paved road."*
* *You prominently display a gift you bought at Graceland.*
* *You've ever worn a tube top to a wedding.*
* *You think Moon Pies and Beef Jerky are two of the major food groups.*
* *Your lifetime goal is to own a fireworks stand.*

THE CHOPPING BLOCK
$1 from Kit Lively, Rt. 2 Box 146, Celina, TX 75009

A zine of rather sick humor, from the boy with a vagina on his knee to the rude notes about people on television, it's also the only zine with the "Valerie Bertinelli Seal of Approval" (someone should let her know). Editor Lively doesn't take himself or anyone else too seriously, so everyone and everything is free game in this journal. The "medical column" and the comics in particular are gross, disgusting and terribly funny. We can't get enough of "Talk of the Town," selections of "quotes" from celebrities like Rob Lowe and Cindy Williams. Another high spot has Ted Bundy appearing on "Hollywood Squares," Marilyn Monroe giving study lessons and a list of "Rejected **Enquirer** Headlines." Kit doesn't care who he lampoons — you may be next.

RECOMMENDED TELEVISION FOR AUGUST
America's Least Wanted: This week profiled are famed irritants Sandy Duncan, Judge Wapner, and the entire cast of "Charles in Charge." Hosted by Bob Uecker, who, last time I looked, was pretty irritating himself.
Gidget Goes Nuts!: When Moondoggie stands up for Gidget for the annual beach barbeque and dead fish throw contest, she becomes a bloodthirsty butchering lunatic, armed with an arsenal of stainless steel cutlery and a hunger to kill that cannot be quenched!

It's a Beach Blanket Bloodbath from the same people who brought you Nursing Home Nightmare Part 2 & 3, and the Wyoming Weedeating Massacre! Filmed in PlasmaVision!

LADIES' FETISH AND TABOO SOCIETY COMPENDIUM OF URBAN ANTHROPOLOGY
$1 from PO Box 542327, Houston, TX 77254-2327

"Ladies" Kathy and Elaine discovered one day that the "weird" was following them — they turned back and made it into a zine. Urbane and altogether irreverent (but true!) collection of real life happenings — from clippings to musings to the retelling of horrendous occurrences (a young woman discovers that her boyfriend is a cross-dresser, for one) to strange and wonderful accounts of highways that mutate numbers, shrines to Harmonicas in Italy, weird headings in the Library of Congress catalog, and much more. They also include other stuff like recipes for Peanut Brittle Salad, the "Continuing Proof of the Theory of Obstacles," and unusual shrines (there is certainly a complex mythology surrounding the ladies and their practices of worship). Some people lead decidedly interesting lives and you'll find a few in here. Real fun but hard to grok.

The Ladies' Fetish & Taboo Society was revealed late in the summer of 1986 to Kathy Biehl and Elaine Gerdine, who did

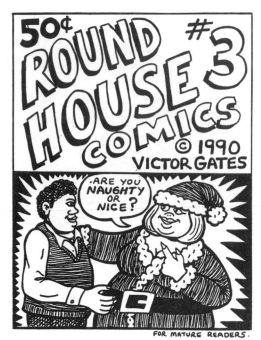

not so much found the Society as append a name to what they had already been experiencing. The Society's purpose is venerating and chronicling our unceasing encounters with the weird. We also engage in devotion to efficiency and strive for that intactness of self known as Harmonica Virginity.

Our members are few, our devotees growing in number and god knows what other ways. Changing from the latter to the former is an ephemeral process that usually makes itself known after the transforming event has occurred. Like so much of life and certain of its attendant carbon-based forms, it just happens.

GUMBO COMICKS/ ZOOMCRANKS COMICS
$1 from Mark Cunningham, 601 S. 6th Ave., St. Charles, IL 60174

Easygoing and "indulgent" comics that come from somewhere inside the recesses of Cunningham's brain. What kind of person would print a cookie recipe involving live slugs? There are also thoughts of Medusa, memories of assembly-line work, a tribute to body movements, giant tapeworms and urban folklore battling it out together. Somewhat disjointed modern primitive comics with

a wild and wooly cast of characters, including the mini about the joys of motorcycle riding to blow off steam, made more curious by the fact that the rider is headless.

NOT AVAILABLE COMICS
$1 from Matt Feazell, 3867 Bristow, Detroit, MI 48212

This is a conglomerate of minicomic publishing. They offer all sorts of titles, and medleys of work from some of minicomics' finest. Matt Madden gives us a Big Boy sunken in disturbing memories of past sexual exploits. Matt Feazell appears regularly with perhaps the two most famous stick-figure comic characters in the country — Cynicalman and Antisocialman. Certainly the best minicomic anthology around.

DR. JOE GUY PAN PRESENTS RALPH AND REGGIE
$2 CASH & Age Statement from 2118 Guadalupe St. #179, Austin, TX 78705

A really weird comic book featuring a rat, a bum, and the spirit of Michael Landon (that were published before his death) in adventures ranging from Heaven to Hell and points in between. Motorcycle madness, devious pigs and a graffiti-drenched art style make this

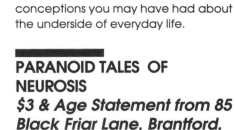

one stand out. It's an adventurous but muddled plot between a man and dog, providence and stand-up comedy. But who's complaining — this is a comic we're reading, isn't it?

THE BEST NEWS OF THE WEEK
$1 from Radio Werewolf High Command, Buenaventura Durruti Column Branch, PO Box 75416, Washington, DC 20013

Calling itself "an alternative press alternative to the alternative press," these folks are "Radio Werewolves" offering broadsheet high political humor and satire. They are so irreverent that they claim anyone is free to photocopy and *take credit* for their work — they even encourage it! Their "God Save the Queen" issue had them poking not-so-delicate fun at Great Britain and its monarch, while the "Two Step Forward/ Twelve Steps Back" issue looks to the day when smoking is blamed for nuclear radiation-induced cancer. They also present views on the programmed sale of videotapes, "Meet the Press" voting procedures, Saddam v. Hitler and lots more political trotting.

PEPG!RLZ
$1 from PO Box 20801, New York, NY 10009

Ready? Anarchist-squatter-lesbian-activist comics from the hothouse of New York City. What a mouthful! Sledgehammer Sue and Co. get off on throwing egg bombs at the cops (recipe included), give tips on how to eat well in jail, and revolt against (you guessed it) The Establishment, armchair anarchists and eventually the artist herself. Wild stuff and certain to blow away any preconceptions you may have had about the underside of everyday life.

PARANOID TALES OF NEUROSIS
$3 & Age Statement from 85 Black Friar Lane, Brantford, Ontario, CANADA N3R 7M2

A collection of dangerous comics with a bent for violence and paranoia. There are bizarre and twisted comic tales of violent rock concerts, horror movies, a man being eaten by his friends —ugh, the list goes on. In one issue Joe reveals the sources of fear in his life and goes off the wall with guns and other instruments of violence — Satan pops up here and there, as well. The artistic style perfectly conveys the heavily bizarre emotional states behind it...

HOTHEAD PAISAN
$3 from PO Box 214, New Haven, CT 06502

A comic centered on a "homocidal lesbian terrorist" and her cat Chicken, though no one actually gets killed here. Instead there is mega-discussion of Political Correctness and tolerating men and true radicalness and bashing men, with an obligatory sex scene and repartee with Chicken the cat. Definitely outrageous and a lot of fun. These women have Attitude.

COLIN UPTON COMICS
50¢ from Colin Upton, 6424 Chester, Vancouver, B.C., CANADA V5W 3C3

Colin produces dozens of mini-comics under various titles and they all contain his certain brand of charm. He draws in a realistic style, concentrating on real life. Some titles include **The Collected Socialist Turtle**, which are the events in the life of a curmudgeonly maxi-mini

socialist turtle whose ideology gets thwarted left and right by commie squirrels, imperialist eagles and a naive fox; **Famous Bus Rides**, where the bus becomes a salon as big as life and with such characters as old hippies and a religious sourpuss; **Happy Ned**, the adventures of a rabbit; **The Granville St. Gallery**, a remarkable series of mall portraits; and **Hotxha the Albanian**, which is something of a backhanded tribute to **Asterix the Gaul**.

PAH!
SASE from Mark Morelli, 702 Mae St., Kent, OH 44240

This is an off-the-wall, one-man humor zine. It usually comes one sheet at a time, with each issue numbered, and is ready to hit on just about anything. Some sheets describe verily weird items and events like the "interview" with the "founder" of Workaholics Anonymous; the experiences of Gepetto, who leaves Pinocchio in the dust to go work for the U.S. government; a wine-buying guide for those whose "6-year statute of limitations on buying cheap jugs of wine" has run out; a harrowing bathroom experience in lower Manhattan, or the discovery that fathers are rapidly disappearing from view as they wield the videocams at family gatherings. The list goes on and on. Excellent humor and tongue-in-cheek asides (like trying to cope with Christmas commercialism at a time that should be reserved for Rudolph specials) from a truly inspired mind.

Nifty Origin #658: "...that face that electric guitar players make has its origins in a West Village club. On July 16, 1954, Bobby Blossoe — who was a guitarist but always just wanted to be a mime — was absently imitating the face of an audience member who was biting into a piping hot slice of pizza..."

NICE DAY COMIX
Free catalog with Age Statement and SASE from Randy Crawford, 911 Park St. SW, Grand Rapids, MI 49504-6241

This is the family name of a whole series of different mini-comic collections from Randy. Titles include **Your Dirty Lil' Comic**, which features among other characters a female private eye who gives her clients their money's worth; **Plain Brown Wrapper Special**, a selection of erotic sketches, paintings and comics; and **U-People**, a 60s Marvelesque look at some all too human superheroes (even the android!). Randy also offers **Paper Doilies**, a paper doll collection of female characters from previous *Nice Day* comics.

KARNO'S KLASSICS
75¢ plus 29¢ postage and Age Statement from Kjartan Arnorsson, PO Box 32292, Tucson, AZ 85751

Animal comics with a difference, the difference being the improbably large and much used sexual equipment the animals have. These intelligently written anthropomorphic romps feature high quality art throughout and stories that are mostly good soft-porn. Very often Kjartan will team up with other comic artists or produce one of his "Karno's Klassic Specials," "Porno Babies" (a kind of soft-porn Muppet Babies adventure) — all with his inimitable and refreshing style.

THE 10 BEST MOVIES OF ALL-TIME? YOU BET!
1. FREAKS— MIDGETS, MONSTROSITIES AND MUTANTS IN HORRIFYING B & W
2. WHERE ANGELS GO, TROUBLE FOLLOWS— GIRLS, NUNS AND A BUS!
3. DELIVERANCE —"SQUEAL LIKE A PIG!" (NEED WE SAY MORE?)
4. MOMMIE DEAREST — JOAN CRAWFORD, MOTHER FROM HELL!!!
5. POSEIDON ADVENTURE — COOL SPECIAL EFFECTS — PLUS SHELLEY WINTERS DROWNS!
6. THE OTHER SIDE OF THE MOUNTAIN — HE DIES, AND SHE MUST FACE LIFE ALONE — IN A WHEELCHAIR!!!
7. FEMALE TROUBLE — DIVINE THROWS TANTRUM AND WRECKS THE FAMILY CHRISTMAS TREE.
8. CAN YOU HEAR THE LAUGHTER? — DOCU-DRAMA ON FREDDIE PRINZE — BUT DOESN'T SHOW HIS SUICIDE...
9. THAT CERTAIN SUMMER — HAL HOLBROOK AND MARTIN SHEEN? NAKED? TOGETHER?! ARRRGH!!!
10. VERY SPECIAL PEOPLE — UNABASHED OPPORTUNITY TO FILM SIAMESE TWINS FOR A "DOCUMENTARY"

Scenes you play back on the vcr over and over
MICHAEL CAINE AND CHRISTOPHER REEVE KISSING — DEATHTRAP
LINDA BLAIR DISCOVERS NEW USE FOR CRUCIFIX — THE EXORCIST
JULIE ANDREWS UNVEILS HER KNOCKERS — S.O.B.
DIVINE DINES ON DOG-DOO — PINK FLAMINGOS

Sports

Every facet of popular culture has coverage in the zine world, and sports is no exception. Oddly enough, professional wrestling seems to draw the attention of more amateur publishers than any other sport. But those interested in other forms of physical activity need not despair, for we've seen publications devoted to baseball, football, basketball and even frisbee and footbag. So if the zine you want isn't in here, keep looking — or start it yourself.

CHOKEHOLD
$1 from Lance LeVine, 507 W. 43rd Pl., Chicago, IL 60609

Chokehold is one of the bad boys of the wrestling zine world, refusing to take anything seriously. Lance knows everyone and makes fun of most, running a mix of serious material and satire that's likely to be baffling to most outside of this particular subcommunity. His autobiographical tales of life on the fringes of the wrestling world are classics in themselves.

Boy, getting here to Hawaii was no easy feat. As you recall, I'm in search of the dreaded Black Kayfabe, the evil dude that tried to send me to prison for some reason. Can you imagine someone hating me that much? Me neither. Anyway, I busted out of jail and began my pursuit with the advice of an ancient Chinese wise man, Wing Yip. All I gotta do is find this chameleon, beat a confession out of him and my name will be cleared. But I've already gone to Las Vegas, where I got some clues, but was told to look around Hawaii next. Which updates you all on our saga.
I thumbed rides through the desert from Vegas through California 'til I finally reached LA. The most memorable leg of that journey was when a van full of Grateful Deadheads picked me up, braided my hair, dirtied my clothes, fed me some weird mushrooms (with a wonderful Chardonnay, however) and bombarded me with stories about Jerry Garcia. Can you imagine the kinds of things a brave person could find picking through that beard of his? Anyway, after I got out of Sunbeam's van, I went into a

full service truck stop and showered in hydrogen peroxide to make sure I didn't catch any of those Deadheads' diseases. Or bad vibes.

WRESTLING PERSPECTIVE
$1.25 from Paul MacArthur, PO Box 401, Camillus, NY 13031

A wrestling zine which concentrates on commentary rather than match results, which they presume their readers can get from other sources. Instead, they invite essays from some of the best zine writers today on likely future developments in the wrestling world, promotional strategies, classic wrestlers, and so on. Rather refined for its genre.

ROD'S REFLECTOR
$12/10 issues from Rodney Leighton, RR #3, Pugwash, NS, CANADA, B0K 1L0

Rodney's been around the wrestling newsletter circuit for a long time, writing here and there and publishing numerous titles of his own. Mostly the **Reflector** acts as a sort of meta-zine, directed at those already in touch with a batch of other zines in the business, interviewing publishers and considering the shape of wrestling fandom. Rodney also reviews whatever other stuff he can get his hands on and always has a variety of complicated swap deals available.

COMBAT SPORTS
$2 from Michael O'Hara, PO Box 651, Gracie Sta., New York, NY 10028-0006

Published since 1978, this is the oldest wrestling/roller derby zine in existence. Though the title indicates a broad focus on all sorts of sportainment, in fact wrestling (due to its overwhelming popularity) occupies the majority of the pages. Michael is well-connected by now, and he presents the latest from the rumor mill in every issue. The zine also tracks title matches and mainstream coverage of the sport. Plus it's an excellent source for wrestling collectibles, including rare older zines.

ROLLER SPORTS REPORT
$2.50 from Fred Argoff, 1204 Ave. U #1290, Brooklyn, NY 11229

You probably know about roller derby, the sport where teams of people skate around a banked track trying to pass one another and beating one another up in the process. But did you know that there have been literally dozens of roller leagues over the years? This zine is the place to find out about them, as it skillfully mixes reprints and nostalgia with news and gossip about the current attempts to revive the sport in one form or another. The talks with some of the older skaters, now retired, about what it was like in the early days (the original Roller Derby was a traveling marathon rather than a team sport) are completely fascinating oral history.

When the derby switched to a game it wasn't so brutal to begin with. It was more of a speed and roughhouse game on the order of hockey — a lot of body checking, a lot of bump blocks. There was none of this hitting a guy from behind, hitting him on the head, kicking him or jumping on top of him or anything like that....But as the years went on, they got used to seeing more fighting...and that's when the violence all started. I think Roller Derby is a sport that wants to please the fans, and that's why they do it. We have 75% bloodthirsty, chilling people for fans. They all say they're peace-loving, but they're not.

TWISTED
$1 from Jamie Early, 11698 Howitzer Lane, Woodbridge, VA 22192

You may not think of skateboarding as a sport, but it is, on both the amateur and professional levels. **Twisted** is one of several skateboarding zines out there, and it's one of the best. The main attraction here is the photos of young men flying through the air on their boards, launching themselves into space from the tops of plywood ramps and troughs. Jamie visits the local places to skate and tells his readers about them, and reviews some of the music beloved of people who enjoy this activity. Inspirational in its enthusiasm even though a lot of the pictures are pretty terrifying.

WRESTLING OBSERVER NEWS-LETTER
$1.50 from Dave Meltzer, PO Box 1228, Campbell, CA 95009-1228.

The **Observer** is widely acknowledged as one of the best of the wrestling zines, or "sheets" as those involved in this branch of zinedom call them. With a worldwide network of informants, Dave's able to give the results from matches all over, from Alabama to Japan and beyond, in his weekly roundup of the news. He's also tied into the gossip chain, so that new promotional gimmicks, rules changes, legal hassles, and similar events get covered quickly as well. In addition to the zine, Dave produces an annual yearbook, a fat compilation of results and news that gets behind the usual hype to deliver a lot of facts on the sport. Occasionally a bit dry but always indispensable. Things like the recent flap over steroid use by professional wrestlers break here long before you'll see them in your local newspapers. An extensive letters section keeps tabs on the grassroots feelings of the fans as well.

Sting kept the NWA title beating Sid Vicious in 12:40. Vicious was cheered by more than half the crowd live. Match itself stunk for a main event, though no fault of Sting. He did a few flying moves, including a dive over the top rope splashing onto Vicious. Sid just can't work, but he looks phenomenal standing still. The finish saw them brawl (if that's what you would call it) to the dressing room while Ric Flair and Arn Anderson came out to divert everyone's attention. Then they got back into the ring, but unbeknownst to everyone, it was Barry Windham dressed up like Sting. Windham collapsed on a bodyslam attempt and Vicious pinned him to apparently win the title. Fireworks went off and balloons started flying everywhere as Sid paraded around with the title with the place popping like a babyface had just won the strap. Then Sting comes out with a rope around his wrist (apparently the story line is that he was tied over and broke free) ran to the ring while the fake Sting ran away (a missed camera shot although a still shot did air during the recap) with the ref watching and he re-started the match. Sting hit Vicious with the belt, splashed him in the corner and cradled him for the win. * 1/2 (The work itself of the match was a dud, although Sting gets 1/2 star for trying those hot moves and the finish gets a star).

WRESTLING CHATTERBOX
$2 from Georgiann Makropoulos, 23-44 30th Dr., Astoria, NY 11102-3252

Georgiann concentrates more on the people involved in wrestling than do most of the other sheets. She seems to be quite a nice gal, which may account for the fact that she's managed to meet and get her photo taken with many wrestling greats. The Chatterbox also reports on match results, but the heart of it is the photos and personal accounts of what the wrestlers are up to these days.

WRESTLING - THEN & NOW
$1.25 from Evan Ginzburg, PO Box 471, Oakland Gardens Sta., Flushing, NY 11364

This is an idea which has taken off rather unexpectedly but has gotten quite good response — a wrestling zine that looks back to the old days, before the gimmick-laden big business promotions that are all the average modern fan knows about. Evan manages, through reprints, hunting down memorabilia and talking to the men who were involved, to present anecdotes and ideas that really get the flavor of classic pro wrestling across. For anyone who wants a sense of the roots of the current sport.

*Sometimes I wish I was a "mark" again, I have very reluctantly assumed the moniker of "smart fan" because I write for some of the newsletters, and owe it to my peers and my readers to be well informed. But am I enjoying wrestling more than I did when I wasn't aware of the implications of TV ratings, house receipts, lawsuits, PPV buy rates, political in-fighting and bookers? I don't think so. I don't knock those who simply enjoy wrestling as dumb entertainment (and it **is** dumb in a sense) without concerning themselves with the reality of it all; nor do I knock those who respect it enough to seriously analyze every aspect of it. I have picked it apart myself. Critical assessment of the sport keeps the powers that be on their toes and gives*

the fans an insight into the business. But I have never liked the arrogant, elitist attitude that many smart fans exhibit. I very rarely enlighten marks unless they ask. What purpose is served by telling a 10 year old kid that his hero is a steroid abuser, a drug addict, a rapist or a philanderer just because I know and he doesn't? Many smart fans are like the first kid on the block to hear the facts of life, who then proceeds to spread all kinds of misinformation to the younger kids because he really doesn't know what he is talking about.

erikkd 9-89

Personal Zines

A personal zine, or perzine, is the most intimate kind of zine. It allows the editor/writer many freedoms, not the least of which is spouting off about anything or nothing-in-particular without worrying about editorial policies and other rules of regimented periodicals. It's also a way of corresponding with any number of people simultaneously while maintaining an aura of intimacy and friendship. And something else to remember as you're reading (or writing) a perzine -- because this intimacy is conducted through the mail, the editor/writer remains faceless. S/he can be whomever they want, without any limit to her/his own unique form of expression.

NOTES FROM THE DUMP
$20/yr from Terry Ward, PO Box 39, Acworth, NH 03601

A zine time-capsule candidate if there ever was one. Longtime zine-publisher Terry Ward began this particular venture while working at the Acworth-Langdon Transfer station — or more precisely, The Dump. It included his feelings about the work and a host of other items that occupied his mind. More recently Terry stopped working at the dump but continues to publish this melange of ruminations about everything from love affairs to cars to recycling to anti-war activism (he was around for the Vietnam stuff). Read about the hard-living folks he has known, struggling with the booze, enjoying peace in the mountains, his '55 Lincoln, even quotes from Shakespeare and Goethe. He writes well, and has enough interests to keep the reader wondering what will be on the next page. Thoughts from out somewhere in the wilderness, waiting to connect with other thoughtful people. "The salt of the earth" is one of those phrases that springs to mind when we read Terry's stuff.

You'll feel better. Well that's what I'm doing as I growl into BF and up through The Square checking myself out in the windows...hmmm...what happened to the Marlon Brando I was as I whipped through the scenic countryside a few moments ago? Hmmm...that guy I just saw reflected in Newberry's window was "Tubby" wrapped in black leather and...hmmm...the freaky long hair flying was gray and the long beard as white as one of those surviving Civil War vets you used to see. Lord have mercy it was me! I

flush with embarrassment and race for the border roaring down the highway and cutting off onto the back roads where there are no friggin reflections and I can continue living my illusion.

BVI-CENTRAL
$1 from J. LeRoy, PO Box 95984, Seattle, WA 98145-2984

One of the longest running and most individual of personal zines. J. LeRoy recently celebrated his 10th anniversary of publishing (not an easy feat by any means) and the foundation of the BVI network (you're going to have to write to J. for the long, sordid history of the network) — which has included in its history separate zines with the BVI-moniker from Seattle to Albany, New York. J.'s contributions are always consistent, never-boring, sometimes-indulgent, nearly-always-inviting social commentary, personal reflections, rants, fiction, pleas for social understanding and a personal battle of ideas with George Herbert Walker Bush (whom he always refers to as such). While many of his editorials speak out against racial and sexual prejudice, he also graces us with eloquent memories and stories of love and friendship. J. also provides his readership with continuing social satire from the universe next door thanks to his alter

BVI central
Issue 10-3

$1.00

Readin' Mool

ego Randall Cantern — a kind of 90's Everyman. A very clever writer, a very impassioned voice, with easy access to his world — all you have to do is write to him or send him transit paraphernalia (his guiding passion). In a recent issue there was a section heading which sums J. up pretty accurately — "Rambling of an Angry Young Man." 'Nuff said.

I have started to write for other people's zines, I'm starting off at this in our "system." Whether all of the underground people want to admit it or not, there is a system that operates like a micro version of the "real" system "out there." The only reason that some of us don't think there is is because it is small, it is more accessible and this accessibility creates the illusion of a really open system. Our system isn't really any more open than the "real" one, when it is viewed in scale.

THE JED YARICK NEWSLETTER
$2.50/3 issues from Jed Yarick, FF Bristol Terrace #215, Lawrence, KS 66049

Tales of life in the cool sector, which, in Jed's case, happens to be in Overland Park, Kansas. Plenty of friendly folks you'll never meet in person here, along with opinions on everything from beer to soc-

cer. You'll follow Jed along his pathway of life — from school to Denny's to the bars, back to Denny's, past graduation to the start of a "real job." Some of his political musings turn out to be fascinating alternatives to the status quo, such as his way to end the wars (a global Battle of the Bands — out-metal the enemy) but then on the next page you might find a handwritten map of his apartment. Jed has gone Andy Warhol one better, proving that with only minimal effort one can garner much more than fifteen minutes of fame.

THE LATEST NEWS
$1 or 4 stamps from Jennifer Payne, 24 Haskell St. Apt. 3, Allston, MA 02134

One of the friendliest personal zines floating around the small press universe. Jen's style of writing is easy and down-to-earth and the zine itself is nicely produced, with scanned photos and a clean graphic look. She writes about the joys of discovering fandom, climbing up Mount Washington, her illustrious past as a local television personality, skipping stones on the water, being unemployed and just about everything you'd want to hear from a good friend. She always keeps up to date with her growing list of correspondents and colleagues and lets us know each time how her move is

progressing, her job is going, or how that picture of her and her sister made her think of a story. This easiness and accessibility is one of the new directions the personal zine is taking and Jen just about has the market cornered.

Walking towards the spot, I played the just-one-more game. You know, the game you play when sitting in front of an open package of Oreos. You make a promise that this one will be the last, as you devour it; but you can't help nibble on just one more. So, even though my pockets were full, I kept searching for one more perfect addition to my collection. Just one more and just one more, until both pockets were full of the best assortment of skipping stones available on the beach.

THE JOE NEWS
$1 from PO Box 153, Back Bay Annex, Boston, MA 02117

One for the books. This is an anonymous personal zine, all about Joe. Who is Joe? Why does he have a zine named after him? Darned if we know. Hipness oozes out of the writing here. With Joe being a rather shadowy figure and all, what else can they rely on? Pontifications on potatoes, a Worst Song contest, pinball, typos, Joe's coffee consumption, fish and chips and hashbrowns are among some of the bizarre attractions. Joe himself is pretty mysterious and his adoring fans write about him in hushed tones, while passing on pearls of wisdom about the state of the cultural world. A unique item.

We need volunteers to help stamp out the unsavory practice of taking JOE's name in vain — an increasingly common & disturbing trend of late. Perhaps the worst example is the all-too-prevalent usage of "Joe Blow," or when denoted as an occupationally derogatory term, such as "Joe Doorman" or "Joe Windowasher." A calm and collected, yet cheekily flippant You-Know-Who says, "Who'd have thought, when I coined the immortal phrase "Joe Cool," that it would come to this?"

BALCONY OF IGNORANCE
$1 or trade from Claude Bottom, 14 Pearl St., Rouses Point, NY 12979

You never know what's going to be in this chronicle of Claude's life. Among other things, Claude almost single-handedly opened up the arena of discussion about those hidden messages in record grooves, together with ideas for making pro wrestling a bit faster moving, rants about "info-mercials" (those half hour ads disguised as programming), and posing lots of burning questions ("Do Austrians actually eat Vienna sausage?") You can also expect to find comprehensive rock trivia quizzes, notes on environmental blasphemy, the bathroom's place in society, or plain old pop culture. He claims to write a personal zine of "slanted egocentrical rantings," but we enjoy this one anyway. What's a personal zine if not slanted and egocentric?

L.A. GANG BANG
$1 from Lee Wochner, 1212A N. San Fernando #244, Burbank, CA 91504

Can a cartoonist/actor, playwright, travel agent and respiratory therapist move from Atlantic City to Los Angeles and find true happiness? A unique entry in the field of personal zines, this is a newsletter from Gary, Lee, Mary and Valorie, four cool people who lead interesting lives and encourage their correspondents to do likewise. Their lives become entangled with ours with such stimulating fodder as **Rocky Horror Picture Show** anniversary parties, turkeys, movies, seminars, bad trips to the dentist, a hunt for iced tea mix, and other lively escapades. Each issue contains, besides the usual talk, a "Topic of the Month" with such social commentary as fads, teachers, road trips as well as "What I Don't Want for Christmas." While they are busy navigating the shoals of modern life, they also actively encourage their readers and friends to send in their own recipes for pursuing fun and gen-

eral hijinx. Every issue becomes a multitude of events and thoughts and before you know it, you're joining the discussion and find yourself helping the gang find a name for Valorie's new baby, relating your own bad dentist experiences, following them to the San Diego ComicsCon and pretty much wishing you lived next door.

Mary: Things are going swell in the new digs. My roomie, Colleen, is an expert marksperson. She goes to the shooting range regularly and brings home her targets. She even sends some to her mom in NY so she can hang them on the fridge. One of our neighbors asked Colleen on a date...she made me go with her. It was great...He tried to impress us by using the word "astronomical" when describing everything from Rodney Dangerfield to editing sitcoms. He then proceeded to do a 40-minute monologue of Rodney. I was so embarrassed for him...

THE SACRED WILDERNESS
2 29¢ stamps from Ann Patterson, PO Box 15266, Santa Rosa, CA 95402

There's a new strain of personal zines these days and this is a good example. Ann writes an "unpretentious journal for women" with a slant on spirituality and self-love. She reviews books she thinks are valuable, reprints letters from readers on subjects such as cosmetics, teasing, movies, and great social inventions, and courageously fights the use of the verb "DO," (as in "do lunch"). A gentle and down-to-earth effort that doesn't exclude members of the male gender despite its subtitle. A feminist, pagan-but-not-dogmatic spirit animates this zine. Ann may reprint Gandhi's version of the seven deadly sins, or offer editorials on matters of choice, healing, and becoming closer to Nature. While much of the content is pagan, it's not exclusively so — there is a general spirituality here that does not insist on any one dogmatic Path, which is refreshing.

Reaching out is difficult, but as a friend

THE SACRED WILDERNESS

July/August 1991   No. 11

An Unpretentious Journal For Women Celebrating Nature and Each Other

of mine said succinctly, "few people are willing to be so open and honest about their lives and their feelings, unfortunately. These are critical times and we have to talk about the reality of what's happening." This includes being honest and open about our pain — how will we know whether anyone is listening if we don't cry out? We just need to make sure we find a safe place in which to make ourselves vulnerable. And as long as you and I are honest with each other, those places will exist — because we continue to create a loving network. Stay in touch.

BVI-PUGET SOUND
$1 from Ann Yo!Rel, PO Box 95984, Seattle, WA 98145-2984

Ann Yo!Rel writes and edits her personal zine with the ferocity of a wolverine. Usually a collection of collage, graphics, posters and personal poetry with lots of her history and current musings included. Not a single emotion is spared as she relates in strategically placed text and photos her life and innermost thoughts. Sometimes it can be quite painful or uncomfortable reading this zine filled with feminism, open relationships, geographical rants, and some of the most intensely personal stuff out there. This is an exploration on paper of human relationships among a shifting cast of people — a blunt and human search for social transactions that go beyond the rigid status quo.

BYOKI
(formerly BRAIN CANCER)
$1.50 from Mike Canich, PO Box 31, Romeo, MI 48065

Raw writing with intense art and other filler — if you're in an end-times mood or just feel like you want some company in your angry moments then Mike is the guy to read. Unlike other, lighter personal zines, Mike takes you right out of escapism straight into his reality — which isn't always that bright and shiny but it is nonetheless compelling. Mike blows off quite a bit of steam over many topics — chosen, it seems, for the purpose; censorship, abortion, even Christianity — using comic book art, prose, and vignettes. His comic series "The Politics of Suffering" slices to the bone, as do some violent love stories and rants about government repression. Sometimes he lets us in on his daily activities, such as the trip to the mall and how that reverberated into a new consciousness about the existence of women, or some facts about his life, including his pierced ear, his mother, or the phonies he knew in school. Curiously attractive and aching at the same time — this is one to really

penny four your thoughts

sink your teeth into.

JASON UNDERGROUND'S NOTES FROM THE TRASHCOMPACTOR
Free from Anarchy Farms Mailorder, 2795 Via Vela, Camarillo, CA 93010

Jason Underground's perzine with a unique Christian anarchist slant — what's that, you say? Write Jason and find out. Mostly it's about the things he's read or thought about lately — and includes inspirational quotes, sly humor, recommendations for things to see and do. He's got reports on the dangers of television and new music, indictments of fashion political correctness as "a sham" and comments on government wrongdoings. He's pretty upfront about his Christianity — but he's got a wide range of interests and opinions. A cooly personable commodity.

As you all know, this is a "personal zine," which means that it is intended mostly for my friends, relatives, and acquaintances. There are only a couple of people receiving this who have never met me. The photograph of Malia Marden by Robert Mapplethorpe (pictured on a previous issue's cover) is one of the most beautiful pictures I have ever seen in my life and that is why I printed it. When I look at that picture and see that innocent little girl, with her moppy blonde hair, her fat, baby legs, and the mid-meander pose she was caught in I experience no sexual arousal whatsoever. It's simply a beautiful picture of a beautiful little girl who embodies all the beauty of innocence.

THE LETTER PARADE
$1 from Bonnie Jo Enterprises, PO Box 52, Comstock, MI 49041

Like a letter from a longtime compatriot, this personal newsletter tracks Bonnie Jo's life and events and thoughts on everything from international politics to gardening. While one tract may reflect her personal vision of hell as it relates to

a garden, another may detail an Eritrean man's exile and asylum in the United States. Then there are views on Kalamazoo's group housing laws, Bonnie Jo's dog (whose past includes a stint in jail), a reunion with someone's sister, a paper pattern for a kayak, or maybe an excerpt from **The Devil's Dictionary**. In a feature entitled the "Monthly World News" there are always oddball news clippings from mainstream publications that sure don't look mainstream. Bonnie Jo has a host of readers and correspondents who love sharing in the mayhem and answer her surveys on such topics as "The Almighty Auto" or holiday overeating and why we do it, or send in their own sordid (and sometimes hilarious) family histories, funny anecdotes and strange clippings. The content always changes as Bonnie Jo Enterprises gets new ideas about what to publish. This one really is quite a bit like a letter, from a correspondent who stuffs odd bits of things into her envelope before mailing it off to you.

What makes a nation? I wonder. Does it require citizens with certain traits in common? A common language? history? religion? A common purpose of some sort? Is a nation a nation if it hasn't been accepted as such by the world community? If we could just get hold of an acceptable definition for a country, we might be able to talk sensibly about the topic...Perhaps a nation is a state of mind....Perhaps nationhood is like pornography as seen by Justice Potter Stewart, and we will know a nation when we see it.

THE LOST PERUKE
$1.50 from PM Kellerman, PO Box 1525, Highland Park, NJ 08904

PM Kellerman — who's written many a verse on the rhyme and reason behind his unpunctuated initials — is another of the classic personal zine editors whose lifeblood is spilled onto the pages by his typewriter, then whisked off to the printer to be shared with his correspondents. PM's zine reads much like a journal — with memories, problems with cable tele-

The Lost Peruke
May 1991   XXX $1.50

vision, abortion, his dog, recollections of times past, familial anecdotes and items like his many reasons for hating summer. You'll find politically-oriented humor that plays to the yuppie generation in one issue and the next will be a scathing media issue containing, among other items, a photo essay of suitable alternative careers for the rich and famous. He's also got his own brand of "save the day" ideology, strange surveys that provide curious insights into New Jersey values and a very strong sense of solitary origins.

So, when I'm watching the news while eating along and a story about refugees or famine comes on the air, I always get up for seconds — or third if I've already had seconds, assuming, of course, that I cooked enough food. It's not that I'm insensitive, but starving people make me hungry. Homeless people make me homesick. Home is where the heart is. Sometimes, home is where the livers are. Ironically, I keep livers in the kitchen, not in the living room. At other time, I chop liver. Meanwhile, on death row, lifers live on liver — but not for long — while other inmates eat banana after banana while they wait for their case to come up on appeal.

MARKTIME
$1 CASH/Stamps from Mark Strickert, 3852 N. Oconto, Chicago, IL 60634

Many zine editors feel limited by editing a tightly focused publication — a personal zine can round out all the corners. Veteran zine-publisher Mark Strickert (who also edits **Decalcomania**) jumped genres by starting his own perzine, taking some of his other zine interests with him. He's got hobby lists, tape trading, sports and map collecting. Also news of what he's been up to lately, which may include family vacations, transit systems, other fanzines, or just about anything he feels like talking about. Which is what perzines are all about.

MISC.
50¢ and SASE from Clark Humphrey, 1630 Boylston #203, Seattle, WA 98122

A single sheet of culture-watching and opinions. Clark dives into such obscurities as the difference between women in punk and women in surrealism, smells of the U.S., local and national press, and the elections in Nicaragua. He is a wry observer of modern life in a progressive city (Seattle) and tells us things we didn't even know we needed to know — like the connection between Teenage Mutant Ninja Turtles and imitation vanilla, or "Nintendo Thumb," — or else digs up an aerobic video game and spills the beans about Boy Scouts selling ad space on their merit badges. Social commentary from the fringe of the Pacific Northwest and beyond, truly these are days of great confusion.

PHILM PHACTS: "The Great Rock 'n Roll Swindle" was cool and quite the nostalgia trip, especially for the kids in the Neptune audience who were still in grade school when the Sex Pistols happened. It was fun to look back at England before Thatcher...when it still had a veneer of respectability to rebel against. But punk was more grassroots than Malcolm McLaren still will admit. None of the hundreds of other bands

were mentioned in the film.

PARACHUTE LIMIT
29¢ from c/o Totoro Hunter Leto II, 10849 Macouba Place, San Diego, CA 92124

The link between a really serious comics reader and a member of the zine community is more than just a chance association. They actually have quite a few things in common. This group personal "weird in a white, middle class yet pleasantly random sort of way" zine is a good example. Four men talk about comic strips, the golden path to graduation, daytime TV (a popular activity for them while anticipating graduation), hanging out and meeting (or trying to meet) women, and serious rants about Japan from their correspondent over there. They hold **Calvin and Hobbes** in great esteem, rate the desirability level of anthropomorphic cartoon femmes (I imagine they would admire Jessica Rabbit), breakfast cereals, more comic strips (and the plots behind them — ever wonder about the family in the syndicated **Fox Trot** or **Adam**?) and women (either domestic or imported coverage from the guy in Japan). There's also good advice for those post-adolescents trying to make it through high school and college from some men who've been there. These pages would make a good time capsule addition to any study of white middle-class post-adolescent America.

THE UNDERGROUND S-CENSORED
Free from Greg Carden, 7216 Briarcliff Drive, Springfield, VA 22153

One of the classic examples of the personal zine and of the kind of passion that causes a person to start one. In the great tradition of underground high school newsletters, this one comes from a student who *already graduated* from the school and is *still* trying to raise its consciousness. Everyone from Eugene Debs to "Bob" Dobbs has their say in here and it usually ends with an ardent call to stand up for your beliefs and

* *

The only thing that's the end of the world is the end of the world.

```
MATH I LEARNED IN HIGH SCHOOL:

There are 3,500 calories in a pound.
If I consume 1,200 calories per day
for seven days, I will lose 2 pounds.
If I lose 2 pounds per week for 10
weeks...I might get a boyfriend.

Remembering the focus of those "bad
old days" makes me glad to be far
removed from the trauma of adolescence.
But I wonder if things have gotten any
better for today's teens.  In 1991,
does being in high school and not con-
forming to certain body types condemn
young women to four years without a
coed social life? After all these
years?  I can only hope not.
```

* *

thoughts. It's a pretty freewheeling venture, printing everything from essays on the cliques at school to Discordian propaganda. Very often you'll find a blank page inserted as a way of hinting at reader participation. Nonetheless, this is a single person's praiseworthy effort.

UNSETTLED
$1 from Donald J. Morrison, PO Box 562, Columbia Station, OH 44028-0562

Donald J. Morrison's is an example of the quintessential personal zine: he just sits down at the typewriter and lets it all spew out. Read about the movies he watched (and hated) recently, his shopping trips, his very own recipe for stage blood, the feeling of being late in putting out the issue, his auditions for coveted theater parts. Donald is not your average zinester — he's much more classically cultured and much more in tune with the higher art forms (but he never lets himself get away from the more, shall we say, *frivolous* artistic pursuits). He shares thoughts on **Rocky and Bullwinkle**, lays out his plans for the Warner Bros. cartoon characters to star in **Les Miserables**, which he knows backwards and forwards. He also buys a lot of videos — and feels the pain of regret after each clunker. His worldly manner and total devotion to the arts makes his ‘zine more of a primer of the arts than just a journal, though he's not a loner by any means. The man has minor anxiety attacks when he doesn't get any mail and feels pangs of guilt over missing his self-imposed deadline. A thespian with a flair for the written word.

I ended up making blood bladders for the play I'm in, and I had to search through back issues...
DON'S BLOOD RECIPE
1 1/2 cups of clear Karo syrup
1/2 cup of warm water
4 Tablespoons of red food coloring
12 drops of green food coloring

WATLEY-BROWNE REVIEW
SASE and a stamp from Kali Amanda Browne, 451 64th St., Brooklyn, NY 11220-4916

We've received only the premiere issue of this perzine, but it demands attention in a big way. The first is a pretty impressive issue from a savvy and hip young woman in New York. Editor Kali takes on the burden of sassing the NYC government, the brouhaha over the "Mother Of All Parades," new subject headings to be found at the library (would you believe "Dreadlocks" and "Chinese American Bullfighters" to name a couple?), the evil conspiracy behind white rap music and the misunderstood hepness of J. Danforth Quayle (she has him auditioning for Spike Lee's next venture). A personal zine that you can't get quite as close to as others in the genre, due mainly to her independent nature. This is one to read, not necessarily to join — but that's only a guesstimate. Thoroughly enjoyable hip whatnot, Kali could easily replace the droning morning TV commentators with her pizazz and slightly askew reality.

Curiously enough, the parallels to Vanilla Ice and new World Language Ethic don't quite end there. I wonder, when Saddam Hussein alluded to the "Mother of all Wars," did he mean the same Mother Ice is talking about when he says "Word to your mother"...Is this "Mother" the same I've heard some mention at the height of passion: as in "Oh, Mother of God!!" Does this have anything to do with the Mother Goose-izatition of Park Slope, Chelsea and SoHo? Puzzling, is it not?...'Course, there are no easy answers to any of these questions. However, it does seem obviously clear that the World is indeed changing...

Science Fiction

Science fiction fandom is one of the longest-lasting subcultures in zinedom, and the one to which many other types of zines can trace their roots. Thom Digby once described a science fiction fan as a person who used to like to read science fiction who likes to hang around with other people who used to read science fiction. In the same way, many SF zines are not about SF, but about the personal lives of their publishers or the state of the world. But despite this many SF fans are perfectly happy to remain within their own subculture. This seems to be changing slowly as a new generation of ziners arises, moving from interest to interest as the mood strikes them. In this section we'll look at some of the zines that are rooted in the science fiction world, and yet open to those outside of this world.

NOVOID
$2 or "The Usual" from Colin Hinz, ASFi Editions, PO Box 161, Orillia, Ontario, CANADA L3V 6H9.

Colin is a fan of many interests. In some ways, as the heady smell of Gestetner mimeograph ink from his zines indicates, he is the very model of the traditional SF fan, cranking out his work by hand and eschewing the modern photocopy shop. Yet he's also interested in mail art and new music and the zine world outside of the SF subculture. Add a heavy dose of dry wit and you have a typical issue of **Novoid**. Every issue is a riot of multicolored mimeography, fabulous artwork, and articles about publishing, politics and even science fiction. A classy zine with modern interests that has not abandoned its rich history.

Frankly, once you've seen hydraulic monsters stalk and spit flame at each other five or six times, you've seen all there is to see. This is the problem of such a spectacle: You have to increase the noise and onslaught by geometric proportions just to maintain interest. We're addicted to spectacle by our passive absorption of intrusive media. Something apparently simpler but ultimately more challenging is really more dangerous; a writer like Jim Thompson at his best, for instance. Jane, who had fewer preconceptions, felt an immense exhilaration at the gouting flames and explosions. Like seeing another kid get away with something forbidden, she knows enough about engineering to have a good idea what it took to make the machines act the way they did, and appreciated that in the same sense a painter might appreciate the brushstrokes on an otherwise failed canvas.

NEOLOGY
C$3.28 in Canada, C$3.50 in USA from ESFACAS, Box 4071, Postal Station South Edmonton, Edmonton, Alberta, CANADA T6E 4S8.

Neology is one of the longest-running clubzines around — that is, a zine produced by (and often largely for) the members of a particular fan group, in this case the Edmonton Science Fiction and Comic Arts Society. They report on science fiction conventions, review books and zines and roleplaying games, and do a certain amount of club business (though like most SF groups ESFACAS is rather laid-back, or even disorganized, in that department). They also print some poetry and short stories and letters from readers.

NOVA EXPRESS
$10/4 issues from PO Box 27231, Austin, TX 78755-2231.

Nova Express is focused on the literary side of the science fiction field, featuring serious talks with authors and solidly polished fiction in its mix. They have done excellent service in compiling bibliographies to go with their interviews, and rise above the usual chit-chat to ask questions getting at the heart of the creative impulse. They also review books on the cutting edge, trying to see where the field is going and why. But never fear, **Nova Express** also retains a sense of humor; a recent subscription offer threatened to unleash the brain of L. Ron Hubbard (preserved in a jar) on the world if they didn't get enough response. A very satisfying read for the lover of good fiction and good writers.

Also I believe there is a certain latent stability to culture. I have a hard time believing that twenty years from now everything is going to be completely changed, because we've gone through periods of upheaval, the Sixties for example, and thought, "My God, history's accelerating and everything's going to change" and then years pass and you realize that actually people are still much the same: couples get married, they bring up children. Religions have a remarkable resilience. Our lives have deep structural similarities to lives in the Thirties, the nineteenth century, all the way back to the savannah. This despite great technological change. It's scary, this inertia, in some respects, because there are things that must change if we're going to survive the next century. But in other respects it can be comforting.

AGONIZER
$10 from Sue Frank, 2508 Pine St., Philadelphia, PA 19103.

Surely **Star Trek** is one of the best-known science fiction works in the world. It's not surprising that there are a lot of fanzines out there devoted to one or another aspect of that show and the universe that it has created. This is one of the most amazing of the bunch, a huge (some issues weigh over a pound) zine for Klingons. These people are *serious*, as one look at the alien script and color photos of them in costume will tell you. Here you'll find notes on Klingon society and weaponry, serious discussions of honor among Klingons, debates on the activities of the Klingon Strike Force, and so on. They get into activities like conventions and blood drives, write stirring communiques, and generally seem to be having a lot of fun. The **Star Trek** universe long ago escaped from the control of its creators; now it's a part of popular culture, and as the **Agonizer** attests, it is popular indeed.

FOSFAX
$2 from FOSFA, PO Box 37281, Louisville, KY 40233-7281.

This is the clubzine of the Falls of the Ohio Science Fiction and Fantasy Association — but that's like saying that **Time** magazine is designed for people in New York City. **Fosfax** has encouraged the art of the loc (Letter Of Comment) to an amazing degree, and its pages are filled with missives by professional writers as well as fans. Each issue starts off with a few articles to stir the pot, dealing with fan politics, new books, scientific discoveries and core science fiction topics. But halfway through the zine it's turned over to the letter writers, some of whom have been cheerfully arguing with all comers for years now. Writing letters is one of the easiest ways to get involved in the zine world, and **Fosfax** is one of the most exhilarating places to get started.

WHAT'S REALLY WRONG WITH THE PRESS (and the rest of the media and a lot of corporations and your elected officials): They think they are a lot more sophisticated than you are. They often <u>believe</u> they are to the left of the general public when they are actually right of center.

They think anything they like is over your head. Network executives were shown MONTY PYTHON'S FLYING CIRCUS back when it was still being made here, thought it was brilliant, but insisted that, see, they were really very sophisticated, but most Americans weren't sharp enough to appreciate it. The press think they are the only people in the country, except for maybe a few professional feminists and lesbians, who believe that maybe women and men ought to get paid the same for the same work, or that daycare might not necessarily be a commie plot — and it's a shame the rest of you are too ignorant to figure that out. Your elected officials are afraid that if they mention Albania, you'll think they're some sort of over-educated rarefied pretentious intellectual. TIME deliberately waters down the contents in its US editions because (as it says right here in the editorial of last week's issue on Germany), Europeans are so much more sophisticated about world affairs than most Americans so, you see, Americans won't appreciate this. (Not, possibly, because they've never even heard about half this stuff, since it's only here in the strange country of Not The US that the TV news and daily papers even bother to mention the existence of some of these countries?)

SCIENCE FICTION EYE
$10/3 issues from PO Box 43244, Washington, DC 20010-9244.

Cyberpunk is currently one of the hottest "movements" in the world of professional science fiction, and (despite the bold heading "BEYOND CYBERPUNK" on one issue) **Science Fiction Eye** has developed a reputation as the place to read about this movement. They go for serious articles and literary criticism, but mix this with flashy artwork and the occasional bit of sheer critical nastiness. Their interests extend beyond SF to "slipstream" literature — novels of the fantastic whatever rubric they may be published under. Recent topics have included the potential links between cyberpunk and feminism, the flaws of "Hippies in Space" novels, and the state of SF critical theory itself. Sometimes the

writers here seem to forget that not everyone shares their obsession for developing the One True Literary Theory, but by and large every issue of **SF Eye** is an exciting foray into new worlds of literature.

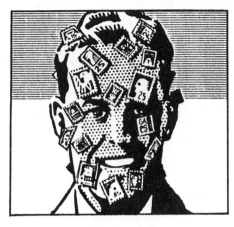

SCIENCE FICTION CHRONICLE
$27/yr from PO Box 2730, Brooklyn, NY 11202-0056.

Regularly published for over a decade now, and nominated ten times for the prestigious Hugo Award, **SF Chronicle** has made itself the essential magazine of record for the science fiction community. Books and magazines are paramount here, with guides to currently published fiction and cover photographs in every issue and lots of short reviews. But they also track the people of this community, reporting on births and deaths, sales and radio broadcasts, conventions and other events. Even lists of fan and pro birthdays and photos of faces to go with familiar names appear here, helping provide the social glue necessary to hold the subculture together. No serious reader of the genre can afford to pass this one up.

STAR*LINE
$10/yr from Chuck and Susan Noe Rothman, 2012 Pyle Road, Scenectady, NY 12303.

This is the newsletter of the Science Fiction Poetry Association, a group devoted to that particular combination of genre and form. They split their contents three ways, between market notes, critical essays, and of course the poems themselves. They also sponsor the an-

nual Rhysling Awards for the best in the field, and publish an anthology of the nominees and award winners.

NEW AGERS ON MARS

Three had been there before,
in their astral bodies.
The trip over
gave them
great opportunities
for group meditation
now that
NASA
had legalized futons.

After
some light chanting
("This place does
great things for your
red chakras, man.")
it was off
to Olympus Mons
to see the ancient
bridge supports
expertly disguised
as natural rock formations

Todd Mecklem

PENGUIN DIP
$15/10 issues from Stephen H. Dorneman, 94 Eastern Ave. #1, Malden, MA 02148.

To take a metaphor suggested by the title, **Penguin Dip** is a mix of fish and fowl — or, in this case, science fiction fandom

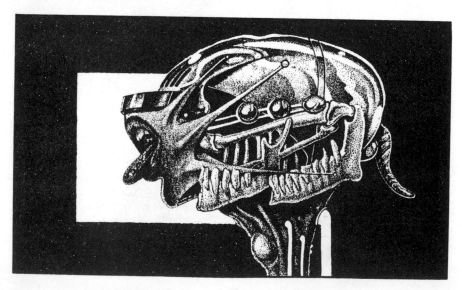

and the postal gaming hobby. Originally inspired by the board game Diplomacy, postal gamers are people who conduct incredibly complicated simulations by mail, with a zine often acting as the central linking point between players. This explains why the back end of **Penguin Dip** is filled with such abstruse notations as "**Russia (Nash)** A Mos-Ukr, A Waar-Gal, F StP(sc)-Bot, F Sev-Rum" and notes from player to player like "Can anyone be trusted? How about for one turn? One half a turn? One army's movement?" The front half of the zine, on the other hand, is more traditionally in the SF zine mold, with letters, book reviews, refrigerator repairs and whatever else catches Stephen's eye.

How to Afford Overseas Vacations
1) Don't get married. For some of you, this may be good advice much too late. For the rest, marriage costs money. I can understand the attraction of getting laid every night, or whatever frequency of sex you have. But consider the virtues of inflatable dolls, vibrators, and other masturbation devices.
2) If you must get married, don't have children. Again, I realize this is easier said than done. My own vasectomy operation was the best $100 investment in my life. I have saved thousands of dollars in child-support payments and other related expenses.
3) Consider sharing an apartment or house, rather than living alone. This can reduce your monthly rent by at least one-half.

4) Don't buy a TV. Period. If you do, sooner or later you will be buying videos, and they cost money. So do Nintendo games and other add-ons to your TV system.
5) Don't even THINK of having any kind of home computer system. If you doubt the wisdom of this, ask a friend you can trust for the _real_ cost of their computer systems after such things as phone bills, software costs, maintenance, and so on.
6) Work overtime, if you have a Union that enforces the time-and-a-half rule for overtime over 40 hours a week.

MIMOSA
$2 or "The Usual" from Dick & Nicki Lynch, PO Box 1270, Germantown, MD 20875.

Even while some SF fans (focused narrowly on their own publishing world) lament the death of the fanzine, zines like **Mimosa** are keeping alive fifty years of fan history. Dick and Nicki go so far as to mimeograph their zine on Twiltone paper, a rough-textured sheet that was used by many classic zines in the field. The contents are a wealth of references that will be as obscure to outsiders as they are delightful to insiders: propellor beanies, "First Fandom," Tuckerization and more. But **Mimosa** is not meant to be an insiders' zine so much as an introduction to the field; in articles and interviews with some of Fandom's Elders, they explore the traditions that have made fandom great, and invite newcomers to join in.

EDGE DETECTOR
$2.50 from 1850 Lincoln Ave. #803, Montreal, Quebec, CANADA H3H 1H4.

This "Magazine of Speculative Fiction" does a great job of exploring the ideas of technology as tool for liberation and threat to survival. Mixing traditional SF, cyberpunk, and wild comics, the authors and artists here create complex and engaging worldscapes to explore. Along the way they also print book reviews and explore topics such as cryonic preservation that promise (or threaten) to bring science fiction into the commonplace. An idea-oriented zine for the technophiliacs among us.

RADIO FREE THULCANDRA
$3 or "The Usual" from Marty Helgesen, 11 Lawrence Ave., Malverne, NY 11565-1406

This is a zine for Christian Fandom, "an interdenominational fellowship of Christians and Science Fiction Fans interested in the courteous and accurate representation of Christian viewpoints in the fannish community." Marty conducts **RFT** primarily as a letterzine, a continuing exchange of comments among many contributors interwoven with his own viewpoints. Doctrinal controversy is discouraged, the question being whether SF stories portraying Christians are doing a good job, not whether the particular doctrine being portrayed is right.

THE NEW MOON DIRECTORY
$3.75 from Eric L. Watts, 346 Carpenter Dr. #51, Atlanta, GA 30328-5030

This is the latest incarnation of a service-oriented zine that's been passed down through a number of different editors. What **NMD** does is keep track of apas — amateur press associations -- which are zines written collectively by "members" who send their material into a "central mailer" who returns finished sets to them. Each annual issue lists well over 100 of these participatory zines with full directions on getting involved on your own. Subjects span the range from science fiction to comics to music to origami.

PERIPHERAL VISIONS
$2 from Rob Sommers, 926-C Waverly Way NE, Atlanta, GA 30307-2551

A zine from the small but feisty fan community of Atlanta, which has been enlivened by fresh blood (including Rob's) recently. He prints short fiction (though a recent "finish the story" contest didn't do all that well), convention reports, and zine reviews, along with the traditional locs and articles. An easygoing zine, fun to read and with some good though rough-edged fiction in it.

YHOS
$2.00 or "The Usual" from Art Widner, PO Box 677, Gualala, CA 95445

Art has been around fandom for a long long time, and he's still publishing a very friendly, traditional fanzine, full of his own life, fandom, and other goodies. You'll find fan fiction here, history of fandom, and one of the most diverse letter columns around. Everything from words to chili seems to interest Art, and he makes them interesting to his readers as well.

Hobbies & Collecting

Some people have private hobbies. Other people love their hobbies so much they are compelled to write about them and find others who want to read about them. Still others find groups of people who enjoy the same hobby and then everyone can write about it. If there's a collector or aficionado of almost anything out there, then there's the need for a zine.

DECALCOMANIA
$1.25 from DecalcoMania Club, PO Box 126, Lincroft, NJ 07738

The newsletter of a club for radio fans, specifically those who collect radio paraphernalia and promotional items. There's an emphasis on stickers and "airchecks" (recordings designed to show the character of a station), market news and assorted radio whatnot. You'll always find some new promo items listed, some swapping of info on stats, and music polls. Tips for those who want to join in are easily available. Past issues have given us such articles as the "Care and Feeding of a Promo Collection," a nostalgic look back to 1990, and a column about the Australian radio scene.

Have you ever noticed how some towns are sticker towns and some towns aren't? I have had the experience with most markets that I've visited that either most of the stations DO have stickers, or most of them DON'T. I almost never find a town where I get about 50% success. F'rinstance -- Las Vegas, San Francisco, Tulsa, Waterloo (Iowa), Detroit, Boston, Lexington (Kentucky), El Paso, Burlington (Vermont), and Cleveland are all sticker towns. Toledo, Cheyenne, Montpelier, and Columbus (Ohio) aren't. Had any similar experiences?

THE POSTCARD EXAMINER
$1.25 from Ann Rusnak, PO Box 4177, Carson City, NV 89702

A zine for the collector of postcards, of course, but also a friendly newsletter bringing a whole lot of like-minded people together. Ann prints contact addresses for fellow hobbyists, discusses (and sometimes reprints) new and unusual finds in the field, chats about National Postcard Week and lists some of the cards she has for sale herself. In some instances the collector is also the producer of a postcard and will get some space devoted to their works. An age-old hobby with some contemporary ideas.

DISASTER POSTCARDS: March 13, 1990: a tornado roared thru Hesston, KS. A dramatic continental chrome by Avery Postcards of Wichita shows the dark funnel over an industrial neighborhood. Sent by Margaret Pittman of Kansas. Hal Ottoway adds that 15,000 were printed in the first edition, but the card was so popular that 60,000 more had to be printed. Avery made a big donation to the Hesston Relief Effort.
October 17, 1989: the Santa Cruz (San Francisco) earthquake awakened a new postcard interest for Max Toorop. Max mailed chromes of the Bay Bridge the

They Came to Mentor, Drawn Like Lemmings… They Left Overdrawn Like Donald Trump

I will always smile when I think of Mentor. The largest gathering of PEZ collectors ever assembled! Virtually every rare PEZ dispenser on display! Hundreds and hundreds of dispensers for sale—sometimes for hundreds and hundreds of dollars! The fun of meeting people I had only spoken to by telephone—the adventure of roaming the halls and finding other PEZ fanatics—the excitement of the air conditioner breaking down in the dealer room!

I arrived at the hotel Friday evening and met PEZ freaks before I even got inside. Once I checked in, I came back down to the lobby, just in time to meet Jan and Dean (*Surf City, Dead Man's Curve*, etc.) as they were checking in. I started roaming the halls and learned the first cardinal rule of the Dispens-O-Rama: If you don't stay at the hotel on Friday night, you only get half the convention! It was a brand-new experience to walk down the hall, see an open door, enter and find PEZ for sale, trade or just for show. Thousands of dollars and hundreds of dispensers changed hands in the rooms that night and trading was still going on at 2:00 a.m. when I called it quits.

Saturday morning, the dealer room opened at eight and soon there were 14 tables full of cool stuff for the PEZzant. One of the few complaints about the convention was that non-dealers could not get into the hall until noon. I allowed about two hours too long for set-up time, a situation

The Optimistic PEZZIMIST   **July 1991**

day after the quake, telling friends he was okay. Now he has found two continental chrome commemoratives ....A dramatic multiview shows the broken bridge, the viaduct of death and two views of tumbled homes.

OPTIMISTIC PEZZIMIST
$3.00 from Mike Robertson, PO Box 606, Dripping Springs, TX 78620

This is a fanzine for the Pez enthusiast — you know, those wonderful candy dispensers you used to beg your mother to buy you at the checkout counter in a supermarket. Well, you shouldn't be sur-

prised to learn that Pez freaks abound and this is the place they meet. If you're one of them, you too can swap collecting stories, find out about auctions, where you can find Pez, discover ways to build a showcase for your collection and if you're lucky enough, get yourself profiled within these pages. There are also notes on new markets, articles such as "Pez That Never Were" (showing dispenser hopefuls such as Pee Wee Herman and Freddy Krueger), and all kinds of other Pezaphilia. Now that you're old enough to buy your own Pez go ahead and do it and find yourself in very good company.

Although most of the "remakes" of PEZ dispensers have involved licensed characters, there are some curious variations of other dispensers. For instance, the Elephant, one of the Circus series, seems an unlikely candidate for much variation. Most common is the Elephant...frequently found with an orange head, green tongue and blue, flat-topped round hat. Less common is the version with a Chico Marx-type hat...which is found in several other colors. Perhaps the rarest of the Elephants is the one...which seems to be wearing a wig of some sort. This one has a yellow face and the pachyderm's toupee is a reddish-brown. This may be a case of using up spare parts by the PEZ company, but I don't know of another dispenser which features a hair-do quite like this one. Any other variations?

GREEN PRINTS
$3.50 from PO Box 1355, Fairview, NC 28730

A lovely diversion into the world of gardening and botany and its relation to real life. Articles and editorials represent true stories and advice, but they always somehow lead one to think that there is much more to loving a garden than just soiled gloves. There's also a spiritual and personal quality to it, mixing gardens with literary efforts. They write about the joys and frustrations of gardening, the love of the land, the people involved and what to expect and hope for from your garden. This is definitely the gardener's diary of experience, thoughts and emotions, with some helpful hints and warm stories.

Saturday's garden cleanup never got finished because I spent more time on recollections than on physical labor. The outside temperature was almost 60 degrees when I went forth with wheelbarrow and tools to lift out the rest of the frost-killed plants. Wind and rain had stripped the peak of autumn color from the trees, but in the sunshine, the warm rust of the oak leaves and the bright yellow of poplars still gave a gold October glow to the whole valley. My vegetable garden is more than a

No. 3 $2.50   AUTUMN 1990

GREEN PRINTS
CHASING THE SOUL OF GARDENING

important projects, to always shoot from your heart and not your pocketbook, to shoot with reckless abandon whenever the need arises, to say nice things to small and old peoples, to wash the dishes at least once a week, to continue to photograph through the storms of indignation and arrive at a cafe that serves hot bagels, to daily forge ahead with camera in hand with a new vitality and inner strength, to sometimes be able to throw guilt to the winds and leave your family for a day of photographing, to have a positive outlook on your road of life and to listen to music that inspires, preferably via portable cassette player while making pictures of the ones you love in the cool twilight.

good day to you, reader of fine foto fanzines. This here is the 20th issue of the magazine that you just can't put down, the journal that won't go away and is definately here to stay. SHOTS twenty is dedicated to a girl photographer from NEW YORK named Sylvia Plachy. She has been the SHOTS spiritual advisor for many years, shoots wonderfully moving pictures with her large assortment of cameras and has a NEW book coming out this fall called UNGUIDED TOUR. She is definately one cool lady. Way cool says Shilo Rose, who's sitting beside me now eating a YELLOW Banana....

plot of land where I grow food. This hilltop space helped me overcome inertia, insomnia, and depression. To begin a new way of living.

SHOTS
$2.50 from Daniel Price, PO Box 109, Joseph, OR 97846

Shots is for the photographer in all of us, using words and pictures to convey a lot of flavor of life in this big wooly wonderful world. The photos here are by real people, using everything from dinky plastic cameras to fancy set ups (and yes, there is some tech talk here, but not

much) and it's all tied together by Dan's backwoodsy, fun and rambling words, announcements and drawings of petroglyphs. A wonderful magazine of honest contemporary photos, printed on chummy newsprint, from plain folks not struggling for prizes, but actually trying to take interesting pictures.

cre - do:

...to illuminate and rejuvenate. to inspire great visions of truth and reveal injustices, to boldly go where no other photographers have gone before, to stand your ground even when mad dogs are biting at your feets, to find open roads to drive down to think of new and

Potpourri — I

The most striking feature of zines is their diversity. This very diversity makes it very hard to get a comprehensive feel for what's going on out there. While some categories do stand out (you'll find them in the rest of this book), many zines remain stubbornly unpigeonholable. This section (and several more later on) is for these weird zines, the one-of-a-kind productions that liven up any mailbox they happen to land in. And remember, for every one we review, there are dozens more just waiting to be discovered, on every subject you can possibly imagine.

MAWEWI
$10/6 issues from Adastra West, PO Box 874, Mahwah, NJ 07430

A selection of light information, astronomy, ecology, current events, social trends and more, all in a friendly, breezy style. These folks collect facts and put them together for those who need a bit of amusement or distraction; one obvious resting place for the zine is the nearest bathroom, for visiting royalty to read while on the throne. Educational and fun at the same time.

Words We Don't Really Need in English
Farhvergnugen (German)
Literally, "driving pleasure."
Do you speak Volkswagen? Do you feel the need to learn a German expression when an English one conveys the same concept? No doubt VW's marketing department was inspired by the success of its original name here — surely more people bought Volkswagens than would have wanted to acquire a "people's car" — but the least they could do is teach us the right pronunciation.

LIZZENGREASY
$2 (no checks) from Dai Ni Kuroda Kopo 203, Funabashi 5-30-6, Setagaya-Ku, Tokyo 156, JAPAN

Named after editors Liz Stumps and Greasy Fletcher, this is a zine written by American expatriates living in Japan. They do a delightful job of chronicling Japanese culture and society for we outsiders, as well as reviewing the occasional US book or record which wanders into their offices. Whether it's Japanese eating habits or the Tokyo public transit system or the fish around the Imperial Palace, you're sure to find wonderful things you never knew about before here.

If we could have come up with some more money when we bought our scanner, Susan would have had an easier time of it. When we got the scanner, however, we could only afford the smallest, hand-held model. If we had sprung for a full-page model, Susan wouldn't have had to slide slices of graphics around to make full-size ones and the magazine probably would have come out a week earlier.
Actually, if we'd just junked the scanner and pasted photocopies of the candy packages to the boards we would have saved a solid fortnight. All we'd have had to do was walk down to the Sun Chain convenience store, dropped Y100 or so into the machine for the copies, and cut and pasted for 40 minutes or so. One wonders why we went through all the aggravation of trying to scan too-large pictures, especially considering that we had to edit half of them pixel-

by-pixel because shaky hands and reflective originals had fouled up the graphic files.

Aside from general stupidity and pig-headedness, I can think of no cause other than our very possession of this here computer. We've got it, so we've got to use it, even if it takes longer than doing it the scissors-and-coin-fed photocopier way. In short, having the computer (which we bought to save time) drives us to use it for everything possible, even if it isn't too well-suited to it. Our intent was to save effort and money by using this thing: we've ended up spending more of both since we got it.

THE DROOD REVIEW OF MYSTERY
$20/12 issues from PO Box 8872, Boston, MA 02114

Like to read mystery novels? Then you should check out this zine for the connoisseur of the genre. Drood's staff ably reviews a batch of new mysteries in every issue, dividing their space between short capsule reviews and longer essays covering more than one work. There's also twice-annual listings of forthcoming books. coverage of important genre conventions, and more.

FUGITIVE POPE
$1 cash or stamps from Raleigh Clayton Muns, 7351-A Burrwood Dr., St. Louis, MO 63121

Life as a librarian need not be terminally dull, as Raleigh proves over and over again in these pages. He recounts strange questions encountered at the reference desk, gives us glimpses of what it's really like in librarian school and suggests ways to discourage masturbation in the stacks. Along the way, bits and pieces of obscure writing are dropped in — almost as much fun as finding them serendipitously among the stacks.

THE PEACEMAKER
$10/yr donation from PO

Box 627, Garberville, CA 95440

This tabloid for people who believe in dedicating their lives to peace, even in the face of a non-peaceful society, has been around for decades and continues going strong. They offer ideas and support for those who engage in nonviolent resistance to the government, from tax avoidance to Plowshares actions (the destruction of military property as a form of witness). There are surely some saints lurking in these pages.

We must continue to press for the admission into our courtrooms of the Nuremberg Principles and International Law. If a court of justice is not the proper forum to advance arguments based on conscience, morality, and principles of international law to defend nonviolent civil resistance actions, then that egregiously illustrates how much ugliness of a barren world, where power and might make right, still predominates. Ironically, this inability to distinguish between the maliciousness or virtue of the goals of our actions is indicative of exactly the type of nihilistic, amoral, solipsistic thinking that existed in Weimar Germany in the 1920's and gave birth to Nazi Germany in the 1930's.

A LONG CYCLE OBSERVER
$36/12 issues from Andrew Ralph, PO Box 4132, White River Junction, VT 05001

A financial newsletter for those interested in exploring the idea of "wave" theory — the notion that there are well-defined long-term cycles which largely govern the behavior of financial markets. Andrew is not a True Believer, but an intrigued Fellow Investigator, looking to share information and check premises with those similarly interested. Reasonably priced and well-written too, unlike most financial advice newsletters out there.

We're a smarter, better-informed and more sophisticated bunch than our poor benighted predecessors in France and England the the Netherlands. Where they could only encompass one mania per country, and those for only a couple of years at a time, we've been running two manias at once, and have kept the ball rolling for a decade, on top of becoming the world's biggest debtor nation and some other follies, and we're only now starting to notice something's wrong. Do we credit progress, or American know-how?
Our manias have been the tangible assets mania, the best-recognized part of which was the real estate mania, and the corporate takeover, or leveraged buyout mania.

THE GAME'S AFOOT
$2.50 from Zirlinson Publications, 1447 Treat Blvd., Walnut Creek, CA 94596

A zine for role-playing gamers, which focuses more on running good games than on any particular system. You've probably heard of the original role-playing game (RPG) Dungeons & Dragons, but there are a lot more of them these days. The best RPGs are run more as interactive stories than anything else, and there's a talent for running them that the authors here try to encourage. Very worthwhile reading for all those involved in the hobby.

SIDNEY SUPPEY'S QUARTERLY AND CONFUSED PET MONTHLY
$2 from Candi Strecker, 590 Lisbon, San Francisco, CA 94112

Candi has been zining for a long long time, and her idiosyncratic interests continue to provide some of the funnest reading around. From thrift shops to virtual reality, computer games to 70' nostalgia, she doesn't seem to be able to write an uninteresting sentence. She's been exploring "lowlife scum" interests, those bits of hip culture shared by many people on the fringes, for as long as I can remember, and I hope she continues to do so for a long time to come. Sheerly enjoyable commentary on the craziness of life. Also available for $4 is the first installment of "It's A Wonderful Lifestyle," Candi's encyclopedic look at pop culture during the "Avocado Decade," a time which it is only now becoming popular to engage in nostalgia over. You can catch the leading edge with this wonderful zine.

Pure communication of true selves requires trust, and I see no reason to think virtual beings will prove more trustworthy than flesh ones, especially when using a medium that, in a sense, is founded on lying. VR may be a safe playground for the moment, when it's only accessible to a few hundred hand-picked people. But the dark aspect of human nature that makes us stomp on each others' sand castles — call it Original Sin, or Will to Power, or selfishness, or crime, or irresponsibility — won't be kept out for long. Perhaps the more dismal possibilities of VR get overlooked because of the reassuring way that virtual acts lack physical consequences, You can tumble your virtual panda-body over Niagara Falls, or send your 747-body crashing in flames over and over again, without damaging your flesh body out there in the real world. But just because acts don't have physical consequences doesn't mean they have no consequences at all. Quickly enough, people will discover how to use the pretty fictions of VR to cheat, slander,

THE OFFICAL STORY WAS THAT JOHN HINCKLEY SHOT PRESIDENT REAGAN TO IMPRESS ACTRESS JODIE FOSTER... IN REALITY, HE WAS OBSESSED WITH BEATRIX POTTER.....

commit virtual rape. Then the virtual world will need all the unpleasant unfree things we have in the real world: rules, laws, police, punishments. I'm particularly troubled by the claims that in VR-land, the people who will be most prized are those with the "most interesting personality." What kinds of people are known for their ability to project a seductive personality? Automobile salesmen, con artists and psychopaths.

NEWS OF THE WEIRD
$10/7 issues from Chuck Shepherd, PO Box 57141, Washington, DC 20037

With three books in print on the subject, Chuck is the pre-eminent weirdologist in the world today. That is, he collects true but bizarre stories from newspapers and magazines, and puts them together in this 4-page zine as an almost overwhelming cascade of wild human behavior. It's hard to believe in a normal world for long after reading a few of these; a real dose of surreality to liven up any humdrum life.

Jason Ray William was sentenced to 90 days in jail in Houston for pleading guilty to shoplifting a $150 ferret from a pet store by putting the animal down his pants and trying to walk out. The arresting officer said he remembered frisking William just a few weeks previous after a report of a suspicious person and

THIS LATE NIGHT SNACK WAS ORDERED BY JOHN WILKES BOOTH FROM ROOM SERVICE THE NIGHT BEFORE THE FATAL PERFORMANCE...

had found a 4-foot python wrapped around William's leg....In March in New York City, Aundray Burns, 26, making a getaway from what police speculated was a crime scene, leaped into the nearest open car and tried to get control of the steering wheel from the driver, yelling, "I gotta go! I gotta go!" The car was a well-marked New York Transit Authority police car, and the driver, Officer Daniel Daly, was in uniform....

POPULAR LIFE
$2 from Lamar, 105 Belmont St., Rochester, NY 14620

A collection of collages and altered advertisements from the past. If there's a single theme here, it's the silliness of our consumer's society, from get-rich-quick schemes to the bowels of fashion. It's a light touch look at modern culture with slices of Americana as seen through those ad campaigns of the past: housewives attached to vacuum cleaners; mail order "micro-fluff," a centerfold with identity-changing glasses to cut out and assemble; making toast pop up properly. They've recently started to add new features, one of them being a NYC report and some recent fashions out of L.A. Scuba diving is explored (one of the undersung cool sports), the urban toothbrush legend puts in an appearance, and what would a modern culture zine be without mention of Spam? (It gets "honorable mention" here.)

MOTORBOOTY
$3 from PO Box 7944, Ann Arbor, MI 48107

A zine of the finer things in life — like rock music, weird artwork, drugs, comics and rebellious youth. Tongue firmly in cheek, they've been known to make fun of the latest hip cultural icons (their Matt Groening spoof was hilarious if possibly actionable) and puncture a lot of balloons along the way. The perfect zine for a sixpack of beer and a long antisocial afternoon.

RURAL SOUTHERN VOICE FOR PEACE
$1 from 1898 Hannah Branch Rd., Burnsville, NC 28714

These people are earnestly trying to urge the world towards peace, justice, and global health. They pass on a lot of information on peace actions, international work, community conflict resolution, and similar activities. Relentlessly hopeful and nonviolent, their commitment comes through on every page.

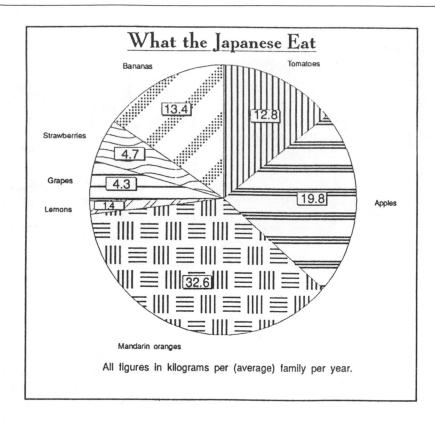

What the Japanese Eat

Bananas — 13.4
Strawberries — 4.7
Grapes — 4.3
Lemons — 14
Tomatoes — 12.8
Apples — 19.8
Mandarin oranges — 32.6

All figures in kilograms per (average) family per year.

THE SACRED COW SIG NEWSLETTER
$1.50 from Barbara Koksal, 3392 Clemens Dr., St. Charles, MO 63301

A "SIG" is a Special Interest Group of MENSA, the organization for high-IQ people, but in this case everyone can join in the fun. The fun consists of wide-open, no holds barred debates — racism, sexism, anti-Semitism and all sorts of other usually forbidden political and social views pop up. Generally the discussion remains friendly, though it is obvious that some of the writers here hate one another pretty deeply. A good zine to dip cautiously into if you enjoy having your own prejudices challenged by articulate proponents of opposing views.

I'm a "racist" because I believe that there are differences among the races of men, and that is is not immoral to discuss these differences. I'm "sexist" because I believe that there are significant differences between men as a group and women as a group, and that ignoring these differences is not only an act of studied ignorance, but a hindrance to the happiness of both sexes.

I'm "anti-Semitic" because I believe that it is not immoral to question the actions of Israel or to debate whether the Holocaust existed, but that it IS immoral for self-appointed Jewish "defenders" to commit arson and assault against those who raise such questions. I'm "fascist" because I believe people have the right to use whatever force is required to defend themselves. I'm "elitist" because I believe that merit and personal charity should be the only criteria for dispensing the rewards of life. I'm "selfish" because I believe that if everybody looks after Number One, then Number Two will very rarely need assistance. I'm "greedy" because I believe that every man has a right to profit by the sweat of his brow and the force of his intelligence. I'm "anti-labor" because I believe that labor and business are just two economic interests which should be permitted to slug it out in a free market without government intervention. I'm a "warmonger" because I believe that the best way to prevent war is to be militarily strong. And I'm "heartless" because I don't think that is is good to feed millions of starving now only so they can turn into billions of starving later.
*But on the other hand I'm **NOT** a conservative because I don't believe that is is the province of government to*

regulate the substances people put into their bodies or the information which they put into their minds.

ROUGH DRAFT
$10/year from PO Box 426392, San Francisco, CA 94142-6390

The newsletter of the San Francisco Cacophony Society, "A randomly gathered network of free spirits united in the pursuit of experiences beyond the pale of mainstream society." They meet for a round of activities including picnics on the Golden Gate Bridge, tours of the local sewers, formal dinner in unlikely places, spectacular desert pyromania, and more. If you're jaded and near the Bay Area, this may be the cure.

Pull on your Pedal Pushers & Bermuda Shorts for the 2nd Annual Great American Backyard Barbecue & Improv Jazz Party. In the spirit of all great cookouts, bring something to throw on the grill & food & drink to share. (Please bring food in your best picnic Tupperware. Don't forget musical instruments & your favorite '50's records & tapes.)

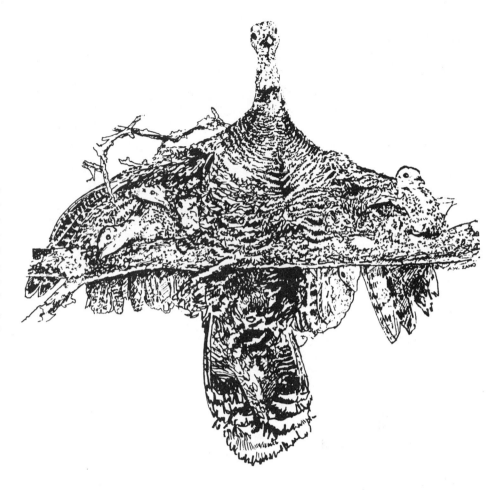

NOTES FROM WINDWARD
$2 from The Windward Foundation, 55 Windward Lane, Klickitat, WA 98628

There seems to be another upswing in the community movement in recent years, as more people construct their own voluntary families and living situa-

tions. *Notes From Windward* provides a handy window into one of these efforts, the Windward community in Klickitat, Washington. With 60 acres, a sawmill, lots of livestock, an induction foundry, a darkroom and tons (literally) of equipment, Windward provides an exciting background to the careful development of a new social system. Though it sometimes seems that *Notes* is about goat farming (one of their major ongoing activities), in fact the goats' antics serve as an springboard to discuss consensus, evolution, planting for the future or any other darned thing one of the community members wants to talk about.

It used to be that people had three main choices. If they found an appropriate mate, they could form a nuclear family. If they didn't, they could try to go it alone. Their third general option was to stay with their extended family and work on the family farm or in the family business. Today our culture doesn't include that option. Now it's either make

it as a couple or go it alone. Looked at from that perspective, Windward is an extended family, a family of choice, that functions in place of the family network that people used to fall back on. The trick is how to form a family without the patriarchal baggage that accompanies the concept of 'family' in most minds We rarely use the term family since most of our people are orphans of one type or another, While blood is thicker than water, so is sewage.

DIARIST'S JOURNAL
$12/yr from 102 W. Water St., Lansford, PA 18232

One of the greatest things about the zine world is that truly new ideas can turn into success stories. **DJ** is based on one very simple idea: publishing excerpts from diaries and journals, written by the average person and the famous alike, with a sprinkling of articles on the practice of keeping a diary. It's relaxed, it's fun, and it works. People-watching on paper.

Random thoughts on a beautiful day in the park sitting by the stream, wind rustling the tall, dry grasses about me and ducks serenely floating past — all effort of movement hidden beneath the water's surface. Mallard I think but I don't know my ducks yet. Need Lynn here. Guess he spotted me perched amongst the rushes — he's scurrying for the other side as fast as dignity will allow. (Just realized I left my glasses in the car. Probably this will be totally illegible. No great loss.) (Of course without my glasses I will probably also be late for class because I also can't read my watch.) Golfers intrude on the horizon.
It's so peaceful by streamside — such a contrast to sitting by the ocean with the surf pounding and the salt spray blowing over you (which I miss). Must go back and reread Especially Maine *which so sensitively describes all the ocean's moods.*

AMERICAN WINDOW CLEANER MAGAZINE
$4 from 27 Oak Creek Rd., El Sobrante, CA 94803

This might seem like an unlikely candidate for inclusion in a zine book, being a trade journal for those who wash windows for a living. But they've stayed friendly and personable and interested in staying in touch with other small publishers, and that's good enough for me. They write of new government regulations and reasonable safety practices (though how anyone can go over the edge of a skyscraper in a bosun's chair is mind-boggling) and competitions and the latest products and more. Who knows, there might even be a new career for you here.

SIPAPU
$4 from Noel Peattie, 23311 County Road 88, Winters, CA 95694

This is a zine for those with a professional interest in the small press, written by a librarian and chiefly aimed at other librarians. Noel has pretty wide contacts, and he scores interesting interviews with regularity. News from the alternative side of the library profession is also frequent, giving a view of a struggle between social activists and conservatives within the profession.

Music

Zines and music seem to have a natural affinity for one another. Although they were not the first in the field, music zines are certainly more numerous than any other type by now. As you'll see here they cover many styles and appear in various formats; what they share is a love of the sonic arts in all their varied and wonderful forms. Some of the popularity of music zines can be credited to the do-it-yourself spirit that pervades punk and other alternative forms of music, but some can only be explained by the deep human need for self-expression. Of course, it helps that music zine editors can get free passes for concerts from record companies hopeful for any publicity!

INK DISEASE
$2.50 from 4563 Marmion Way, Los Angeles, CA 90065

This is one of the long-term classic Los Angeles punk rock zines. Although it comes out infrequently it has always been reliable, sticking with loud sounds, centered on hardcore, but with a sense of style and humor that indicates the writers are more than just groupies for noise. In format they have (along with **Flipside**) set a standard for many other punk zines, leading off with interviews and band photos and closing with a bunch of short reviews of records and tapes. One of the must-have zines for every punk.

SANTIAGO: After our set Steve took a couple of cases of band beer that was in the back and started flinging them at the crowd.
*STEVE: That was good...handing out free beer to a bunch of teenage Belgians. That really got 'em going. We stole all the beer from **The Mission**. We stole like 4 cases of beer from **The Mission** and I pissed in their amp cases. Boy...**The Mission**...they really blow. You looking for a band that blows? Try **The Mission**.*

INTENSITY
$2.50 from John Book, 2502 W. Opal St., Pasco, WA 99301-3352

Pasco is in the Southeast part of Washington State, and this is a good example of a regionally-focused music zine. John Book focuses his coverage on bands from Washington who haven't yet made it big, giving them some space and perhaps even a bit of a boost. He's got eclectic tastes (developed by writing material for a bunch of other zines) ranging from garage-punk with 60's influences right over to thrash metal and other hard genres.

JERSEY BEAT
$2 from Jim Testa, 418 Gregory Ave., Weehawken, NJ 07087

Jim's zine has gone from a small review of New Jersey alternative bands to becoming one of the most thoughtful new

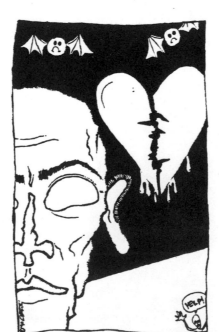

music zines in the nation. Though he retains his local focus (on the greater New York and New Jersey area), **JB** is impressive as a place to catch the important trends and changes in the alternative music world. Its reporting on major music events (such as the NMS and SXSW trade shows) is second to none, and their continuing coverage of the tension between major labels and indie bands will make any music fan think twice about being spoon-fed ideas on what music is worth listening to. All of this is wrapped around a collection of interviews and reviews and fabulous NY area live show coverage, to make a consistently entertaining and enlightening package.

I have been railing against the way major labels have been co-opting the "alternative market" now for about a year, but lately it's really been getting me down. "Alternative," as we all know, is what major labels call acts who aren't going to sell as well as their mainstream bands. But if there's a friggin' penny to be made out there, the majors want to be the ones to make it. So after eight years of doing this fanzine — of doggedly and sincerely trying to promote the cause of "alternative" music — I suddenly find myself and everything I believe in lumped in with the likes of Michelle Shocked, The Cure, Depeche Mode, and all kinds of other dreck, bands that are selling 2 million records and still appealing to the college kids and post-mods by wearing the "alternative" label. I'm sick of this shit, really.

MTV's "120 Minutes," at one time the only two watchable hours of programming they produced, has tightened up its playlist and fills a good third of the show with "Alternative Sales Charts," college radio charts, and interviews with major label bands. What could possibly be more FUCKING stupid than an "Alternative Sales Chart?" The whole POINT of being "alternative" is supposed to be music that's measured on originality and merit, and not on mass market appeal. And I'm even less enamored by "fanzines" that spend 3/4 of their editorial space interviewing major label bands, as if the only music interesting enough to spotlight is music that sells a couple million records. You still don't see the majors advertising in any of these zines, do you? So it's the cream of the indies — Touch & Go, Caroline, Relativity, even, god bless 'em, Dischord — who are paying for the ink and the paper that's being filled with features on the Beastie Boys and Poi Dog Pondering. Wake up and smell the coffee, kids. They're buying your soul for the price of a couple of lousy CD's.

UNBROKEN CHAIN
$2 from Laura Smith, PO Box 8726, Richmond, VA 23227

There are a few bands out there that have inspired an entire community of people. The Grateful Dead have to be at the top of the list, and it's no surprise that there are a couple of zines out there devoted entirely to the Deadhead community. **Unbroken Chain** is one of the best, a friendly zine with the feel of a letter linking together members of one big sprawling family revolving around this band's music. They reprint mainstream Dead coverage, give fans the

set lists for various shows, look at the tensions surrounding vending and camping outside of shows, and generally help people keep in touch with one another.

VICIOUS HIPPIES FROM PANDA HELL
From John, PO Box 34, Portland, OR 97207

Like most zine titles this one doesn't really *mean* anything but it sure is great. Printed on a variety of brightly colored paper, **VHFPH** is relentlessly free; even when queried for this book, John wouldn't provide a price, though he certainly wouldn't mind a few stamps in the mail. It covers life in the Portland new music scene with a mix of beer, quick interviews, short reviews and generally bizarre writing with a youthful edge.

Speaking of **Beat Happening**, the Feel Good All Over label has released a cd retrospective called 1983-85 that documents their start as the ultimate DIY band. Lotsa hard to find tracks all on one cd, if I had a cd player I would've kept it even.

WHAT WAVE
$5 from Dave and Reno O'Halloran, 17 Erie Ave., London, Ontario, CANADA, N6J 1H9

A zine for people who love the music of the Sixties, all fuzz guitar power pop and rockabilly and dripping with coolness. There are still a lot of bands producing this sort of thing — The Fleshtones, The Flamin' Groovies, The Cramps, Link Wray, Hasil Adkins, and many more — and they all show up here. The **What Wave** crowd is super-dedicated, and most recent issues have included a hard vinyl 45 or a compilation tape as a bonus and a way of spreading the music. They also spend some ink on related topics including surfing, wrestling, and comic books, and for some reason carry a continuing series on nifty garage music from Italy.

SLUG & LETTUCE
SASE from Chris Boarts, PO Box 2067, Stuyvesant Sta., New York, NY 10009

Chris is doing something unique here, promoting the DIY (Do It Yourself) music scene with free classified advertising accompanied by reviews and good-looking photos from live shows. She's quite into helping projects like Squat or Rot and ABC No Rio (a pair of activities organized by NYC punks). A cool little zine worth a look.

STILL NO SYMPTOMS
$2.50 (no personal checks) from Liz Colker & Dave Cunningham, 542 Haight St. #202, San Francisco, CA 94117-3407

A music zine which dwells on some of the more questionable and challenging bands, people who use death and sex as routine imagery. There is still raw power in a lot of music that can't get out in the mainstream media, and you can find some of that power here. They're also fascinated with some other arts, including tattooing.

SPILLED GUTS
$1.25 from Chris Wagner, 12 White Oak Way, Trenton, NJ 08618

A zine fueled by proximity to the hard music scene of New York City and environs. They're into classic punk, but also newer, more bizarre acts such as Gwar, whose blood and guts spectaculars tend to cross the line from music into performance art. Small but feisty, with plenty packed into each issue.

STRESSED OUT
$1 from Pauline Poisonous, 96 Hilldale Ave., Ormond Beach, FL 32174

This one is punk in many ways without necessarily focusing on the music (though there are bands and records and tapes and zines aplenty here). Pauline gets into snappy punk artwork, helping people avoid the draft, social justice movements, and more. Punk as a way of life.

SUBURBAN VOICE
$3.50 from Al Quint, PO Box 1605, Lynn, MA 01903

No-nonsense punk coverage with a pretty long pedigree, now incorporating metal as well as frequent free hard vinyl EPs with recent issues. Al has been around for years and knows most of the bands that have hit the Northeast, and every issue shines with his in-depth interviews with the more important punks. Plenty of reviews and excellent live coverage show up here.

Poopshovel occasionally hint at brilliance and manage to generally overcome some spotty material as well as some silly lyrics ("African Bees"). Metallic and muscular, as well as some

jazzy dissonance, squealin', chugging guitars anchoring the sound. "Ouija Board" cranks it up furiously. Enough sparks to bode well for the future. One suggestion — get rid of the trumpet.

TECHNOLOGY WORKS
$2 from Paul Moore, PO Box 477, Placentia, CA 92670-0477

There is a lot of rough new music out there, with heavy rhythms, distorted bass lines, dance-oriented synthesizers and sampled sonic mayhem in general. It goes by names like dance-industrial and technobeat, but whatever the precise genre, you'll find it in **Technology Works**. Started a couple of years ago to track this particular movement, **TW** has grown into the best source for info on new music in the field, as well as a home for interviews with bands like KMFDM, Front 242, and Consolidated.

Sasha: KMFDM was, after doing music for about twelve years, I met En Esch and we got along in a way that I haven't experienced before. We got along doing things like me giving my part and him giving his part and together we just experienced the sensation of creating something that you feel is hot. Before, I thought that I was just copying something, being inside of something, and all of a sudden I felt this lift, being a little out of convention, out of tradition. And that just made me believe in the seriousness of what I was doing and the moment and that's how. It's got a lot to do with the physical reaction. When you listen to your own music and you get totally high from it, then you think this is good. And you develop the energy to do more and to go out with it. Since I'm doing KMFDM I can go out on stage and I don't feel adrenalin anymore. I'm just excited but I'm not scared. Because I know what I do is what I want to do and if you don't like it, fuck you.

THE MANDOCRUCIAN'S DIGEST
$3.25 from Niles Hokkanen, PO Box 3585, Winchester, VA 22601

This is (as far as we know) the only music zine in America focused exclusively on the mandolin. Well, actually, they also address other semi-obscure folky stringed instruments. They interview widely-known players, review records, and generally promote "mandomania." New players will appreciate the extensive selection of sheet music in each issue, designed to help the reader master some of the finer points of the instrument.

MIDI GUITARIST
$2 from Warren Sirota, PO Box 21354, Oakland, CA 94620

MIDI is an acronym for Musical Instrument Digital Interchange, a way for various electronic instruments from synthesizers to drum machines to exchange information via computer cables. This specialized zine is for those playing guitars with MIDI capability — you can think of their instruments as crosses between traditional guitars and synthesizers. It's a highly technical production, full of articles on which knob to twiddle in which direction to get what hot new sound, and seems to be right on top of the field.

MONTHLY MUSIC REPORT
$6 from all genre, 738 Main St. #387, Waltham, MA 02254-9038

One of the few music zines out there that is actually doing anything truly new and different with the format, MMR includes a "Just Listen" cassette music sampler with every issue. The tape has music from four or five bands who are featured in the zine, and the bands get total creative control over their own segments. MMR also includes listings of new music and the record companies putting it out, plus thoughts on the shape of alternative music and the industry surrounding it. A direct connection to the grassroots.

For about a year now I've been seeing SST's motto on bumper stickers and ads — "CORPORATE ROCK SUCKS". I have never asked someone (for fear of embarrassing myself) what exactly "corporate rock" is. Every time I think of "Corporate Rock" I start picturing a bunch of accountants taking the stage at a local club. If you know, maybe you could let us know. Once I figure that out I might be able to spend some time wondering why a record company feels that their main goal is to destroy another kind of music. I guess labels can now be either in the business of creating or destroying music. Makes for interesting competition.

MUSIC SCENE MAGAZINE
$24/12 issues from Larry & Diana Freed, PO Box 4661, Annapolis, MD 21403

The emphasis in this zine is on getting out to hear some of the great new music that plays every night throughout Maryland and the surrounding states. They publish extensive listings of clubs and the acts booked into them, and constantly encourage people to support their local musicians. There are also editorials on the shape of the music world and interviews with some of the hottest local artists.

GAJOOB
$3.50 from Bryan Baker, PO Box 3201, Salt Lake City, UT 84110

"Cassette Culture" is one of the great unknown musical developments of our time. There is a whole world out there of people recording cassette tapes at home, packaging them up more or less professionally, and sending them out to a network of people linked by zines and a love of music. Gajoob features the most encyclopedic coverage of this world, with hundreds of tapes spotlighted in every issue — and even then they only scratch the surface. In the true DIY spirit they even invite tape producers to write their own review, allowing readers to see what the artists were thinking behind the music (or noise, as the case may be). Bryan also talks to some of the most fascinating people in the field, features numerous columns, and acts as a central clearing house for information on underground projects new and old. If you've ever had the urge to go hunting for non-corporate music or produce some of your own, this zine is a must-have.

HAWAIIAN BOOGIE DISEASE
$2 from Steve Franz, PO Box 3276, University City, MO 63130-0676

Despite the obscure title this one actually has a simple mission, to be "the Consumer's Guide to Blues Music on CD." It's mainly reviews, of classic music being re-released in the new format as well as new stuff recorded directly for it.

HEARTSONG REVIEW
$4 from PO Box 1084, Cottage Grove, OR 97424

This is a central clearing house for reviews of "New Age Music of the Spirit." They focus on recordings that have "both social and spiritual consciousness" and "consciously celebrates higher truths and speak directly of the many ways that human beings relate to the Divine." The result is a very focused review publication, cross-indexed as to particular uses for the music, from meditation to just keeping the kids happy. One nice touch is the inclusion of notes on technical quality in each review, along with the critique of the music itself. Performers also get some space via interviews, and there is the occasional article on subjects such as the healing power of music.

THE BIG TAKEOVER
$3.50 from Jack Rabid, 249 Eldridge St. #14, New York, NY 10002

This is one of the original punk zines (they had their tenth anniversary issue not too long ago) and still one of the best. Jack Rabid does an amazing job of compiling information and opinions on hundreds of live shows and recordings in every issue, now covering all manner of alternative music with style and vigor. The zine is fueled by a straightforward love for music and the hope that other people will discover great new stuff through its pages, rather than by graphic pretensions or mouthy opinions. A welcome beacon in the confusing world of new music.

Most of today's indie bands wouldn't know a well written, catchy song if one shot them in the balls they think they have so much of. Following Sonic Youth (a great band aurally, but not exactly classic songwriters), most of the indie scene can't, or more likely won't write songs that are worth singing along to. Their indie offspring are far worse, far more annoying, celebrating noise, volume, distortion, offensiveness (much like the fanzines that support them) and

Matt Towler

just making a godawful racket as great music. Sometimes it is, with powerful results, a kick in the ass (from Big Black to the early Nihilistics), because the riffs are there hiding in the background, and thus the chaos is liberating rather than just noise for noise's sake. Mostly, it's merely irritating, a headache producing blitz not unlike the Con Ed man ripping up the street with his jackhammer after the latest water pipe rupture.

BLONDIE FANZINE
$1 from Robert S. Robbins, 1997 Misner Rd., Williamsport, PA 17701

Another zine for those who like a particular artist, in this case Debbie Harry, better known to most as the lead vocalist for the band Blondie. They print little tidbits about the blonde singer's continuing career, dress the zine up with computerized photos, and have done such bizarre things as calling her parents for an interview.

BORDER X-INGS
$2.50 from Mary Ann O'Brien, PO Box 5173, North Bergen, NJ 07047

The "Fanzine on Irish Rock Groups and Celtic Life" starts out with megastars U2 (who are at least mentioned in every issue) but branches out from there to feature many of the other fine Irish musi-

cians whose music is hitting these shores. They also expand further, into publicizing Amnesty International (one of U2's pet causes) and commenting on the pan-Celtic movement, where to stay in Dublin, and other cultural matters.

BREAKFAST WITHOUT MEAT
$3.50 from Gregg Turkington & Lizzy Kate Gray, PO Box 15927, Santa Fe, NM 87506

Sometimes it's hard to know what to make of **BWM**. Mostly they are into rough punk music and noise put out by outfits like Caroliner, surely one of the most abrasive groups recording today. But then they'll turn around and feature an apparently-serious interview with the company that produced all those schmaltzy 101 Strings records. Of note also are the record reviews by Gobo, just about the only reviewer out there with the guts to say all those nasty things the other reviewers are scared to tell their audience.

BUTT UGLY
$1 from 408 E. Roberta Ave., Waukesha, WI 53186

There's a "scene" in even the smallest towns, it seems, and the punk and hardcore kids in Waukesha are the target audience for **Butt Ugly**. They review local shows (one in the editor's living room while his parents were out of town) and interview anyone they can snag in person or by mail. There are hundreds of this sort of zine fermenting across the USA, proving that the urge to write is still alive and well and catching more kids all the time.

CONCERTINA & SQUEEZEBOX
$6 from Joel Cowan, PO Box 6706, Ithaca, NY 14851

No points for guessing that this zine is devoted to concertinas, accordions, bandoliers and other wonderfully squeezy reed instruments. There are bunches of people out there still playing these things, in styles from traditional to rock, and it seems that sooner or later they all turn up here. Interviews and transcribed music rub elbows with reviews of music and instruments, news from the squeezebox community, and lovely advertisements for the classy little things.

Just to reinforce Stinson Behlen's comments about leaving accordions in cars in the hot sun (of which we have much here in Australia), the following story may amuse, worry or sicken your readers. A customer recently brought to me a Hohner Corso, complaining that it had suddenly become unplayable. Upon opening the accordion, I found that the reed wax had melted, run all over the reeds and valves, and created a real nightmare. The customer readily agreed that it had been left in the rear window shelf of his car on a recent hot day, whilst he had been away from the

vehicle, but was most indignant about my opinion that this was what had caused the problem with his accordion, stating that his dog had been in the car for the same length of time and had been perfectly O.K.

CURIOUS GOODS
$2.25 from Jerry Rutherfod, 3754 Almond Dr., Oxnard, CA 93030

One of a growing number of zines devoted to heavy metal and its offshoots (such as thrash), **CG** does a good job of mixing coverage of new demo tapes with interviews from older established bands. (They are not exclusively metal, giving some space to hardcore as well). Forthright reviews and a penchant for many short interviews instead of just a few blockbusters make them a good survey zine, a place to turn to first when you want the best possible chance of finding something new and interesting.

Picture this: you wake up after a long night (it doesn't matter what you did), and your stomach is making weird noises. Your brain clicks, and makes you think "damn, I am hungry/thirsty!" Opening up the refrigerator all you see is a Coca Cola can (empty), an apple (brown and crusty), a slice of cheese (purple), and a shiny glass of milk. It looks good, and you immediately chug it down like there was no tomorrow. You don't even think, so you just swallow the whole thing until there's a milky residue on the bottom of the glass. You place to glass in the sink, and then you breathe. You smell something funny, your mouth tastes very foul, and you realize the milk was four months old! You throw up all over the floor, jacking your body into mysterious positions. Now remember the faces you made when you threw up all of that milk. Those are the exact faces I made when I heard a ten song cassette by UNCLE SAM called "Letters From London."

CUT
$2.50 from Steve Erickson, 11 Julian St., Norwich, CT 06360

Some zines are stamped very strongly with the personality of their editors, and **Cut** is one of them. Steve covers much of the most visible new indie music (i.e., the stuff from labels big enough to send out promo copies) and does it well, putting records and groups in some sort of perspective developed over years of dedicated listening and trying to figure out what the heck is going on. He also throws a few interviews into every issue, chatting with interesting noisemeisters from Sebadoh to Courtney Love.

It's like this: Punk's corpse has been rotting for at least 7 or 8 years. 'Alternative music' is nothing but a marketing term, and the same goes for any similar phrase. At one point I listened to almost nothing but white boys playing loud guitars on independent labels. My taste has changed a lot in the past 6 months and (I hope) it's reflected in the issue that follows (tho I don't think it's reflected to the extent I'd like it to be.) Listening to 90% of the records that I get in the mail seems to be a game of cataloging minor variations in the same 2 or 3 themes.

1/1
$4 from The Just Intonation Network, 535 Stevenson St., San Francisco, CA 94103.

These people are interested in somewhat experimental music, based on the notion that notes on the scale should

stand in simple integer ratio to one another, rather than being offset from those ratios as they generally are. They publish scores, notes on various tunings, theoretical articles and features on particular musics from around the world. A somewhat technical but excellently produced reference for the seriously thoughtful musician.

YOUR FLESH
$3.50 from PO Box 25146, Minneapolis, MN 55458-6146

A fat zine of new indie music distinguished by colorful cover art assaults, loud bands that take no prisoners and continuing contacts with other creative endeavors (they've done more to publicize selected outrageous performance artists, including Annie Sprinkle and Frank Moore, to the music community than anyone else). Every issue features dozens of interviews and a hundred or so reviews, most written for those who already have some inkling of what's going on with the cutting edge and can follow the references. A document of the times that tends to be a bit ingroupish but is definitely worth pursuing for the clarity of insight that comes with understanding the vocabulary.

ROGER MILLER Xylyl/A Woman in Half CD — I've always had a soft spot in my heart for Herr Miller; from Mission of Burma to Maximum Electric Piano to No Man, he's

always been too damn smart for both the world he lives in and his intended audience: Sampling oil drums in his basement, pounding the shit out of a Fender Rhodes, Miller has consistently pleaded, cajoled, threatened, and enticed in an effort to lure pop culture-opiated audiences into new territory, where they might have to use their tiny little reptilian brains to process something more complex than a three-minute pop song. He's often frustrated himself horribly in the process: A Maximum Electric Piano performance at Nazareth College in Kalamazoo, MI — attended by three or four Miller fans and about twenty nuns — resulted in disaster when the Penguin Contingent fled one by one, fingers in their delicate Christian ears. Poor Roger's frustration mounted steadily until he was allowed to escape to the sanctity of the Holiday Inn bar. Despite it all, Miller persists. Someday, perhaps, he'll get the respect he deserves.

THE NEW MUSIC INFORMER
$1 from Chris Murtland, 3514 Millhaven Rd., Winston-Salem, NC 27106

The nice thing about covering "new music" is that it means you can tackle just about anything, from synth pop to garage rock to Mitch Easter. The overall slant here is towards new progressive acts, but even that is a wide arena. Chris does a solid job of reviewing new releases in a fashion straightforwardly guided by idiosyncratic personal tastes.

THE AFFILIATE
$3 from Peter Riden, 777 Barb Road, RR#1, Vankleek Hill, ONT, CANADA, K0B 1R0

The Affiliate is a grassroots music magazine put together by a man who is something of a social visionary. In addition to making his color-photocopy pages available to lots of writers, he prints pages and pages of contact addresses for those involved in indie music. Peter also hosts various events at The Grand Barn, a rural convention facility dedicated to his vision of the world as one happy place full of joyous sounds.

THE NOISE
$10/yr from Timothy Maxwell, 74 Jamaica St., Jamaica Plain, MA 02130

Long-term (over 100 consistent issues to date) coverage of the relatively cool Boston music scene by local mediamonger T Maxx and his crack crew (including gossip hounds Rita and Lolita and the wonderfully talented cartoonist Fitz). The format is solid and predictable, with a few pages of scene news and silliness followed by interviews and reviews. Plenty of later-big names have shown up in these pages, and the scene is still simmering, so keep an eye on it.

OUTLET
$6 from Trev Faull, 33 Aintree Crescent, Barkingside, Ilford, IG6 2HD, Essex, U.K.

The scope of **Outlet** is mind-boggling, as Trev first came on to the music scene in the Sixties, listened to a ton of stuff from the Fifties and has kept in touch right up to the Nineties. So you never know what to expect here — obscure British discographies, a sweeping look at the current state of indie music or a history of English rock and roll. Whatever he publishes is mixed with a fat pile of reviews, all written from the standpoint of encyclopedic knowledge. Some groups, such as The Residents, he keeps special track of; not surprising, as they are practically a musical encyclopedia in their own right.

FLIPSIDE
$2.50 from PO Box 363, Whittier, CA 90608

A stalwart of the punk scene, **Flipside** has been around seemingly forever (more than a decade, in any case, which is a barrier very few zines of any type pass). Nowadays their issues are the size of **Time** magazine and a whole lot more interesting, still filled with punk music and still finding new bands to write about. With cheap classified ads and an extensive letters column, they help knit the punk community together, not only in Southern California but anywhere else the mails reach. What's best about them is that they've steadfastly refused to stagnate and decide that any particular era of music is the end of the road. Despite those who wish it was still 1976, Flipside follows the punk feeling wherever it goes, even 15 years later.

FILE 13
$2 from Mark Lo, PO Box 175, Concord, MA 01742

Talk to music zine editors for a while and Mark's name always seems to come up as one of the great indie music reviewers of our times. He, along with the rest of his staff, displays that skill here while dealing in some of the more interesting crannies of new music and the surrounding culture. Not flashy, but you can always expect a good read out of a new issue, and some serious thought on the part of the writers.

ANCIENT GRANDMA SECRETS
$1 plus 50¢ in stamps from Libby Gilbert, PO Box 42691, Tucson, AZ 85733

A music zine skewed towards unknown/ underground releases and away from CDs. This puts them into music that's even stranger than most indie labels will touch, and harder to find (fortunately the reviews provide ordering information). Libby also does a good job of covering shows that come her way, expressing the total experience rather than just focusing on the bands on stage.

PORTRAIT of the ARTIST

..(.sonG fOr carl).

THE ATHENS RECORD
$2 from 330 Clover St., Athens, GA 30606

With a thriving new music scene, Athens is perhaps best known as the hometown of the relatively successful band R.E.M., so it's not surprising that they get the lion's share of the ink here. Every issue has the latest R.E.M. news, divided between legitimate recordings and bootlegs. They also cover other area acts, including Indigo Girls and Chickasaw Mud Puppies, providing a window into a musical area worth keeping an eye on since Athens is one of the hot music towns of the 90s.

BACTERIA OF DECAY
$2 from Curt, 63 Lennox Ave., Buffalo, NY 14226

Yes, Buffalo has a scene too, although it's not as active as the live reviews here might at first lead you to believe, since a bunch of them are sent in by California friends. This is a classically "punk" looking zine, packing reviews and interviews in via reduced photocopying, and not worrying too much about the aesthetics of the end result. But it's thoughtful and concerned and even fun to read.

BANZAI
$2 from PO Box 7522, Overland Park, KS 66207

Heavy metal shows up everywhere — even in Kansas. This zine covers the local heavy metal scene and visiting acts, giving space to all variations of the genre. It's put together with plenty of club info and looks like a useful guide to those wanting to sample that scene. They also do reviews for those out of the area, with a slant towards Kansan acts.

EAR OF CORN
75 cents from Dave, PO Box 2143, Stow, OH 44224

I don't know if there's a real "scene" in Stow, or just one incredibly prolific guy. In addition to his work with **EOC**, Dave runs the Wheelchair Full of Old Men line of tapes and works with his own band Sockeye, who have a dozen or two releases out. These are all rock bottom DIY projects, full of energy but sometimes shaky on the quality. The zine part of Dave's media empire exists mainly to publicize other underground and personal projects, and you'll never find a major label release here.

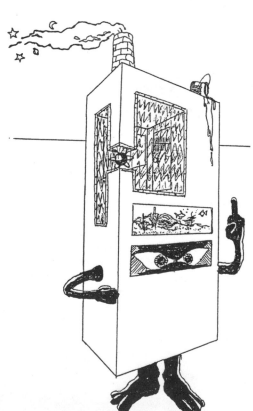

ELECTRONIC COTTAGE
$3 from PO Box 3637, Apollo Beach, FL 33572

This is the best zine around for making contact with the people of the "cassette culture" scene — home tapers and producers and musical experimentalists who engage in grassroots trading and communication. Many of the big names (if that's not an oxymoron) of the scene can be found here, writing or talking about what they do and why they do it, from analog synth musicians to far-out noise artists. Editor Hal McGee has been involved on all levels himself, having previously recorded music and run his own small tape company. Now he's drawing on his manifold contacts to capture at least some of the spirit and energy of this vigorous musical offshoot.

The indie home taper scene is bursting at the seams, ready to explode. There are more people than ever before doing that home taper, do-it-yourself thang! Needless to say, there will always be a lot of us who will get discouraged, overwhelmed by the sheer breadth and weight of a subculture that cannot be contained. How can anyone possibly keep up with the whole thing? It's so big that no one could ever possibly listen to all the home-produced tapes being made out there. Almost every day when I pull the mail out of my post office box there's a letter and/or a tape from someone I've never heard from before, or a newcomer to the scene, looking for a path in. It's thrilling and exhilarating, and yes, a little scary and mind-blowing. But I'm certainly not one to run away from a challenge. Are you? I love the life I'm leading, in the swim and thick of the home taper scene, and I've learned to let the current carry me where it will. And if I did not enjoy what I'm doing, if it did not fill me with excitement I would quit. I have said it before, and I will say it again, you gotta have FUN doing this home taper thing. Sure you can be serious about it — I consider it not only my life's work, but my lifestyle and way of life. But on the other hand, I think it is important not to be too self-serious. Straight up — I do not think there is any

Dangerous Liaisons...

room in the scene for snobs, hypocrites and would-be rock stars. I suggest you go peddle your wares elsewhere. Got it? These types will be left behind anyway, discarded and cast off, bowled over by the cassette culture comet as it hurtles into parts unknown. This is a society of doers, of producers — not passive consumers with a remote control couch potato mentality. Everyone produces; everyone beats the tribal drum — not just a select few.

EXPERIMENTAL MUSICAL INSTRUMENTS
Sample on request from PO Box 784, Nicasio, CA 94946

This is a prime example of the sort of thing that exists only in the zine world, a professional journal for a very narrow specialty — in this case those who enjoy constructing and using their own nonstandard musical instruments. Every issue is packed with articles both theoretical and practical, construction plans, photos of strange instrumental art objects and more. They also make available recordings from these creations, mention goings-on in the experimental world, and give some notion of how to use music in a classroom setting. Always a fun and unusual read.

THE CUTTING EDGE
$1 from Dan Kennedy, 8303 Hilton Way, Orlando, FL 32810

Christian music is one of the genres which seems livelier in the zines than in the mainstream music press, probably because the big guys consider it too marginal to be of more than occasional interest to their readers. Well, this is an entire zine devoted to Christian music (and it's far from being the only one) proving, among other things, that there is a lot of it out there. They review material in all genres from rock to rap, commenting both on musical and spiritual quality as they go along. Each issue also has an extensive list of other Christian music zines.

I would like to clarify the meaning of our song "Mark My Words," which was in question, because of lyrics concerning 'pride.' I think it would be best if readers know what message we were trying to convey. The song is a direct reference to the scripture Mark 2:17, in which Jesus states "It is not the healthy who need a doctor, but the sick." He was being scrutinized by the scribes and Pharisees

for hanging out with sinners. We wrote the song in response to all the criticism we've received from Christians in our area (Bible Belt) about playing in secular clubs where alcohol was being served. We feel God has called us into the ministry of playing in bars and secular clubs. Our message is not watered down either. We talk as we feel led, and each person who sees our show leaves knowing where they stand and that Jesus is the Way, the Truth and the Life.

DAMP MAGAZINE
$3.50 from Kevin Kraynick, PO Box 613, Village Station, New York, NY 10014

A wildly idiosyncratic music zine that can spend one page worshiping the

genius of Captain Beefheart and the next telling you why you should like sumo wrestling. In and amongst this there is plenty of indie music, with Kevin's contacts and strong sense of style leaving no secret as to what he likes and doesn't like. A genuinely interesting zine that does a lot to break out of any mold the unwary reader might try to force it into.

SINGING SPOONS, Resin Cabin (Manufacture) — The erratically "painted" cover of Resin Cabin led me to believe that the Singing Spoons would be plucking and guffawing within the framework of the lopsided rock aesthetic that I am so unnaturally fond of, but instead it turns out to be chock full of relatively uncatchy Bob-Mould-with-a-sinus-infection punk pop sung by fellows who should learn the difference between the expressions "so bad it's good" and "so bad it's bad." Maybe next time.

PROFANE EXISTENCE
$2 from PO Box 8722, Minneapolis, MN 55408

A heavily political music zine with ties to the Anarchist Youth Federation. Much of the zine is political coverage, with an emphasis on fighting injustice *now* around the world — they are in contact with the Warzone Collective in Ireland as well as Britain's Class War group. The bands interviewed tend to be politically conscious outfits with an emphasis on hardcore.

PUNCTURE
$2.95 from 1592 Union St. #431, San Francisco, CA 94123

"A Magazine of Music and the Arts", though the biggest difference between Puncture and many other music zines may well be the impeccable layout and design. But they don't let form dominate content, ranging from analyses of black rock to an interview with the outrageous Genesis P. Orridge. They do an excellent book column and venture afield into photography and the criticism of rock critics as well.

WAKE UP
Face the Music

STOP BEING SEDUCED BY THE INSIDIOUS MEDIOCRITY THAT IS WESTERN TONALITY. THE BEETHOVEN ROLE OF TOILET PAPER HAS ALREADY BEEN USED UP. WAGNER DREW IT OUT; MAHLER AND STRAUSS QUICKLY FLUSHED AWAY THE LAST FEW SOILED INCHES OF IT IN A LOGICAL CONCLUSION WHICH COULD NOT BE REVITALIZED BY ANY SERIALIST BEATING OF A LONG DEAD HORSE. WHY WAS BERG--THE ONLY MEMBER OF THE SO-CALLED "NEW VIENNA SCHOOL" TO QUESTION SCHOERNBERG'S FASCIST IDEAS--SHOT TO DEATH IN HIS OWN HOME? A RANDOM WARTIME CASUALTY? OR JUST AN EARLY EXAMPLE OF THE WOLRD WIDE CONSPIRACY TO PERPETUATE WESTERN TONALITY AS A MEANS OF DEPRIVING CITIZENS OF THEIR GOD GIVEN RIGHT TO SPIRITUAL NOURISHMENT THROUGH MUSIC? NOT POSSIBLE YOU SAY? THEN

--WHY DID YOUNG AARON COPLAND SUDDENLY ABANDON HIS INVESTIGATIONS INTO NEW TONAL STRUCTURES AND BEGIN WRITING TRITE JINGOISTIC SCORES LIKE "BILLY THE KID"?

--WHY ARE THE INSTRUMENTS OF HARRY PARTCH--WHO DIED MYSTERIOUSLY AT A YOUNG AGE--NOW LOCKED UP BEHIND THE DOORS OF PRIVATE INSTITUTIONS?

--WHY ARE THE MICROTONAL INTRICACIES OF ONCE CULTURALLY VITAL JAPANESE MUSIC FORMS NOW ONLY UNDERSTOOD BY A SMALL AND WEALTHY ELITE?

--WHY WAS CHARLES IVES FORCED TO SQUANDER HIS CREATIVE ENERGY SELLING LIFE INSURANCE?

--WHY ARE 'MINIMALIST' COMPOSERS PHILIP GLASS AND STEVE REICH NOW MAKING MAJOR RECORD DEALS WITH A CERTAIN RECORD COMPANY--THE SAME COMPANY TO CO-OPT THE ONCE CONTROVERSIAL LAURIE ANDERSON--WITH NEWLY ANNOUNCED PLANS TO SELL-OUT THEIR EARLIER SENSIBILITIES FOR COLABORATIVE PROJECTS WITH POP STARS?

COINCIDENCE?? NOT LIKELY. YES, CERTAINLY THERE WILL CONTINUE TO BE NEW EXPERIMENTS WITH POLYRHYTHM, INSTRUMENT BUILDING, ALTERNATE TUNING SYSTEMS, STRATIFICATION, ETC. BUT SUCH DANGEROUS PURSUITS ARE QUICKLY DROPPED IN EXCHANGE FOR TAWDRY CAREERS WRITING TV JINGLES & TEPID ROCK SETTINGS, ONCE WOULD-BE INNOVATORS DISCOVER WHAT IT IS TO PLAY HARD BALL WITH THE BIG BOYS.

BUT THE PROBLEM ISN'T THE RECORD COMPANYS. THE PROBLEM ISN'T MTV. THE REAL PROBLEM IS YOU. BACH ONLY USED OUR HACKNEYED SCALE-SYSTEM FOR LACK OF ANYTHING BETTER--BUT YOU HAVE A CHOICE! STOP SINGING CHRISTMAS CAROLS. REMOVE YOUR SONS AND DAUGHTERS FROM THEIR BAND AND ORCHESTRA CLASSES. THROW OUT YOUR RADIOS, MELT DOWN YOUR RECORD COLLECTIONS, AND TAKE A BULK ERASER TO YOUR TAPE RECORDINGS. ACT NOW BEFORE IT'S TOO LATE.

Food For Thought

REAL LIFE IN A BIG CITY
$10/year from Debi Dip, 6520 Selma Ave. #332, Los Angeles, CA 90028

This monthly zine has its own distinctive format, opening with a single extended interview (usually with an unsigned but fun band) and then moving into absurd humor, the comic adventures of Stubo (the cat with no paws) and a batch of reviews. Debi always keeps things light, with the exception of the spotlight interviews which tend to be long and rambling.

ROCK & ROLL CONFIDENTIAL
$24/year from PO Box 341305, Los Angeles, CA 90034

A zine that has gradually backpedaled head critic Dave Marsh's music coverage in favor of dealing with a more pressing matter: attempted censorship

of rock music. Marsh and **RRC** have been at the forefront of the fight against labeling various records as obscene, and their booklet "You've Got a Right To Rock" has rallied numerous others. Usually the first place to read any news of music-related assaults on the First Amendment.

ALTERNATIVE PRESS
$4.50 from 1451 W. 112th St. #1, Cleveland, OH 44102

AP looks a lot more like **Spin** or **Rolling Stone** than most other zines, but it doesn't have their megabudget. What it does have is colorful covers and a lot of words about what's hot in the college/independent music circuit. Often their coverage is a bit lacking in depth, but it more than makes up for that in breadth. Their coverage of demos and Jack Rabid's continuing news column help keep them in touch with the grassroots as well.

FORCED EXPOSURE
$13/4 issues from PO Box 9102, Waltham, MA 02254

Due to longevity, heft and hipness this remains one of the prime music zines on the market these days, anxiously awaited despite long breaks between issues. Besides plenty of music coverage (which often tells you what to think instead of what the reviewer thinks) they get into weird science fiction, reviewing porn movies, splattering indie music in-

jokes across their pages, and investigating avant garde video. Sometimes difficult to penetrate, but practically required reading for today's music moguls.

BLACK SPOT: **Flaps Down** *LP (BIG MONEY)*
...Mr. Ron Lessard (of RRR fame) had a loft party a few months ago in downtown Lowell, which featured an unbelievably maxist sheet-of-sound performance by Merzbow. Because the volume level was excruciating, and since one of Ron's neighbors worked as a caterer, he decided to have some chips 'n dip to accomodate any potential noise grumblers. He also had a bunch of cheap record players rigged up all over the place, "playing" various anti-records (if you have to ask...). The player nearest the dip table actually had this Black Spot LP on it. In the middle of the disk there was a great gob of onion dip and crackers and other food aids. The needle, caked in this shit, grated along beautifully, and I can assure you it sounded "great." Unfortunately, I only have an expensive stereo, one that I am quite unwilling to dump any kind of food onto, so I've been unable to replicate this experience in the privacy of my own home. The electronic charges this disk is pushing through my $100 needle right now, devoid of creamy dip and dusty cracker, are very very sad. Dullish hard rock, with that vague, "well produced" Minneapolean funky varnish, and unbearably "howled" vocals. If you know this sound, I'm terribly sorry. For you and for me.

THE ALTERED MIND
$1.50 from PO Box 1083, Claremont, CA 91711

The zine seems interested in a number of different musical subcultures, sticking to the newer ones from punk to Goth. They take the space they need to deal with each album, whether that's a paragraph or a page, and print in off hues of purple ink. The staff seems truly interested in the music, not just in being known as zine mavens.

When you were about eight years old, did you ever take an old tape recorder and the cheapest tapes available and record your singing? If you recall the sound quality, then you know what this sounds like. Did you ever spend seventy-two hours in two motel rooms and write songs about lower-middle-class existence? Didn't think so. Well, Paste have saved you the trouble.

THE LIL' RHINO GAZETTE
$2.75 from K.K.R. North, PO Box 14139, Arlington, TX 76094-1139

A music zine of mostly reviews that seems relentlessly cheerful and upbeat, probably because they can always find lots of music they like to write about. Content definitely comes ahead of form here, with interviews and reviews slapped on the page along with phtocopies of whatever amusing band photos they can find. Stylistically they range from industrial to pop to who-knows-what, trashing the occasional album that really deserves it while saving most of the space for pointers to the really fun stuff in the underground. Their interests range wider than music, with comics interviews and a page or two for poetry and other creativity, but the sheer joy of making independent noise is what fuels the writing.

THE BEST WAY TO PRINT UP COPIES OF YOUR 'ZINE IS...
A.) "With a number 2 lead pencil."
B.) "With a state-of-the-art home computer laser-printer."
C.) "At a copy shop that will give you a good rate on bulk printings."
D.) "On the copier at work with company paper joined with company staples, mailed with company envelopes and using the company's postage meter when no one's looking, whenever possible."

Science & Beyond

Science and engineering and technology being as important in the "real world" as they are, it should be no surprise to find them in the zine world, too. The selection ranges from relatively mainstream topics with a limited audience (how many neon tubebenders are there, anyhow?) to the sort of Weird Science-UFO-and-perpetual-motion stuff that draws condemnations from the establishment and laughs from experienced fringewatchers. Whether or not you find a lot of breakthroughs out here, chances are you'll develop a new respect for the complexity of the world.

2600
$18/yr from PO Box 752, Middle Island, NY 11953.

This is a magazine for hackers and phone phreaks — those people who wander around on the leading edge of technology looking for security holes and interesting quirks. Unlike the media-portrayed hackers who, armed only with a computer and a paper clip, are out to bring down Western civilization and destroy your credit rating, these are sane and sensible people who are fascinated by the systems controlling our lives. A typical issue might explain a common computer operating system, contain a history of payphones, pass on radio scanning information from a reader and report on the latest arrests of purported hackers by Federal agents. Fascinating reading for the electronically-inclined.

When you first put your coin in the slot, it is tested for size, weight and material. Size is determined by the size of the slot the coin passes through, as well as the coin chute it slides through in the phone itself. A coin that is too large is not allowed into the phone itself, while one too small just falls through without having accomplished anything. Material is identified by the use of magnetic fields; slugs will be deflected, while coins will not. If the coin is right, it is allowed to hit a sprocket, which when hit by the coin, spins a certain amount of times, determined by its weight. This spinning of the sprocket controls a tone generator within the telephone, which creates the coin deposit tones, which in turn, the exchange then interprets to determine the amount to credit the customer.

JU'I LOBYPLI
Intro packet $4 from The Logical Language Group, Inc., 2904 Beau Ln., Fairfax, VA 22031-1303

This is the technical journal of a bunch of people working on a new artificial language project. Lojban, their language, is a descendant of the original Loglan project of a few decades back. The goal is to create a logically-designed language and use it to test the Sapir-Whorf hypothesis that our languages shape our worldviews in critical ways. It's an exciting prospect and one which these people, using computer mailing lists, meetings, classes and plenty of good old-fashioned letter writing, appear to be making good progress on.

CRYONICS
$3.50 from Alcor Life Extension Foundation, 12327 Doherty St., Riverside, CA 92503

Alcor is one of the groups at the forefront of the cryonics movement, actually freezing people after their death in hopes of future reanimation and cure. They have a number of members already frozen and more signing up all the time. This zine presents a little of everything: progress reports (medical and legal) from the front, philosophical considerations, speculations on future medical technology and advice on how to financially prepare, for example. Sure, it's a long shot, but it's the only game in town, and this seems to be the best-prepared bunch of players.

UFO
$5.45 from PO Box 1053, Sunland, CA 91041

This is getting towards the upper range of what can be called a zine, being slick and professionally produced. However it's definitely far out of the mainstream, being serious consideration of all facets of the UFO phenomenon — not just lights in the sky, but abductions, hypnosis, missing time, alien babies, secret under-

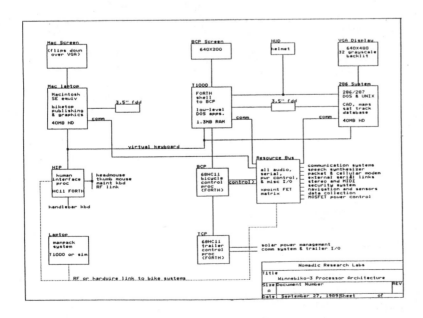

ground government bases and coverups, and more. These people live in a strange world indeed, well removed from the everyday reality of the daily paper. But it does seem like there must be *something* going on to account for all these stories, doesn't it?

THE INFO JOURNAL
$4 from PO Box 367, Arlington, VA 22210

This is the newsletter of the International Fortean Organization, so named after Charles Fort, the indefatigable researcher who chronicled hundreds of odd occurrences, from rains of frogs to sightings of sea monsters. Modern Forteans continue to explore the inexplicable, though often they turn up a prosaic explanation and go on to the next mystery. UFOs, strange rock formations, mysterious archaeological remains and prehistoric animal survivals are among their major concerns. A solid and non-sensational effort.

THE RECUMBENT CYCLIST
$3 from 427 Amherst St. #305, Nashua, NH 03063

The newsletter of the Recumbent Bicycle Club of America. You may have seen such bikes—very low to the ground, with the rider leaning further back than on an upright bike. Proponents say they are superior in many ways, mostly in ease of traveling long distances with less effort. There's plenty of news here, from product reviews to the latest results of pushing man and machine to their limits.

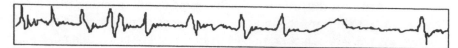

These are the brain waves of a normal American teenager.

These are the brain waves of the same teenager after hacking.

When you hack, you're overusing your brain and are liable to find out things you shouldn't.

THE PARTNERSHIP FOR A HACKER-FREE AMERICA

TRAJECTORIES
$6 from PO Box 700305, San Jose, CA 95170

Robert Anton Wilson — author, rogue, futurist and heretic — is the moving force behind this zine, which explores some of the wonderful upbeat things we can look forward to as the century turns. He's into mind machines and virtual reality and world power grids and life extension — in short, things to make our lives better by revolutionizing our world. He also throws in hefty doses of the amusing teaching writing that he's so good at, while keeping the personal touch. A cantankerous guru for your mailbox.

Personally, I see the ultimate implications of Virtual Reality as Techno-Zen — a comment that probably needs some explanation.
The most important discovery of the modern neurosciences, I think, consists of the fact that every "reality" we perceive has emerged from an ocean of more or less random signals, which our brains have edited, organized and orchestrated into glosses, or sets, or grids, or (in Leary's wonderful term) reality-tunnels. Becoming conscious of the process by which we generate these reality-tunnels out of a potential chaos definitely liberates us from many forms of unconscious bigotry and unexamined assump-
tions. (This awareness of our role in creating our individual Virtual Reality may even cure neuroses, as Korzybski thought.)
Unfortunately, until the invention of this new Head Hardware, the methods of becoming aware of ourselves as co-creators of our "reality" have had major drawbacks. Some of these methods come from shamans or yogis and arouse the violent prejudice of Fundamental Materialists, who never cease attacking research in this area. The other method of awakening from conditioned perception relies on psychedelic drugs, and it seems not only impossible to explain this to most people, it has even become illegal to continue the research. "Drugs" and "mysticism" serve as potent thought-stoppers for most of the educated and uneducated fools in the world — in other words, for the majority. Virtual Reality hardware and software, however, teaches the same lessons as yoga, Zen, and LSD — the brain, guided by a deluge of photons and other energy-blips, creates a Virtual Reality which, in most cases, we believe literally; and, just like Yoga and LSD, this new technology forcibly reminds us that any Virtual Reality, including Consensus Reality, contains elements, colors, structures, meanings, etc., put there by our brains.

ALGORITHM
$5 from PO Box 29237, Westmount Postal Outlet, 785 Wonderland Rd., London, Ontario, CANADA, N6K 1M6

Words and pictures from the lighter side of the home computer revolution grace the pages of this zine, edited by A.K. Dewdney, who once wrote on recreational computing for **Scientific American**. You'll find fractals and chaos here, billiard tables and strange mathematical puzzles, virtual aircraft and extensions to the game of life. But this is not just a journal displaying results but an invitation to get involved, as these programs are presented from the bottom up and readers are encouraged to read, run, and improve upon them. A cheerful alternative to trying to computerize your recipe index or wondering what you bought the darned machine for.

NOMADNESS
$3 from Steve Roberts, PO Box 2185, El Segundo, CA 90245

Steve owns a bike — which is like calling the Mona Lisa a painting. His bike is a seriously high-tech recumbent, with "105 speeds from 7.5 to 122 gear inches, 82 watts of solar panels, over 300 meg of hard disk, a SPARCstation linked by ethernet to PC and Mac environments, HyperTalk graphic user interface to a trio of FORTH control systems, a satellite earth station, cellular phone with modem and fax..." and lots of other bells and whistles. He's built this thing with industrial sponsorship while developing his own nomadic high-tech lifestyle and writing about it on the computer networks and in this zine. It's an inspiring and (at least to this engineer) seductive

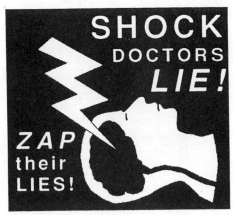

project, a real step towards playing for a living. Subscribe and you can hit the road too, at least in your own imagination (and perhaps some day in the flesh as well).

One of the most common questions I hear about the bike, now worth somewhere near $1 million, is: "Mah gawd, man, how do you LOCK that thing?" Well, I do have a cable lock, but it is seldom used. Instead, there is a very robust security system that includes 7 levels of sensors, opens voice and data links to my backpack during an alert, and even beacons latitude and longitude on ham packet frequencies if the Trimble GPS satellite navigation receiver starts reporting changes in coordinates without the right password. It can lock its own wheel, call 911 and deliver a synthesized message if it thinks it's being stolen, and even do a few things I probably shouldn't write about.

DENDRON NEWS
$1.50 from PO Box 11284, Eugene, OR 97440

Psychiatric liberation is the theme here, as people who have been through the psychiatric system (or who are still en-

meshed in it) try to find more humanitarian alternatives. Their main campaign these days is directed against electroshock therapy, which has been making quite a comeback in recent years despite a number of serious drawbacks. They support a growing array of events, resources, and connections between people, and demonstrate that mental health can be successfully left in the hands of mutual support groups in most (all?) cases.

Lie: "We've tried all the alternatives. And that leaves ECT."
Zap: *Shock doctors usually just try drugs and traditional talk therapy first. Countless empowering, healthy alternatives to shock are working for people every day. The psychiatric profession — based on control and emotional repression — has largely refused to learn from these successful mutual support peer groups, retreats, advocacy programs for basic human needs, user-run community & residential centers, wholistic approaches (such as meditation, massage, exchange counseling, nutrition, exercise), etc. Therefore, it is up to all of us to demand these less harmful alternatives be made readily available to everyone who chooses them.*

IRON FEATHER JOURNAL
$2 from Stevyn, PO Box 1905, Boulder, CO 80306-1905

A zine for hackers and other folks who like to hang around the fringes and have illicit fun. They talk about computer programming and viruses, mild explosives, and ways to screw up your school system. They're a good source for phone numbers to interesting BBS systems, with some tilt towards the C64 world. An outpost from a usually-hidden underground.

A milk carton bomb is relatively simple and safe. It's only purpose is to create a loud noise. The ingredients needed to make this are few and easy to acquire. You will need a plastic milk carton, lighter fluid (type used in cigarette lighters), a piece of paper, and a pair of

chopsticks. If you cannot obtain chopsticks, it's okay to substitute them with something that can hold the paper and is long enough so you won't be harmed by the flames. After acquiring all the ingredients, you can now start to make the bomb. The procedure is easy. First, puncture a hole at the bottom of the milk carton with a screwdriver or equivalent. Next fill one-fourth of the milk carton with lighter fluid. Place the milk carton in a fairly large area outside. Hold a piece of paper between the chopsticks and light the paper with a match. Cautiously place the lighted paper under the hole of the carton and BOOM! You have your loud explosion with little damage to the surrounding area. It would be a good idea to have some water handy to extinguish any flames. Be careful when doing this and have fun.

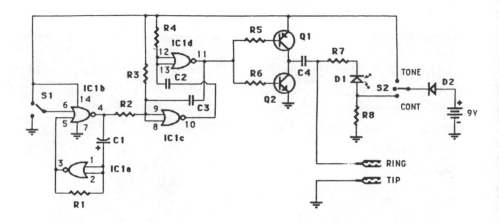

PARTS LIST:

C1-	.47µF electrolytic	R1- 1M 1/4 W
C2, C3-	.01 µF monolithic 20%	R2- 470K 1/4W
C4-	.1 µF 100V	R3, R4, R5, R6- 100K 1/4W
D1-	standard LED	R7- 1K 1/4W
D2-	1N4004	R8- 8.2K 1/2W
IC1-	4001 CMOS quad NOR	S1- SPDT
Q1-	MPSA92 PNP	S2- ON-OFF-ON
Q2-	MPSA42 NPN	

Additional parts: large alligator clips, modular phone plug, 9V battery and clip, IC socket, enclosure, PCB.

TONE TRACER SCHEMATIC DIAGRAM AND PARTS LIST

THE GATE
$2 from PO Box 43518, Richmond Heights, OH 44143

A Fortean zine which concentrates on collecting reports of oddities and mysteries from the mainstream press, wandering from weird science all the way to hauntings and like phenomena. They do give attributions but often these are just to newspapers rather than primary sources. Somewhat light but full of hints that the universe is not so simple as we like to think it is.

Scuba divers in Sydney, Australia have discovered the remains of creatures unknown to science. Experts are baffled by initial examination of photos of the

monsters from an underwater cave off the Fijian island of Matagi in the Pacific. "They bear no resemblance to any marine animal I know," said diver Kevin Deacon. The two largest skeletons are 30-feet overall with yard-long skulls.

EXTROPY
$4 from PO Box 77243, Los Angeles, CA 90007-0243

The one and only zine (so far) for extropians, a group interested in providing a philosophy for the future. They're very much into rational use of technology, and write of artificial intelligence, life extension, space colonization and nanotechnology as well as the morality of the future and the irrationality of irrationality. Within their own reality-tunnel they are quite ruthless about examining their assumptions, though using technology in the service of human liberation is probably their #1 preoccupation.

THE EXTROPIAN PRINCIPLES

1. BOUNDLESS EXPANSION - seeking more intelligence, wisdom, and personal power, an unlimited lifespan, and removal of natural, social, biological, and psychological limits to self-actualization and self-realization. No limits on our personal and social progress and possibilities.

2. SELF-RESPONSIBILITY - both moral and cognitive; critical examination of all assumptions and models. Taking charge of one's own life. Political self-responsibility includes the idea of spontaneous order: rejection of central control and unnecessary limits on freedom. Fostering of diversity.

3. DYNAMIC OPTIMISM - promotion of a positive, empowering attitude towards our individual future and that of all intelligent beings.

4. TECHNOPHILISM - affirmation of the role of science and its offspring, technology, guided by extropian values, in realizing the optimistic, dynamic value-perspective of extropianism.

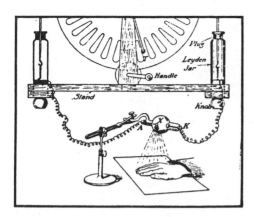

STRANGE MAGAZINE
$5.95 from PO Box 2246, Rockville, MD 20847

A very well-produced Fortean zine with lots of photos and the resources to do some original investigations. They've been especially active in the field of cryptozoology, trying to track down animals which are unknown to science although there are reasonably credible reports of sightings. They also cover a lot of traditional Fortean themes, from UFOs to strange things falling from the skies to analyses of the crystal skulls.

THE NEON NEWS
$4 from PO Box 668, Volcano, HI 96785

A spirited and informative journal for people who work with neon — "benders," as they call themselves. It began in 1989 as a venture in which shop tips, personal experience, ideas, opinions and even gossip could be passed along from one bender to another. Contributors range from the *artiste* to the technologician; there are safety tips, legal responsibilities (a bender discovered faulty neon and fire hazards in a local restaurant), and guides to understanding this delicate art. From transformers to "mean free paths" (the average distance traveled by a molecule between collisions), it brings camaraderie to a select group of working artists.

Dean Blazek, who taught me neon a decade ago, demonstrated what he called "the installer's test" wherein he would drop a student's glass masterpiece onto the work table from a height of eighteen inches or so. This, we were quick to learn, showed where the bad bends or welds were, as well as showing us what our friends the installers would be doing to our work in the future. Then he'd say, "Any questions?" Nope. But I've never met an installer yet who has broken a single piece of neon — none that he'd admit to anyway. The other day one of my installers, who we'll call Irwin came in with four broken units.

ME: FOUR broken pieces? You broke FOUR pieces of my neon?

IRWIN: Not me, I didn't break them. You know I don't break neon.

ME: Well, what happened to it then?

IRWIN: Beats me.

ME: Yeah, I'd like to.

IRWIN: What?

ME: Oh, nothing.

The closest thing to an admission of guilt I've ever gotten was this call:

IRWIN: Boss, can you make me another four-foot "B"?

ME: Why? What happened to the one I made?

IRWIN: I think the gas musta leaked out.

ME: Oh, just bring it back then and I'll repump it.

IRWIN: Uh, I don't think that's practical.

ME: Why not? ...Say, exactly how did it lose its gas?

IRWIN: Well, it musta been right at the end of that two-story fall from the roof we was on.

ANY QUESTIONS?

Reviews

Factsheet Five has always been a unique reference tool in that it reviews zines of all genres — no matter the content or nature. But there are also review publications which specialize in reviewing only particular types of zines. These focused review forums are as essential as the broader-based review zines, as they can spend more time on the various periodicals and participants in their area, catering to a more select crowd.

OBSCURE PUBLICATIONS AND VIDEO
$1.50 from PO Box 1334, Milwaukee, WI 53201

A zine of news and reviews from the small press world and the people behind it. Editor Jim Romenesko skims the cream off the alternative and underground press and looks at the work in depth. He interviews publishers about their lives and zines, reviews notable publications and videos and concentrates on spotlighting only a few in each issue. An essential for anyone who wants to know more about the zine world, and very fun.

I've been interested in the "small press" ever since I was eight-years old and putting out a family newspaper. I have five sisters and four brothers and there was always a lot of news: someone falling into the toilet, the dog biting the mailman, or maybe our favorite television show getting cancelled. Whatever it was, I was there to record it. One time, my tooth fell out while I was printing (literally) the latest issue of The Family News and blood spattered on the frontpage. Rather than throw the paper out, I turned it into a story about my tooth loss. I circled the red spot and noted to my readers: "actual tooth blood." I guess that was my real start in the grisly, gory and sometimes bloody world of journalism.

Since then, I've worked on a daily newspaper and a monthly magazine. I began OBSCURE because I wanted to write about the many interesting and colorful 'zine editors around the world. They have varying interests: film, politics, sex, music, gore, relationships, literature, and the list goes on. Some are sane — others, maybe borderline and beyond. I'm not here to pass judgments, and

perhaps I'm the last person in the world to assess one's character; I published a book of morgue reports called DEATH LOG, which some people think shows me to be borderline or beyond. I don't think I am — just as I don't think Mike Diana, who is profiled on the cover, is a disgusting person. He is merely expressing himself and maybe venting some frustrations about society and religion. That's what everyone in the 'zine world is doing — writing about their various passions. It sure beats watching television for seven hours a day, which is supposed to be the average viewing time for Americans.

SMALL PRESS REVIEW
$20/yr from PO Box 100, Paradise, CA 95967

A staid but never stuffy zine of reviews of small press items, primarily books but with an eye towards the periodical world as well. It's a close inspection of the small press with honest reviews and commentary, in addition to classifieds, announcements, upcoming publications and various articles about the equally various aspects of the small press world and publishing in general. Feature articles have included an assessment of the feminist press, the decrease in cogent and capable literary publishing after the 80s, or questions about the total self-interest of many would-be contributors to literary magazines. The stuff you find reviewed in here should eventually reach the mainstream (hopefully with its integrity intact).

Politics

There's an old joke that says two anarchists placed in the same room will create three groups and five publications. Political zine publishing is an active field, and not limited to the left. There are conservative zines and even a few middle-of-the-roaders, though the bulk of the underground political press does seem to be on the more radical edge of things — hardly surprising as we go through a conservative period in history. There are more leftists than rightists in the zine world, probably because they have a harder time getting a hearing in the mainstream media.

FIFTH ESTATE
$1.50 from 4632 Second Ave., Detroit, MI 48201

Fifth Estate has been around for over 25 years, gradually evolving from a relatively standard underground newspaper to a thrice-yearly questioning of almost everything. Often accused of being anti-technology, they are in fact sophisticated theorists and observers, equally at home condemning the mega-machine and the macho excesses of redneck environmentalists. The writers here are activists, putting their bodies on the line in front of garbage incinerators and other unsavory manifestations of technology. **FE** also remains one of the main watering holes for the anarchist movement, reporting on what's going on across the country and around the world and publishing letters from comrades with something to say.

What would an authentic Earth Day look like? Wouldn't it look like a general strike, a moratorium on production, a reduction of mechanical movement and with it of the industrial noise that drowns out the wind, when all of the former cogs of the megamachine take a long look at the world, perhaps for the first time, and begin the process of becoming living subjects once more? Wouldn't they engage one another in a face-to-face discourse for the first time, taking stock of hands and feet and head and heart as the real material bases for a new society? Wouldn't they simply ignore the television stations, rather than attempting to capture them to broadcast the pronouncements of the latest revolution-

ary-industrial junta? Wouldn't they begin to retrace their steps, back away from the edge of the precipice, turning things off and beginning to rely on their communities and their own human powers to meet their few trifling needs so as to get on with the real adventure of living, of singing, of dreaming? And that first night — wouldn't the sky be dark and beauteous and studded with stars for the first time in memory? Wouldn't a different language, spangled with eternity, find its way into daily discourse as the conditioning of industrialism and manufactured values began to be

shed?
Couldn't it be, rather than one more supervised saturnalia for the inmates, a festival of the oppressed capable of bursting its limits and calling a new culture into being? (And who might be the oppressed? Surely not only human victims, but all the branches of life's tree. The very stones groan under this civilization's weight.)

LEFT BUSINESS OBSERVER
$2.50 from 250 W. 85th #75, New York, NY 10024

A newsletter which might even be too serious to call a zine — if not for the fact that editor Doug Henwood seems happily interested in keeping in touch with real people rather than just suit-and-tie executive types. As the title says, the viewpoint here is decidedly left, taking on the financial establishment and explaining its impact on regular folks in straightforward terms. Whether it's the M1 money supply, the death of social democracy in Sweden, or the effects of mortgage rates

Nobody keeps his campaign promises.
Nobody deserves to live off your taxes.
Nobody can legislate your freedom.

NOBODY IS THE PERFECT CANDIDATE!

If *you* think that Nobody represents your interests,

VOTE FOR NOBODY

If *you* think there's no difference
between political parties,

VOTE FOR NOBODY

If *you* think Nobody should run your life,

VOTE FOR NOBODY

If you *think*,

VOTE FOR NOBODY

---

on the rest of life, LBO is an educational and provocative read.

Capital has pulled off a magnificent PR coup: it has convinced most of the world, including a few timorous lefties, that the market is the ultimate form of social organization, while managing to export, displace, or evade most of its problems. Apologists can point to the undeniable prosperity enjoyed by a privileged sliver within the world's rich countries, for example, while denying any responsibility for the Third World's endless depression. In the U.S., money's publicists can explain the fiscal crises now affecting every level of government by blaming the allegedly congenital inefficiencies of government — what else could you expect from the public sector, after all? Homelessness, crack, AIDS, and busted S&Ls, all of which are pushing public budgets deeper into the red, have nothing to do with laissez-faire.

LIGHT & LIBERTY
$1 from Lawrence E. Christopher, PO Box 33, Woodstock, NY 12498

A chameleon zine balanced between the libertarian and New Age worlds. They're interested in things that can be done to experience freedom in the here and now, on all scales from political action to metaphysical understanding. Pantheism,

decentralism, libertarianism and anarchism are among the threads woven together here to try to present a multifaceted picture of individual liberty.

LIVING FREE
$1 from Jim Stumm, PO Box 29, Hiler Branch, Buffalo, NY 14223

A zine of self-reliance and freedom, with a generally libertarian editorial viewpoint. Jim Stumm discusses ways to become free here and now, from raising your own food in the backyard to equipping a van for stealthy mobile living. This is one of the best places to read about vonu, an idea that had a vogue in underground circles in the Seventies. The basic premise of vonu (an acronym of sorts for "voluntary and not vulnerable") was that one could drop out of society completely and live off the land, taking forays to the edges of civilization for more goods only when absolutely necessary. The originators of the idea eventually vanished, and no one knows whether this was due to success or being eaten by bears.

THE MATCH
$3 from PO Box 3488, Tucson, AZ 85722

Peppered with articles like "Religion as Rabid Madness", **The Match** represents a no-nonsense, crusty approach to anarchism and atheism. It defies and reviles authority whether found in church, state, or landlord (the publisher has had several run-ins with the latter species, and writes amusingly of them). It also has little patience for cloudy thinking and romanticism within the anarchist left. Every issue is sure to have at least a few cantankerous blasts at others less certain in their opposition to the state, as well as plenty of news and opinion that shows just what a rotten idea government really is.

A kind of mass insanity grips America every four years — not the insanity of wild enthusiasm over the presidential so-called elections, but the insanity of pretending that there's wild enthusiasm. In truth, nobody really gives a damn, but the media like to make it seem that all the fore-determined empty hoopla is of vital concern in everyone's eyes, and the reason they do so is that by commenting on it, traveling around busily to it, and appearing in it, they'll seem that much bigger and more important.

Bad as this situation is, a still further fact that you're probably not aware of is that by federal law all periodicals devoted to a dissident point of view are required to be as ugly and unreadable as it is possible to make them, and real experts, believe me, are operating in this field. You've probably wondered why it is that magazines and newspapers expressing any opinion to the left of Adolph Eichmann are almost invariably typewritten, poorly photocopied, laid out in a confusing manner, etc., and this little known statute is of course the reason. The law specifically provides, I think, for bonuses in certain cases that must include: starting an article on the front page and making it jump to page six where it still does not end so that it has to jump further to pages nine and twelve; placing headings, paragraphs, pictures and so forth at various angles so the reader gets an impression of hopeless, drooling stupidity; and, almost needless to add, such publications MUST be set in typewriter-type complete with strike-

overs and lines crossed out in felt-tip pen. Penalties for violating any of these rules vary, but will include sanctions such as postal harassment and misdelivery, refusal of other periodicals to review your issuances, and denunciations by overnight-created 'movement heavies' who ALWAYS turn up to speak at widely separated demonstrations and events.

THE INFINITE ONION
$1 from Dave Fischer, PO Box 263, Colorado Springs, CO 80901

An anarchist zine of the younger generation, very concerned with fighting racism in the punk movement, multinational employers, and other forms of repression outside of the traditional government sphere. Produced by a collective, **The Infinite Onion** goes to show that anarchist thought is not the exclusive domain of aging groups of leftists, but continues to grow and evolve as it is discovered by new groups of people. They pay

less attention to layout than to content, cramming in graphics swiped from all over and bits of opinion and news wherever they will fit.

Here's how I define anarchism in my own life. I will live how I please to the fullest extent possible, only taking authority into consideration because it is forced upon me. I will do as I please as long as I don't harm others intentionally. I will not give in to mass culture conformity and the idiocy that it breeds since I am my own person. This does not mean I will not work with others. I'll do what I have to, to survive in this system which includes working and paying unavoidable taxes but at the same time I will fight the system to make this an easier place to live in and I will fight the system to make my life less dependent on the factors the system forces on us such as work, legal restrictions and all the ridiculous attitudes imposed on us. I've realized that my life belongs to me and nobody else and nobody has the right to control me without my consent.

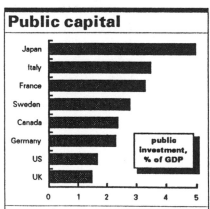

Public capital

public investment, % of GDP

	0	1	2	3	4	5
Japan						
Italy						
France						
Sweden						
Canada						
Germany						
US						
UK						

It's little wonder that the public spaces of the U.S. and Britain feel like they're falling apart. GDP is gross domestic product, which is GNP less net income earned on work or investments abroad. GNP is the value of a country's output of goods and services. Data: OECD.

INSTEAD OF A MAGAZINE
$2 from Mike Ziesing, PO Box 433, Willimantic, CT 06226

Founded in 1980, **IOAM** has concentrated more on thinking about anarchism and spreading anarchist ideas than on slick production or increased circulation, thus retaining a friendly, homey feel. Their views are influenced by the great American individualist anarchists of the 19th century including Lysander Spooner and Benjamin Tucker, though they're not stuck in an historical straitjacket. Common concerns for **IOAM** are prisoners' rights, nationalist struggles around the world (they support efforts to break down existing states, if conducted with non-statist methods), the punk movement, and fighting racism, classism, sexism and other forms of repression wherever they occur. Thanks to Michael Ziesing, who coordinates the zine's production, they also focus strongly on Taoism and other natural philosophies that have some kinship to anarchy. Much of the zine is reader-written, and it's encouraging to see just how many independent thinkers there are out there.

JERICHO NEWSLETTER
3 first class stamps from Michael A. Stephens, ASPC - PO Box B-82951, Florence, AZ 85232

Jericho is a publication focused on the problems of the U.S. prison system — from behind the prison walls. The U.S. has a higher proportion of its citizens behind bars than any other nation in the world, including South Africa and the USSR, and the situation only seems to be getting worse. This zine provides legal news for prisoners, a place for them to put penpal listings, and continuing notes on the overcrowding, prejudice and other injustices in our current legal system. Editor Michael

Stephens is doing time, currently in Arizona (he's been transferred from state to state several times, as his political activities don't set well with prison administrations).

Your day begins at 5:30 A.M. with bright lights shining in your face and a guard shouting over the PA system that it's time to get up and go to breakfast. At 6:00 A.M. your cell door opens with a loud bang and you move into the stream of men moving to the chowhall to eat. In

the chowhall you are herded through a line along with 500 other men and given a plate of food that is often inedible. The day's frustrations are already beginning. The noise in the chowhall is nearly deafening as 500+ men voice their frustrations while a score of surly guards try to maintain a semblance of order with threats of punishment for every minor rule infraction. As the day progresses, the frustrations and attitudes of guards and inmates worsens.

THE KANSAS INTELLIGENCER
$12/year from R.W. Clack, Rt. 1 Box 7A, Morganville, KS 67468

A "monthly polemic" for people who believe in representative self-government, the free market, and "the conviction that human intelligence is more than a Darwinian fluke." Most issues are one legal-sized sheet, with

the commentary of editor R.W. Clack on our military adventures, scandals in Congress, funding for obscene art, tax revolts, and much more. Clack's position is generally conservative, though he's not much of a fan of big government or our current representatives. I find the **Intelligencer** to be a good read, especially recommended to those on the left who are convinced that there are only stupid people who oppose them.

Federal Judge Richard Rogers found for the plaintiffs in a recent case. The plaintiffs are inmates at the Kansas State prison at Lansing, Ks. Plaintiffs claim, on Constitutional grounds, cruel and unusual punishment — overcrowding. The State, in response, is proposing to build a $58 million prison to house 768 additional prisoners. Let's see now: that comes to a tad over $75,000 per bed. The projected operating costs of this prison is $16 million per year or about $21,000 per prisoner per year or about $57/prisoner/day. It would be cheaper to send them to Harvard. And more appropriate too.

TURNING THE TIDE
$1 from P.A.R.T., PO Box 1990, Burbank, CA 91507

People Against Racist Terror (P.A.R.T.) are one of several groups formed within the punk community as a reaction to the rise of racist violence in the skinhead movement. They represent a movement policing itself, and stand strong in their opposition to white supremacists and other racists throughout society. Their insistence that racist literature is not a free-speech issue is troubling, but overall their organizing and educational activities seem to have a positive response.

The KKK/Nazis have no right to carry out organizing campaigns, spout their vile racism on TV or cable, or march and burn crosses. These actions are not speech, but simply the above-ground activity of factions that have always been committed to secretive violence and terror and para-military operations. Groups like the ACLU that go to court to win parade permits for the Klan when communities try to stop their marches are misguided. Their racism is not a matter of "expression"; it's part of a strategy to legitimize and intensify racist terror.

THE UPRIGHT OSTRICH
$3 from Peggy Poor, PO Box 11691, Milwaukee, WI 53211

Something of the **Ostrich's** editorial stance can be gleamed by noting that they express their prices in "FRN's" instead of dollars — maintaining that the Federal Reserve Note is not in fact a lawful dollar under the Constitution. With other Constitutionalists, they argue against a government grown too large and unresponsive the the People, who have a duty and a right to trim it down to size. Their content ranges from esoteric legal theories designed to prove that the income tax is illegal, to notes on suppressed super-weaponry, to the latest theories about what the conspirators behind the New World Order are really up to. While some of their stuff is pretty far out, they've done very good work reporting on little publicized government abuses, such as those surrounding prison privatization.

THE VOLUNTARYIST
$2 from PO Box 1275, Gramling, SC 29348

Voluntaryists might call themselves libertarians were it not for the actions of the Libertarian Party, which supports governmental action. These people believe that "If one takes care of the means, the end will take care of itself," leaving people who are free to negotiate with one another freer in other respects as well. They publish short snippets about the absurd actions of government along with long, chewy essays about subjects like renouncing your citizenship or the state control of weights and measures.

Editor Carl Watner draws on a rich variety of sources in his quest to promote education and self-sufficiency as strategies for removing the state from our lives.

WORLD PERSPECTIVES
$2.25 from PO Box 3074, Madison, WI 53704-0074

A collection of "Alternative News and Analyses from Shortwave Sources." Though it does get off into other areas, mostly this zine is very political with a leftist bent, reporting the news as seen by outfits like Radio Madrid International, Radio Sofia Bulgarian, and the Voice of the Andes. They provide a valuable alternative to the standard news media in this country, which tend to share a common set of biases.

ZENDIK FARM
$2 from Star Route 16C-S, Bastrop, TX 78602

The Farm in question is a commune that dates clear back to 1969, with plenty of new people still joining even today. They are into changing the planet, not just themselves, and see

themselves as a Warrior Tribe, ready to band together and fight against those destroying the planet. Music, respect for nature ("Eco-librium"), and above all the pursuit of the truth are their driving forces. They remain resolutely opposed to corporate DeathKultur, providing an alternative for kids in trouble and helping those they can reach think about the world and their place in it. Though overtly political, this is a different kind of politics than you'll find in most zines; they're into living their convictions, not just exploring and explaining them.

A NEW WORLD RISING
$1 from Box 33, 77 Ives, Providence, RI 02906

NWR is politics as filtered through the spirit of a Grateful Dead concert — indeed, concerts are one of the prime distribution points for this free tabloid. Their main reason for existence is to

People who want to go into the wilderness and live off nature are anti-progressive.

They could stay in the system, become farmers and kill insects and small animals in the earth.

They could work in slaughterhouses and on fishing boats and kill cows, pigs, chickens and sea life.

They could work for industries that mine the ground and kill and displace the creatures there.

They could join the armed services and kill humans.

You see? There are plenty of choices.
—Felice

promote all the good old hippie values of peace and love and understanding, and to network people together. They print a lot of short letters and addresses in each issue, urging people to get together and work together to change society.

We want a world of Peace and Love and Liberation. Whole Earth Harmony and Healing. Music and Dance. Flowers and Cosmic Powers. Creation not Destruction. Applying all of our varied talents to Meet the Needs of Everyone. It's Time. We are Developing the Vision. We must Create the Reality.

NO LONGER SILENT
$1 from Eliza Blackweb, PO Box 3582, Tucson, AZ 85722

This is one of the crop of newer anarchist zines being put out by young people who constitute the bulk of today's "movement" — an amorphous mix of those who see anarchy as fashion with those who have a deeper commitment. NLS is definitely in the latter camp, using poetry, art, and essays to argue for thoughtful action, avoiding the twin problems of mindless vanguard violence and pointless armchair theorizing. A richly alive zine.

BABYFISH LOST ITS MOMMA
$3 from PO Box 11589, Detroit, MI 48211

Babyfish is a celebration of life, a collection of poetry and music reviews and political articles and reports on actions taken to stop the megamachine from killing us all. The writers here aren't afraid to stand up for what they believe in, whether it be the cleansing power of punk music or the sublime release of "dangerous" drugs. This is a product of the new generation of activists, women and men who see even the traditional liberal peace movement as an inadequate response to a deadly situation. Coming from Detroit's Cass

Corridor, home to food co-ops, free concerts, and strange people, **Babyfish** is a uniquely inspirational experience.

Sunday in the park...the day of networking and play...we exchanged addresses and ideas. I was soon drawn in by the ever-growing free-form music jam. I have been at many of these tribal events, at rainbow, in nevada, in detroit. but never did it reach the level of power i saw that day. i know it had something to do with the nature of this gathering and the intention with which we began to move. some drummed. some strummed. some banged. some played crazed sax or clarinet. jazzpunk survival. some danced. i danced. i shook. i ended up on the ground groping rhythmically in the grass. Other bodies came to the ground with me. we rolled on top of each other, crawled on each other. symbol of love making. we touched each other in love as we simultaneously touched the earth. the noise went through many a rise and fall...coming in and out of climax several times. we came into further cleansing.

JAG
On Request from JAG, Inc., 10 E. Charles, Oelwein, IA 50662

R.S. Jaggard, MD, has been putting out this broadside for decades now, dedicated to "Individual Moral Responsibility and the Free Enterprise

System." The most intriguing part about his libertarian ideas is that he's actually putting them into practice, refusing to accept government payments while still providing affordable medical care to his patients. Yet paradoxically he makes his ideas available to all for free, taking donations from those who wish to make them and plugging away at the idea that we should all be responsible for our own actions.

The income tax steals from the workers for the benefit of the moochers. Social Security is a swindle. The goverment of the United States is morally and financially bankrupt. The income tax must be abolished.

GREEN ANARCHIST
L8/10 issues from Box H, 34 Cowley Road, Oxford OX4, ENGLAND

These people combine "black" and "green" points of view to produce an anarchism with a distinctly apocalyptic, ecological feel, ready and eager to drag down industrial civilization in the hopes of a better world to come. They are a great source of information on alternative goings-on in the British Isles, including the annual alternative festival at Stonehenge, often the site of police violence against partiers. There's plenty of information on animal rights here as well. Each issue contains a lovely centerfold poster suitable for framing or propagandizing.

KICK IT OVER
$7.50/4 issues from PO Box 5811, Station A, Toronto, Ontario, CANADA, M5W 1P2

A long-running anarchist zine from Toronto, which has a continuing reputation as an anarchist center. Unlike many far-left journals, KIO remains critical of the macho violent posturing found in the anarchist movement, and has devoted considerable space to examining the

internal dynamics of alternative groups as well as larger political issues. They also remain strongly committed to feminist and ecological points of view. Prisoner support and third world coverage underline their commitment to the dispossessed and repressed everywhere. Despite all these formidable ideas, it's also a fun read, with the art integrated into the text and particular attention paid to being accessible. If you want to explore the anarchist movement this is a good place to start.

From the beginning it has been one of the commonplaces of anarchist thought that men and women are naturally social; that left to themselves people will develop voluntary associations to meet their social, economic, and cultural needs; and that if these needs are met there are no strictly political needs that go beyond them, since freely organized institutions would make government as we know it, with its rigid laws and systems and bureaucracies, entirely unnecessary. Human societies, the theory goes, took a wrong turn long ago, about the time human beings shifted from a simple tribal or early urban community, with their folk moots and their citizens' assemblies organizing everything from below by direct participation and mutual aid, to the imperial or feudal model in which the social pyramid was reversed, everything was arranged from above rather than at the ground level, and the necessities of power brought in coercive institutions.

THE SHADOW
$1 from PO Box 20298, New York, NY 10009

It's not stretching things much to say that there is a war on in New York City, with the Lower East Side being the battleground. Housing and homelessness are the chief issues, and ever since the Tompkins Square Park riot a few years ago, **The Shadow** has been the best source of information from the streets. Police brutality and political lying continues to be rampant in the area, with squatters and activists routinely roughed up, and the editors

of the paper even having received death threats from the cops. If you think civil unrest died out thirty years ago, you haven't been paying attention.

PRACTICAL ANARCHY
SASE from Chuck Munson, 16 N. Butler St. #2, Madison, WI 53703

Chuck is one of what seem to be the new breed of anarchists: people concerned with right livelihood in the world today, trying to live by their principles and exploring what this means. He's into cooperative living, setting up grassroots social systems, and making a difference in people's lives today. His thoughts are presented intelligently and concisely, with none of the bafflegab that makes some "Movement" publications difficult for newcomers.

I feel that anarchy is a viable way of living everyday. Too often anarchists are accused of being too "utopian" or "unrealistic." Anarchy is a realistic, practical way of looking at the world and changing it. I believe that we shouldn't wait for that magical moment when anarchy "takes over." There are many things each of us can do every day to make changes in our world, our lives, our communities....I believe that most anarchists agree that we don't have the answers or solutions to all the world's problems. Even more, there is constant disagreement as to how we should travel the path to a better world. I personally do not feel comfortable with those who would offer strict plans or agendas — I am more confident about the abilities of the "average" person to make choices about change.

Potpourri — II

More zines from the outer reaches; you never know what is waiting for you on the next page.

MADWOMAN
$4 from SisterSerpents, 1138 N. Wolcott 3R, Chicago, IL 60622

"True confessions from women who laugh in the face of patriarchy while fighting against the horrors of misogyny." This is news from the cutting edge of angry radical feminism. It's a mix of horror stories — it seems like most women have some — and creative fighting back, from altered billboards to physical violence. As they say on the cover, "GETMADGETEVEN!"

My phone rang one Sunday morning and a young woman's voice tells me she's doing a survey and would I answer some questions? I ask who this is for and she waffles and asks me my age. I demand more information and she replies, "shut up bitch and answer the goddamn questions!". We both laugh and she hangs up. They hit redial and apologize for swearing at me. They are three teenage girls who have had a sleepover and are now making prank phone calls. They have a list of questions starting with age, occupation, model of car, various like and dislikes on down to explicit questions about social life, birth control, sexual habits and everything they can think of. They've been at it all morning and so far no woman who answers will let them get to the first question. The men, on the other hand, have answered all the questions without embarrassment. They had just finished talking to one guy for half an hour. Often the men wanted the girls to come over and meet them. They got as dirty and explicit in their questions as possible and they never managed to find a question the men refused to answer. Eventually the young women had to end the phone calls when their curiosity got exhausted!!

UNDERGROUND BEAT
$5/4 issues from Beat Club Productions, 1718 M St. NW #154, Washington, DC 20036

A zine of free expression and dissent with solid production and a wide range of interests. They carried especially good coverage of the protests against the war in Kuwait, and in the same issue explored the frontiers of cyberspace and at hacker issues with John Perry Barlow. Interesting graphics and a commitment to building a new Movement that's inclusive and oriented towards real people and real issues make this a joy to read.

BACKWOODS HOME MAGAZINE
$4 from PO Box 2630, Ventura, CA 93002

The "magazine for people who value their independence" is full of ideas for those who want to get out of the rat race, move back to the land, and enjoy life. They start with constructing your own house, look at getting power and water for it, and go on to cooking, raising livestock, making soap, homeschooling your kids — in short, learning to be a modern pioneer. There's a fiercely independent spirit here that is very attractive, and every issue sets me to dreaming of the days when I can follow in the footsteps of these writers.

Anyone can do it — motivation is the main thing. It's lots more work than comparable frame buildings and takes considerably more time, but I've seen very few commence a log building and fail to finish it. Previous experience with carpentry or other building methods has less to do with success in log building than you might think.
Nor do you have to be large and strong. In fact, from my work with students I have observed that women do some of the best work on logs and sometimes learn chainsaw techniques more rapidly and safely than men do. Paradoxically, this is probably due to women's lack of previous contact with chainsaws and consequent absence of need to shed any negative habits prior to learning to use this important tool safely and effectively.

NEW SETTLER INTERVIEW
$1 from PO Box 702, Mendocino, CA 95460

Some zines seem to be imbued with the spirit of a particular place. This is one of them, a zine of the people and land of northern California. Editor Beth Bosk has developed the art of interviewing, picking wonderful people — activists, scientists, feminists, craftspeople, growers — and talking with them about their lives and works. There's a decidedly rural spirit here — agriculture, forests, and

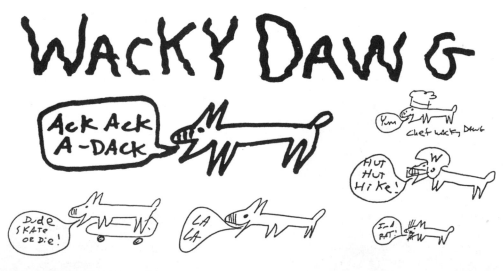

plenty of time for a good chat on the porch. In addition, there's a rare quality of *hope* that runs through many of the interviews, the idea that the future can be better and that individuals can make a difference.

CHRIS BRENNAN: The first hogs were actually brought over on Columbus's second trip and released in the Caribbean. In California, there has been some sort of pig running loose since the Spaniard days. They released them on the Channel Islands off southern California as a food source out there for sailors. Most of the pigs up here on the north coast came during the homesteading days. People would let their pigs loose in the mountains, notch their ears, which was a type of brand, then round them up whenever they wanted to sell them or needed meat. Many of these hogs escaped in the woods and have been there ever since, over a hundred years. In the 1920's, a guy named Moore, who owned a giant ranch in Monterey county, imported wild boars from Europe and Russia and released them, and they interbred with the feral pigs that were already in the mountains. Now we have a kind of mixture. From Monterey county, hunters caught pigs with that blood line and introduced them to different mountain ranges where there might have been feral pigs. So in northwestern California we have a mixture of feral pigs with a little bit of European wild boar in them.

THE PRAIRIE RAMBLER
$1.23 from PO Box 505, Claremont, CA 91711-0505

Editor Jerry B. haunts the libraries and bookstores, collecting bite-sized bits of humor and wisdom from everyone from Samuel Pepys to Malcolm X and beyond. Then he distills these into an 8-page zine together with a bit of his own commentary on the times. The result is easy and delightful reading, bits and pieces suitable for dipping into at your leisure — a bit like the bottoms of the pages in **Reader's Digest** without the bother of all those insipid articles taking up paper above them.

If once they become inattentive to public affairs, you and I, and Congress and Assemblies, Judges and Governors, shall all become wolves.
Thomas Jefferson
And they sure as hell did!

JUST KILLING TIME
$1 from Eddie Banay, 14227 Eventide, Cypress, TX 77429

A zine for those fascinated with the downside of life in human society. It's made up of newspaper clippings and magazine articles (all apparently photocopied without permission) about mass murderers, poisoned Halloween candy, and similar gruesome topics. As a sideline, the publishers sell video compilations of celebrity-nudity and women-in-prison films.

KELTIC FRINGE
$3 from Maureen Williams, Box 251 RD #1, Uniondale, PA 18470

This zine is devoted to exploring the heritage of the Celtic peoples of the world — the title comes from the fact that the Celts (or Kelts, the spelling preferred by some traditionalists) have ended up settling the lands on the fringes of the British Isles. They publish notes about current politics and celebrities, bits of history and myth, stories and poems. Language and culture remain enduring fascina-tions here as well, and the emphasis is on the similarities of the various Celtic cultures rather than on the promotion of any one at the others' expense.

Kelts were great conquerors, taking their spoken language with them as they spread across Europe. But this vast collection of loose-knit tribes was never a unified nation able to consolidate the power displayed in battle. Eventually they were driven out by unversed though more united tribes, pushed to Europe's western shores, & about 500 BC, across the North Sea into the British Isles. Kelts made this land their own over the next century, until a succession of invaders, from Vikings to Romans, drove Keltic tribes to the fringes of the islands - Scotland, Man, Ireland, Wales, & Cornwall - & centuries later, Angles & Saxons caused some Kelts to flee back to France, where they settled an area they named Brittany, or Little Britain.

DO IT YOURSELF

[NORGE]

GRAFFITTI FRIDGE

SCRIBBLE UNLIMITED PRESENTS
$1 from Miles Polar Bear, PO Box 415, Rutherford, NJ 07070

As the title might suggest, this is a home for a variety of writing. Sometimes they stray into structured articles such as a history of punk rock, sometimes they publish stories or poetry. But the most intriguing parts are the scribbles, bits of graffiti and marginal conversations between staffers. A chameleon zine capable of publishing almost anything.

FAGAGAGA
"Free as always" from PO Box 1382, Youngstown, OH 44501

This one is actually a project in the mail art sense rather than a zine proper. "Mail art" refers to the practice of sending artwork through the mail, as a way of democratizing the art process, and an extensive network of people has sprung up around this concept. FaGaGaGa (a mysterious entity composed of one or more persons) participates by sending out a series of original absurd postcards, some inviting art submissions, some featuring the latest received, some with obscure slogans and stickers.

ANTHEM
$1 from Keith A. Gordon, PO Box 158324, Nashville, TN 37215

A zine of popular culture (having expanded out from a music-only base) that's coming up on a decade old now. You never know which way Keith and company are going to leap, from a comparative review of men's magazines (**Playboy** and **Penthouse** at the top, poor old **Oui** at the bottom), to the evils of anti-home taping legislation, to strange missives from some of the loose cannons of the underground. Published irregularly but consistently, **Anthem** may take a while to get to your mailbox but is likely to be a delightful surprise when it does.

MSRRT NEWSLETTER
$15/yr from MLA/MSRRT, c/o Chris Dodge & Jan DeSirey, 4645 Columbus Ave. S., Minneapolis, MN 55407

The newsletter of the Social Responsibilities Roundtable of the Minnesota Library Association, a group of librarians who believe libraries have distinct responsibilities to be on the cutting edge of reforming society. Each issue opens with some news and opinion, divided between doings in the library world and commentary on the wider intellectual issues of the day. But the bulk of what's here is reviews, mainly of preiodicals and books that might be overlooked by more traditional library publications, including a fair sprinkling of zines. Women's issues, media analysis, regional culture and the Third World are among their wide-ranging interests.

For those caught up in the arguments against "political correctness" and "liberal thought police" we have this to say: The so-called free marketplace of ideas is a myth—wishful thinking at best, dangerous delusion at worst. Dozens of biographies ignore or severely downplay the less pleasant ramifications of Columbus's journeys, but when a handful of them dare to reveal another aspect of the story (as in Hans Koning's Columbus: his enterprise) they are railed against. When one cultivates a garden, one sees the weeds are kept under control. Should it be different in society? Ours is polluted—engorged with lies, half-truths, shams, and frippery. How to deal with a society which considers artificially-colored and sweetened carbonated beverages to be superior to fresh water? Which considers all manner of schlock between two covers, regardless of content, to be a worthy book? To cite the C. Wright Mills epigram again, "In a world of widely communicated nonsense, any statement of fact is of political and moral significance." We refuse to modify our vision and will continue to illuminate the truth as best we are able, as long as we speak, write, breathe.

MUSEUM INSIGHTS
$5 from PO Box 313, North Amherst, MA 01059

Nancy Frazier, author of **Special Museums of the Northeast**, discovered that she loved traveling to museums and writing to them. The result is **Museum Insights**, for people delighted by all the oddball little museums that are out there, from small art museums to "living museums" to really strange fun places such as the Dalton Gang Hideout Museum. Nancy has an appreciative eye for these places, and the only drawback to her reviews is that they make the average reader wish for an unlimited budget to go visiting. A welcome introduction to a lot of unusual aspects of our culture.

So far the nation's first and only tenement museum has raised enough money to rent the ground floor spaces and establish offices and a theater there. Though not yet fully operational, they do present an ongoing series of exhibits and guided walking tours that highlight neighborhood life and history. Supporting this organization financially has its benefits — tangible as well as spiritual. They publish a paper, **Tenement Times**, that keeps you in touch with their progress. But, that's not all. In a column devoted to 'Soups from Tenement Kitchens' recipes were included: Dee Dee Daily's West African Chicken Soup, Malachy McCormick's Irish Boiled Chicken and Broth, Rosa (Loh Mooi Kwei) Ross' Cantonese Chicken Soup, Hortense Kreukels' Bavarian Chicken Soup and the broth that cured a million colds, Rebecca Arnowitz's Hungarian-Jewish Chicken Soup.

N D
$3.50 from Daniel Plunkett, PO Box 4144, Austin, TX 78765

Daniel covers a lot of art frontiers in his zine: mail art, performance art, cassette-based noise and more. **N D** gives an excellent feel for the international scope of these democratized forms of artwork production, with interviews and articles spanning the globe. It also participates in the network, with stickers and cassette releases and more. A great way to make new acquaintances, with extensive review and contact sections in every issue.

ND: Do you think the term "mailart" is too confined to describe what is all involved?
Lon Spiegelman: That's a very timely question, because there is presently a schizophrenic debate of sorts transpiring within the eternal mailart network whether to call the lemon a lime, or the lime a turkey. Actually, it's more like, "should we refer to all of this mailing that is going on as 'mailart' or 'networking' or perhaps 'networking art,' or maybe even 'networking correspondence art'."

The majority of mailers still prefer the time-tested term 'mailart' to refer to what they see showing up in their mailboxes every day. However, the term 'networking' is appearing more and more to refer to the same thing. Only time will tell which term will survive in eventually describing our activities. Or, perhaps something that hasn't been presented yet. It will probably be a concensus derived from general usage, and in this, each player has input.

S.E.T. FREE
$1 from Steve Wagner, PO Box 10491, Oakland, CA 94610-0491

Subtitled "The Newsletter Against Television," this zine comes from the Society for the Eradication of Television, a perfectly serious group of people. (You can tell they're serious because Dear Abby has seen fit to devote two columns to railing against them). They promote the idea that TV rots your mind and give lots of ideas on what to do (with yourself and with your kids) if you do take the drastic step of getting rid of your television.

TORN SCROTUM
$2 from PO Box 1523 Bonaventure, Montreal, Quebec, CANADA, H5A 1H6

"A quarterly excretion" of stuff that fascinates the editor: reports of unusual religious fetishes, autoerotic hangings, legal ways to get high, nasty poetry, and dangerous pictures, to name a few. This is the sort of thing that your mother would have stared at with shocked horror when you were back in high school.

THE UNMENTIONABLE
$2 from Miss Kelina, PO Box 7219, Santa Cruz, CA 95061

If **Ladies Home Journal** was put out by mutants from the nineteenth dimension it might be something like this. Miss Kelina prowls through the modern world in search of odd facts, activities for the home, and strange things you can get through the mail. Every issue includes some recipes and some ideas for making your own clothes, as well as other

ideas for staving off boredom. Some interesting lives are lurking behind this one.

Get a partner and make a baby. NO DON'T DO THAT! Find a sock, and some buttons, a ping pong ball, yarn, plastic eyes, and make puppets. If you don't have spare socks, there will probably be extra ones at a laundry mat. Cut the bottoms and sleeves off of tee-shirts, and make hairbands. Make pillows and sachets. Eat a lot, then put your finger at the back of your throat and then make throw up. Decorate hats with ribbons and fake flowers. Make fart music. Pull wax out of your ears, and make wax figures. Make bubble gum people and leave them wherever you go. Plant corn or wild flowers in every available patch of dirt. Other people will begin to recognize the places you have been. This is the best tag there is if you live in a place where plants are likely to survive. If you're lucky you might come back a few years later and find it still growing there.

If you think of anything else to make, or to do that I have forgotten, please tell me about it.

FARM PULP
$1.50 from 1404 N. 41st St., Seattle, WA 98103

Some zines aspire to a near-perfect level of inscrutability; this is one of them. **FP** is mainly composed of reprints from all over — community papers, other zines, mainstream magazines, and who knows where else. It also features snippets of original art and writing, which, like the pirated material, seem generally intended to amuse with a skewed picture of America's stranger side. Run modern culture through a food processor and carefully pick over the resulting shreds

and you might end up with something like **Farm Pulp**.

SCAVENGER'S NEWSLETTER
$1.50 from Janet Fox, 519 Ellinwood, Osage City, KS 66523

This is the number one essential support zine for the writer interested in placing stories in the fantasy, horror, and science fiction small press. Janet produces a constantly-updated listing of markets looking for new work, and if that were all she did it would be useful. But **Scav** also features a very active letter column where small press writers and editors meet to discuss problems and solutions and learn from one another. There are also some "how-to" articles, reviews of new publications, and a chart tracking the response times of various editors. On the lighter side, Janet also produces an annual "Killer Frog" anthology of deliberately bad speculative fiction which is generally quite hysterical.

JAYNE'ZINE
$1 from 512 N. 42nd, Seattle, WA 98103

A collection of rubber stamp and collage art, strange history, and popular culture. Jayne seems to have a lot of fun with life and the main purpose of this zine is to pass that fun on. It's impossible to know what you'll find on the next page — an anti-war statement or a history of forks — but it's likely to be light and unexpected.

DR. JAYNE'S CURE FOR THE BLUES
(Be they of the Sunday, Monday or Sadderday Variety)
1. Get an old T-Rex record (preferably that doesn't skip).
2. Put it on the turntable starting with something lively like Telegram Sam or Get It On. Work up to Lean Woman Blues & Main Man.
3. In the mean time you've heated some water, filled the melitta with a powerful blend of overpriced java & should be ready to conjure up a good strong cuppa.
4. If it's available dipping chunks of

fancy expensive chocolate in the coffee is sometimes advised.
5. It is also advised to have a little project to work on. Stress little.

ARTPAPER
$2.75 from 2402 University Ave. W., St. Paul, MN 55114

Every decent-sized city has some way for the arts community to come together and keep track of itself. **Artpaper** performs this function for the Twin Cities, but it also goes above and beyond the usual call of duty in putting art in a context of activism and community and social organizing. In addition to the usual reviews and listings of who is exhibiting at which gallery, they carry articles on zines, traditional crafts, the corporate and political uses or misuses of art, and other topics. Sporting a roster of writers from across the country, the **Artpaper** crew is doing a good job of exploring the meaning and purposes of art.

POTATO PLAYS HOOKY The potato is not in school. Its history is not taught. Students never learn that their McDonald's fries come to them through the hands of brown-skinned Indian farmers, Irish refugees, and Chinese peasants. They are not taught that the food they eat, the clothes they wear, even the words they use come to them imprinted with the stories of many peoples over the centuries; that the candy bar at lunch is descended from chocatl, the aphrodisiac beverage of the Aztecs (who also developed the cotton in their T-shirts); that they owe their daily-bath ritual to Pueblo Indian, Arab, and East Asian traditions; that the architecture, art, and urban design that surrounds them is in debt to the genius of Africa, Islam, and Native America. Young people are not aware of the thousand invisible threads that connect them at every turn to people they have never thought about, perhaps never heard of. It does not occur to them that this isolation leaves them vulnerable to the demagogic militarism that passes for patriotism. They don't suspect that they are likelier to go marching off to fight foreign peoples with whom they feel no connection.

Hip Whatnot

These zines are a cross-section of hipness and modern culture — with a healthy does of controversy and the ever-popular rant thrown in for good measure. They also represent the cross-pollination that zines make so happily available.

COUNTER CULTURE
$4 from Sean Wolf Hill, 42 Cold Brook, Hampden, ME04444

The premiere zine of diner appreciation or *dinertude*, as it now can be called. Sean and company write lovingly of diners across the US, reviewing them and listing them in a "diner-ectory." They continue their love affair with the diner by saying goodbye to old favorites and panning the phony diner-wannabes that are spreading across the country like a fungus. There are also Top Ten Jukebox favorites, diners on film, pictures, post-cards and enough diner memorabilia to satisfy any diner lover's appetite. Want to know where the best and worst chicken soup can be found? Where the endless cups of coffee originated? Past issues have included poignant essays on the past andfuture of the beloved diner in the face of ever-burgeoning fastfood locations, the history of the Harvey House (from whence came the first waitress), and explorations of the dimensions of dinertude.The list of fans is growing, thanks in no small part to Sean's devoted attention to this bit of Americana.

This journal has always been about the Real — about the significance of the true working class American Diner as a living pattern, not merely as an archetectural curiosity: We have talked a lot about What is a diner? There are still arguments between the Purists who insist a "diner" is a prefab affair only, and the Atmospherists who claim that Dinertude is the feeling of a place. We have all (with varying degrees of intensity) felt uneasy about the fake or borderline diners; the places that either pretend to be diners or may truly be former diners but shun the working class. I've called the former Faux Diners & the latter Yuppie Diners. Neither are diners.

11TH STREET RUSE
50¢ from Sparrow, 322 East 11th St. #23, NewYork, NY 10003

An idiosyncratic litmag with a strange sense of humor. It's a small zine of fun writing, obscure vocabulary and unexpected features like speculations about sheep in the subway, the perfection of the Russian language, an "interview" with Saddam Hussein and other bizarrities. The assorted essays are a mix of the real and the fantastically unreal — the problem lies in deciding which is which. What can we make of the Bhutan travelogue or the recounting of a voyage within to visit a Wise Woman? Which, if either, is real and what is real anyway? Don't miss their customary vocabulary corner and occasional quizzes, either.

BABY SPLIT BOWLING NEWS
$3.75 Cash from BSBN Publishing, PO Box7205, Minneapolis, MN 55407

This zine does for bowling what **National Geographic** did for young schoolboys' imaginations. Here it is, folks: The Zeitgeist of Bowling. This is truly a visionary look at the makeup of the world through the eyes of Bowlers — from the Deviant Bowlers of America, to How to Find a Wife (through bowling, naturally), bowling hygiene, famous bowlers in history, and the list goes on and on. Each issue

presents an alternative theme; a satirical focus on Jesse Helms, the separation of Church and Bowling, nude bowling, New Age Bowling (complete with instructions on how to get that crystal to fit into the finger holes of your ball), and even poetry devoted to the quintessential American sport. Also for sale is a list of products for those worthy of calling themselves Bowlers.

Wonderful Thoughts About Wives:
Every wise bowler loves the wife he has chosen. (Homer)
No wife is ugly if she bowls. (Tertullian)
Two things doth prolong thy life —
bowling and a loving wife. (Thomas Deloney)
Wives are young bowlers' mistresses, companions for middle age and old bowlers' ball carriers. (Francis Bacon)
A cheerful wife is the joy of bowling. (John Ray)

Happy is the man who has a good wife. He bowls twice as good. (J.W. Goethe)
A good wife and bowling is a man's great wealth. (Old English Saying)
Every bowling man should believe there's but one good wife in the alleys, and that's his own. (Jonathan Swift)

BUFFALOON NEWSLETTER
$1.50 from Raisin Blowme, 31 W. Northrup Place, Buffalo, NY 14214

A mix of collage, media reviews, and outrageous nonsense dealing with modern culture. It's also a collection of rants, art and zine reviews. There are photos of famous people chopped out of other sources and enhanced by the addition of speech balloons; editorials such as the joys of cable for avoiding the war, bathroom reading (books to take in small doses, that is), and lots of free speech and First Amendment stuff — Raisin even asks that you send your own epitaph for reprinting here. The collage is manic, combining of mainstream media images with words to make spiritual points. A rather tongue-in-cheek publication.

THE CHRONICLE
$3 from PO Box 80721, Fairbanks, AK 99708

The exceptional college zine that gives itself a new adjective with each issue and theme. In the past, there have been "The Conspiracy Chronicle," "The Constitution Chronicle," and "The Commercial Chronicle," to name a few. And calling it a college zine doesn't really do it justice, anyway. These are the best and the brightest of the younger marginals who tackle such weighty topics as censorship, the debate between Liddy and Leary, just what "politically correct" means in the Green Party, hemp legalization and Ed Gein all at once, while throwing in a hefty dose of movie, zine, music and cult reviews. The folks up Alaska way are not afraid to jump off the margins and see the underbelly of reality — they give a firsthand report from the Exxon oilspill (they had the advantage of geography), an article on a conspiracy at Disneyland, Nazis in your home town — and much more. A zine that spits in the face of its elders and dares them to make something of it.

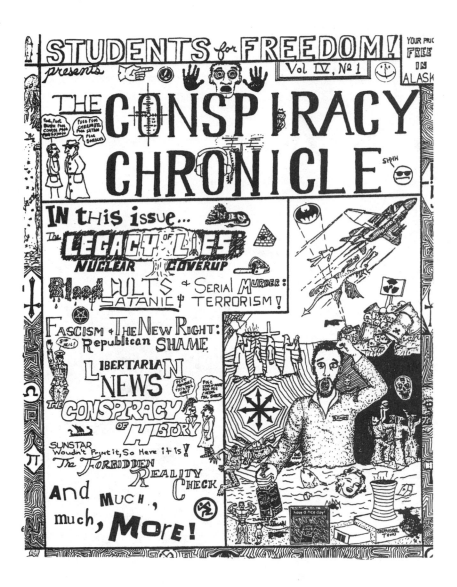

TOURIST TRAP
$1.50 from Keith & Kevin Kinsella, PO Box 1033, Newport, RI 02840

This is an unusual zine in that it comes to us from two brothers — who each have their own distinctive voice but also share many of the same alternative ideas. The editorial subjects range from phony righteousness to phony record collectors and always include a hearty dose of features from contributors ranging from Paul Weinman's ubiquitous poetry, to guides to lobbying for causes in your state, to some unusual perceptions on the homeless. Dedicatated and honest material.

AS IT COMES...

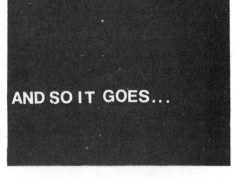

AND SO IT GOES...

Conspiracy. There is some who say that every conspiracy that could ever be imagined is going on right now. What about the unimaginably covert plots? What about Satanism and the Military Industrial Complex? What about the oil companies' five year plan to undermine the national economy? How many more deaths are necessary before we open our eyes and realize the currents of malign conspiracy are lapping at our heels? Mad dogs and company men! The collegiate weasel elite versus underdog and the press brigade in sixteen rounds of sophomoric scuffling related to ambiguous wording and lingering hard feelings. Yet here we are. Perhaps a higher purpose awaits. Just what are we up to?

NO BS
$2 CASH/stamps from Brian Wayson, 555 Buckingham Way, San Francisco, CA 94132

A four-color zine of clippings from "legitimate" sources which are out to prove that life is so absurd that there's no making sense of it — so just relax and enjoy it. And you can do that, too, just by reading one thwarted suicide attempt after another, followed by the letter about coffee enemas and a testament to buttocks biting. The editors have a keen eye for the absurd and a healthy sense of fringe humor.

ercase letters at all times) writing is both bizarre and clear — and it leaves us wondering what's going on. It certainly operates from a higher level of consciousness — on matters of consensus reality, multidimensional thinking, and the breakdown of reality in a media sea. There's also bizarre advice, short fiction, and a strange sense that this all somehow makes sense once you really think about it.

BLACK LEATHER TIMES
**$1 from Deirdre Williamson
2905 PineyGrove Ct.,
Fairfax, VA 22031**

A zine of all sorts of wild stuff with a different theme each time — from the "Valentine's Day/Deviant Sex" issue to one on Japanese culture. The former contained notes on crossdressing, a "lover's lexicon" (what he really means when he says he'll call you sometime), a crossword puzzle for sexual deviants and the like. The latter issue contained some stuff I'm sure the Japanese aren't quite aware of yet, such as etiquette that tell you to take advantage of being a rude "gaijan," Japanese sex aids and assorted sushi reviews. In addition to all this fun stuff, they also give helpful hints for dealing with the family during holidays (including what to do to hide strange hairstyles and tattoos) and a great advice column (although the people they ridicule and attack may not think so).

None of us say exactly what we mean. So here is a little B.L.T. directory to help you decipher your sweet lovemuffin's sensitive words.
"I never meant to hurt you." (I didn't think you'd catch me.)
"Sure I'll call you sometime." (Hell could get chilly. It could happen.)
"I think things are moving too fast." (I haven't exactly broken up with my last boyfriend.)

tab to block bicuspid
**$2 from blackhumour,
PO Box 315, Station A,
Vancouver, B.C.,
CANADA V6C 2M7**

A zine of writing that marches not only to a different drummer, but a drummer playing a clarinet. blackhumour's (low-

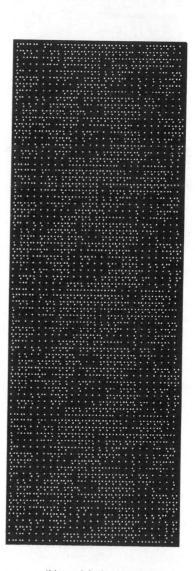

one possible model of a thought-shape conceptualized by d.t. candide while in the process of separating the plywood from the dinosaurs.

Literary

Literary magazines are one of the mainstays of zinedom — indeed, this area is so well-populated that it supports several review publications of its own including **Small Press Review**. The urge to write poetry and fiction at times seems near universal, and people are willing to have their work published without pay just so they can share it. The zines in the field typically differ from the usual run of College English Department publications by being more willing to consider and run experimental work, though as you'll see below the variety is as wide here as anywhere else in the zine world.

UNSHAVED TRUTHS/BARE-FACED LIES
$4 from 2507 Roehampton, Austin, TX 78745

An Austin-based litzine with a unique flavor driven by the on-line (via computer networking) connections of its writers and editors. There is some traditional (and very good) storytelling here, but there are also jarring snap-action pieces that seem to partake of the rhythms of electronic writing. An experiment worth monitoring.

FORBIDDEN LINES
$14/6 issues from PO Box 23, Chapel Hill, NC 27514

A professionally-done SF zine with pieces ranging from something close to Golden Age hard SF to modern splatterpunk.

They also find room to interview some unusual folks such as Dr. Sheridan Simon, who makes a hobby out of designing planets and solar systems. Big names are unusual here, but good solid writing isn't.

FISHWRAP
$1 from 912 1/2 24th Ave., Seattle, WA 98122

Four tabloid pages of confusing self-referential poetry, veiled social activism, and stories that do not behave precisely as they should. They sprinkle in oddball graphics, and generally wander around the cutting edges without devolving into complete nonsense. An occasional read but a fun one.

On the Importance of Getting Published

*To ask if you should write poetry
even if you cannot get published
struck Poem at first like asking
if you should get laid
even if you cannot get it
on tv.*

*Then he saw that poetry
as donation sans recipient
is hardly comparable to two-party sex.*

*But so what? Pumping jizz
into one's own kleenex
is still better than no sex at all,
or getting published
even if you cannot write poetry.*

—Bob Grumman

unconsciously scurrying to climb on the horror bandwagon. In one sense horror is the literature of fear, but fear comes in all sizes. Most people are fearful of something each day, whether it's a small fear like asking for a raise, stage fright when we have to speak in person, feeling a need to conceal what we've done to someone, or the outcome when we're found out. The ongoing unconscious fears of aging and death are monsters that not only dwell within ourselves, they are ourselves. But there are a hell of a lot more! Driving to work on snow and ice, turning in a report to some authority figure, asking for a date, wondering how our kids will cope with the drug problem, seeing our parents grow old before our eyes. Monstrous problems, these are, terrifying ones that all people face. The magazines that say we're all terrified of getting nuked or AIDS are actually more escapist literature and less realistic than anything any pro in horror is writing. It's not that we don't fear such things. It's that we have so many more immediate perils to confront and somehow deal with. Horror fiction tries, attempts over and over, to deal with these really personal, ongoing questions and problems.

BELLOWING ARK
$2 from PO Box 45637, Seattle, WA 98145

Bellowing Ark has broken a lot of litzine rules (if there are such things) and gotten away with it admirably. They're tabloid format on newsprint rather than some elegant folded pamphlet. They publish a mix of things, from short poems to serialized epics and even novels. And they hop with ease from local nature poetry to large issues, from confessional pieces to off-the-wall humor. It succeeds with style and grace, exposing some truly great writers to the world and having a batch of fun in the process.

EUTHANASIA ROSES
$1 from Yehudi Niemand, 759 Cranberry Ridge, Fairbanks, AK 99712

Mostly poetry, the few bits of short prose thrown in are poetic themselves, in their desire to capture an image or a moment. Yehudi lays it all out kitty-corner across the page, mixed with doodle-like art and occasional bits of Jack Chick comics. The odd music or zine review sneaks in as well.

CEMETERY DANCE
$4 from Richard Chizmar, PO Box 858, Edgewood, MD 21040

CD is a magazine of horror fiction specializing in the dark mystery end of things — traditional horror with an enhanced air of suspense. In addition to publishing a good mix of stories from big names and newcomers between slick, colorful covers, Richard manages to print a lot of writing about the field and the people in it. Every issue contains a couple of interviews and profiles as well as book reviews and editorial matter on the progress of the horror field. Chilling and enlightening by turns.

J.N. Williamson: When horror pops up in Broadway shows and commercials, rather than suggesting it is passe, it provides a perfect example of the way writers and producers of all kinds are

iMPORTANCE OF CHEAP ART

A   CHEAP ART IS NOT IMPORTANT

B   CHEAP ART DEFIES, RIDICULES, UNDERMINES AND MAKES OBSOLETE THE SANCTITY OF AFFLUENT-SOCIETY ECONOMY

C   CHEAP ART IS LIGHT, LITTLE, QUICK AND EASY TO DO, MOSTLY MADE FROM SCRAPS AND JUNK

D   CHEAP ART IS A MOVEMENT

E   CHEAP ART FIGHTS THE BUSINESS OF ART

BOGG
$4.50 from John Elsberg, 422 N. Cleveland St., Arlington, VA 22201

A rather serious small press litzine that splits its pages between British and American poets and writers, with the occasional Canadian, Australian or other far-flung Commonwealth writer for a bit of variety. The contrasts are sometimes startling, especially since it isn't always the Brits doing nature poetry or the Yanks stuck in seedy bars. Though poetry makes up the bulk of the contents, **Bogg** also publishes some short prose as well as reviews and interviews with those prominent on the small press scene.

ASYLUM
$3 from Greg Boyd, PO Box 6203, Santa Maria, CA 93456

Asylum explores the edge of the literary world without (most of the time, anyhow) falling off. Greg picks a mix of experimental literature for his mainstays; dreamlike explorations, deliberate distortions of language and syntax, unusual subjects rendered with painful realism. Amongst this we find criticism of the field from writers (such as Bob Grumman) who are inventing the new language needed to deal with these new forms, and the occasional translation or semi-academic essay.

PAPER TOADSTOOL
50 cents from Duncan, 4946 W. Pnt. Way, WVC, UT 84120

This small zine integrates art much more into its vision than do most these days, balancing strange stories, small poems, and lovely stippled drawings (many by Duncan himself). Most of the work here has a wondering, life-positive feel to it, the expression of a natural high, looking around the universe.

YOUR ELBOW
$3.50 from Kelly Green, 1765 Randolph #2, St. Paul, MN 55105

A poetry zine which sticks to new and raw, rough voices: sandpaper over the skin of denial which keeps us from seeing the nasty parts of the world. Whether a look at frat boys or a scared vet and a screwed-up shrink, the writers focus in on repression and depression and dissect it in all its ugly glory. A few rays of hope shine through as well, chiefly when the natural world rather than the human one gets into the act.

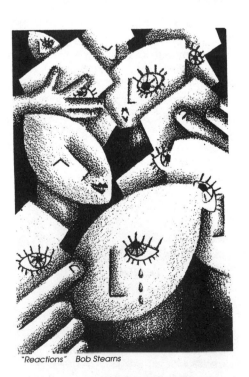

"Reactions"   Bob Stearns

time delay

sitting at a bus stop
all alone
not waiting for
anything
writing it down
by the light
of a convenience
stop sign
an old man walks up
and asks for a smoke
i pretend not
to hear
he calls me a
son of a bitch and
walks away
for some reason
i feel he is
a genius
but they say it takes
one to know
one
and even if it mattered
i don't care

A Razor

EVEN PARANOIACS CAN HAVE ENEMIES
$2 from Tom Long, 1122 1/2 N. 13th St., DeKalb, IL 60115

It's difficult to know just what to do with this disturbing zine, composed as it is mostly of uncredited reprints and photos, yet with a creative spirit expressed in arrangement and juxtaposition, Certainly it is not for the faint of heart, containing everything from rude sexual descriptions to photos of gruesome bullet wounds. In general Tom seems fascinated by the muddy side of the world, perhaps even haunted by it, and determined to spread his own bleak visions even further.

WORDBURGER
$1 from Boris, 1107 Alabama, San Francisco, CA 94110

Mostly this is Boris's own personal rantzine, though he'll reprint other people's work if he thinks it's cool enough (given his high opinion of himself, that doesn't happen all that often though). He's cynical about everything, including life, punk, and cynicism itself. Once his prose gets rolling it has a tendency to steamroller everything in its path, burying it under gross images and skillful scorn.

RULES FOR BEING HUMAN
1. You will receive a body. It is the only one you get and you must do everything possible to destroy it as soon as you can...
2. You must act as foolishly as you can all the time. NO exceptions!
3. Life is a full time school. There are many lessons to be learned. Just like real school, there are only two options: Cop-out and be a miserable failure. Sell-out and sacrifice your ideals.
4. NOTHING you can do will make you happier, more satisfied, improved, or pure. There will always be someone better off than you, so you can never be completely happy. The grass is greener.
5. There is no higher order! There is no meaning to your existence. No answers. No afterlife. When Scruffy died — he was gone. Everybody hates you!
6. Good Luck!

LIME GREEN BULLDOZERS
$3 from Alaina Duro, 1003 Ave. X Apt. A, Lubbock, TX 79401

Heartfelt poetry in a zine that refers to its poets as "soulworkers." The comparison is apt, for these are poems of the inner world rather than copybook descriptions of flowers and horses. Overall, although the folks here have no illusions about the world, they manage a hopefulness not often associated with youth any more. Very forthright.

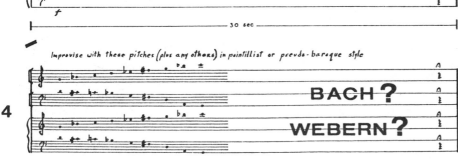

LOST & FOUND TIMES
$14/5 issues from John M. Bennett, Luna Bisonte Prods, 137 Leland Ave., Columbus, OH 43214

Some zines are stamped very strongly with the editor's personality, and this is one of them. Bennett creates strange rhythmic poems that cross the boundary between reality and nightmare, and delivers them in a variety of formats including bizarre idiosyncratic calligraphy. Along the way he's picked up a stable of the underground's most rule-breaking poets, including Al Ackerman, Stacey Sollfrey, Malok, Jake Berry and many more, who work in similar obscure formats. Collaborations take up much of the space here, as two or more subconsciousnesses get together for an afternoon of demolishing the language.

SPEAKING

That cheese glowing from fire within or rot's my brain knowing what I've got's just leased and the rent's hotter and
hotter. What I've sired's spent and my growth's thin, like milk on a mound of dirt, skin and meat slumped on a bone. Will this leaking shirt pay my debt? Can I spend sounds chewed on a phone?

John M. Bennett

FOCUSING IN ON THE MAN IN THE MOON
$1 from Sal Robert Pauciello, 9 Stanley St., Irvington, NJ 07111

A rather politicized zine of poetry and essays. Occasionally they throw in a comic strip as well, usually something leftist and polemical. Of rather uneven quality, this is one of hundreds of small zines around the country which publish a wide selection of work from the grassroots.

FREE LUNCH
$4 from PO Box 7647, Laguna Niguel, CA 92607-7647

One of the finer poetry zines around, featuring a mix of carefully crafted and more or less traditional poetry. They feature a mix of relatively well-known small press poets (Gerald Locklin, B.Z. Niditch, and Lyn Lifshin, to name a few) and new voices, some of whom they deliberately encourage with their mentor program of encouraging established people to pick new ones for showcasing.

NATURAL SELECTION

They powerwalk in matching sweats following a light breakfast

to curb the enemy from within. The knack for synchronization

must evolve slowly, must accumulate like speech, or like cellulite,

the same insidious way a husband and his wife become twins.

Alison Kolodinsky

GYPSY
$7 from Belinda Subraman, 10708 Gay Brewer, El Paso, TX 79935

A solidly established litzine that features a good mix of poetry, short prose and well-reproduced artwork. They tend to print work which explores and dissects human emotions, going for moving, fresh material that steers clear of the more usual sentimental themes. But they've also been very willing to experiment with special issues, including a lovely audio compilation of strong poets reading their own works.

WE MAGAZINE
$3 from PO Box 1503, Santa Cruz, CA 95060

A nice, rather collegiate poetry zine

which concentrates on pushing the boundaries, but not *too* hard. They've done a lot of fun things including silkscreened covers, an audio issue and poetry readings. Many strong voices check in here, with a general clarity that can be at times rather astonishing.

SCORE
$1 from Crag Hill, 491 Mandana #3, Oakland, CA 94610

A lush home for much visual poetry, language poetry, essays on unmeaning, and other curious forms of nontraditional literature. Over the years **Score** has existed in every form from a thick magazine to a postcard, all peppered with words and letters exploring the connection between form and meaning. Lately they've been issuing single sheets, some with new poetry or visual works, some with reviews of material in the same vein from other presses.

If you have any interest in this new world, where a letter may be a glyph devoid of meaning or a picture may be an essential part of a word, **Score** is one good place to start trolling for contacts.

SHATTERED WIG REVIEW
$3.50 from Rupert Wondolowski, 523 E. 38th St., Baltimore, MD 21218

A litzine that tends towards the surreal not just in the material it prints but in the way it prints it — sometimes it is hard to tell just where one writer's voice leaves off and another begins. In prose and poetry they explore a world where anything might happen, childhood fears manifest themselves, people engage in notably insane public practices, and the hidden machinery of paranoia becomes obvious. Sometimes one will find a bit of color photocopy or a poem on shards of cardstock, waiting to be rearranged, hidden inside an issue. Art, wonder, confusion and more.

Things went on like this for several weeks, and before long everyone on the ward was calling me "Eel" — a nickname they had thought up for me in honor of how my bus accident had tapered and elongated my skull so that a sneeze or sudden forward motion could throw the top of my head into my eyes. The insensitivity of this name nettled me a little, but not much. Mostly I stayed busy either dozing in a stupor or worrying about how I was going to earn a living when I left the hospital. This last was a real problem to me because somehow when you're in the scissor-sharpening business and you have to approach perspective customers with "Today sharpened scissors any need you do?" (meaning "do you need any scissors sharpened today?") you can't expect

many of them to want to put a pair of scissors (or a pair of anything sharp) within your reach. So what was going to become of me in the business world? This question was one I spent hours brooding over in my dull fashion and I got nowhere fast with it. The future was looking bleak indeed. Thank heaven Vice President Dan Quayle heard about my case and came around in the nick of time to offer me a job writing all his speeches.

AFTER HOURS
$4 from 21541 Oakbrook, Mission Viejo, CA 92692-3044.

Billing itself as "A Magazine of Dark Fantasy and Horror," **After Hours** stands out from the pack by insisting in its writers' guidelines that all stories take place after dark. Editor William Raley is partial to dark fantasy and horror, but also ventures into lighter science fiction and fantasy material. In addition to stories and solidly scary artwork, **AH** also offers interviews with well-known small press horror writers and some market information.

2AM
$5.95 from Gretta M. Anderson, PO Box 6754, Rockford, IL 61125-1754.

As the subtitle suggests, this slick-covered zine contains "Horror. Fantasy. Science Fiction" in roughly that order. The writers tend to be some of the top names in the small press, people like Wayne Allen Sallee, J.A. Salmonson and Avram

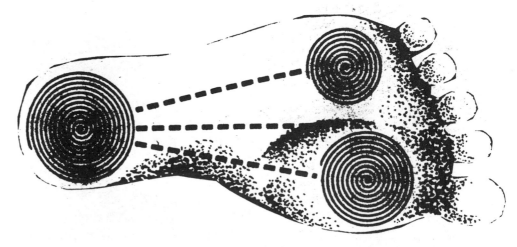

Davidson to name a few. They also run several columns that help readers keep track of the small press, including market news and reviews, and thoughts on the business of writing for the genre. A very professional publication that keeps alive the spark of new writing.

BLIND IGUANA PRESS
$5/6 issues from Dan Breen, 513 Corby Ave., South Bend, IN 46617

A small zine (now up from one sheet of paper to two) with a finely-honed selection of material. Each issue features a single short story plus a spattering of poetry. They go in for exploring inner thoughts of people living close to the edge, field trips of God, and other esoteric subjects. Classy stuff in a small package.

FISH DRUM
$3 from Robert Winson, 626 Kathryn Ave., Santa Fe, NM 87501

One of the best literary zines around comes out of the dry air of Santa Fe, an unlikely collision of zen, quiet desert spaces and gentle art. Poets like Leo Romero and Miriam Sagan shine here, their strong voices cultivated apart from the mainstream. The zine has done several lovely theme issues, including one featuring work from a women's writing workshop and another, combating the general uselessness of the genre, composed of short "How To:" essays.

(excerpted from)
Book of Esther

Friday night shul, Santa Fe, New Mexico
Among the Ashkenazim who travelled mountains and rivers
To arrive in the synagogue of desert air, or evening
In a country of cabelleros, men in black on horseback.
And I am all dressed up for shul
Looking like my grandma Esther
In a black silk dress with a gilt bead necklace
Well dressed for the Ukraine or South Orange, New Jersey
Sweating in my nylons in the heat.
Here in exile we have lost our wildness

Miriam Sagan

EOTU
$4 from Larry Dennis, 1810 W. State #115, Boise, ID 83702

Experimental and esoteric fiction and poetry in a variety of theme issues — although the cover theme is often esoteric and experimental itself. Lots of classy work has appeared here, with amusing touches such as a medley of different definitions of the word "eotu" itself. Always fun to read, and featuring work that doesn't have much chance of appearing elsewhere.

BAD HAIRCUT
$4 from Ray & Kim Goforth, 3115 SW Roxbury St., Seattle, WA 98126

Poetry and the occasional bit of short prose in a generally socially conscious vein. The writers here really seem to believe that their words make a difference, enough so that they are willing to appear in the small press where only a

few people will see them. Certainly those who are fortunate enough to find a copy of the zine will be treated to many things to think about, from war to illiteracy to consumer culture, sensitively presented by a variety of bright new voices.

U.S. 1984

Forget the Gulag
welcome to MX country
and if you don't agree
you must be mad or unpatriotic
we give you Valium (or any narcotic)
and you thinking we are not
like our enemies
became ever more alike
thoughts were inspected
mail, petitions, passports

Joe McCarthy rose
inauspiciously out of his grave
into the news establishments
and all the while we are told
we are in the head of the free world.

B.Z. Niditch

MIDNIGHT GRAFFITI
$6.95 from 13101 Sudan Rd., Poway, CA 92064

A slick-covered zine of "Dark Fantasy" that ranges across many media, with special issues on everything from dinosaurs to the end of the world. They feature short stories (including some by big names), interviews, comics, television and movie coverage, book reviews, poetry, and lovely art. They also slide very close to the edge of what's acceptable, with some of the stories in particular going to great lengths to be gut-wrenching. A great zine, but not one for the squeamish.

CRAMPED AND WET
$2 from Rob Treinen, 1012 290, Sioux City, IA 51104

"A Punk Approach to Writing, Art and Music." This zine has plenty of reviews (more of written work than music), plus a

good deal of edgy writing. The idea of punk literacy may seem odd to some people but it works well here, with the anger and hope for change channeled into somewhat more traditional forms than the music which spawned it. Lots of interesting graphics as well, including some suitable for use as posters to disturb people in the business district.

(excerpt from)
The Next Stop

i still play my punk records on the stereo
when I get the chance and although
the energy is still there, the urgency
intact,
an edge I can't explain has filled.
at twenty-four i find myself mellowing
with age—
not to the point where i listen to elevator
music
or "lite" music for "post-rock adults"—
but i'm no longer the nihilist i once was.
the pessimistic cynic has become more
of a
disappointed idealist (of which i can live
with),
but the question is: where's the next
stop?

John McKinley

CHIRON REVIEW
$2 from Michael Hathaway, 1514 Stone, Great Bend, KS 67530-4027

A tabloid of contemporary writing, mainly poetry with some short stories thrown in. Almost every poet featured here gets a full page, with photo and plenty of room to display a few works. The zine also holds yearly contests, publishes small books of poetry, and features interviews and an active review and news section. They have done very good work in helping to create a new literary community as well as promoting new material such as Namvet poems.

TEMPORARY CULTURE
$5 from H. Wessells, PO Box 43072, Upper Montclair, NJ 07043

dubitare...

ergo sum

Literature on the borders between fact and fiction. Wessells and his collaborators produce discursive pieces that blur the boundaries, sometimes sinking into a language of dream, sometimes exploring everyday life with a cold clarity. You'll hit your share of the unexpected here, as the pages of each issue unfold to form a temporary oasis of unique culture.

———

We dream of eating asphalt and automobiles slow delicate steps taken at molecular levels. Workings of plant mind revealing in change. Host and parasite meaningless in the now of bacterial mutation spawning and dispersing to the four winds keyed on steel fiberglass aluminum polyvinyl-chloride. Grackle and pigeon passing seeds bearing potential of soils germination awaiting

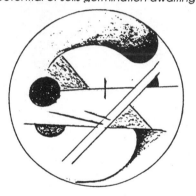

trigger. Drift of locust pollen on fragrant and corrosive winds unnoticed in plume and leach of smelting ovens or gnash of motor. Cottonwood snow and milkweed parachute miles above plain and swamp. From dream to action in deliberate warmth of sun nourishment and multiplication.

TRAY FULL OF LAB MICE PUBLICATIONS
$2 from Melissa & Matt Jasper, PO Box 356, Durham, NH 03824

A home for oddball writing and poetry that takes a variety of forms. They've put out a matchbook of poems (with words glued painstakingly on each paper match) and hand-painted fabric, for example, although mostly they stick to paper (even so, the annual zine is special, with gilt edges and bound-in color plates). The poems tend towards the surreal and the unbalanced, demonstrating and wallowing in a fascination with the bizarre. They've also taken an interest in reprinting such unusual marginalia as the Kirby vacuum cleaner song book and the revelations of Dan Scott Ashwander.

———

Sunlight floods the room. Three are drowned.

*I am out of sight
I am out of mind
I sadly fear my mittens
I am lost*

*The sign says—DON'T WALK
I crawl across the street
The secrets I think of
Begin to think of me*

*I am the man on the window ledge
who jumps out the window for some air
I am not an actor
But I play one on tv.*

*I feed the hand that bites me,
feed gravy-soaked sponges to every dog
I have created god in my own image
He approves of this*

Matt Jasper

HEAVEN BONE
$5 from Steve Hirsch, PO Box 486, Chester, NY 10918

A high-quality litzine featuring fine poetry and short stories, as well as a classy layout and nice art. They go in mainly for work that seems well-crafted, with a mix of modern and traditional work. There is an underlying religious feeling to some of the writing, but it doesn't get in the way of the reader's enjoyment.

THE VOICE OF ZEWAM
$2 from Brendan Donegan, 15 Main St., Dobbs Ferry, NY 10522

A journal inspired by the work of Zewam Amola (1895-1957), Labrador native and influential (if little-known) surreal/visionary writer. In addition to containing the only new translations of her work available, it includes poetry from others, offbeat news clippings, and music criticism. Every issue seems packed with emotion, ranging from high joyous laughter to the isolating feel of a cold winter in the undeveloped north.

———

FOR THE NORTH COAST

*My dream unwoven by the willowbushes
I turn my windburned face
to the coast sketched by my thoughts.*

*Wash flapping on the clothesline and
spindly potato plants
and black pines and frustrated children
and
ruddy old men on the road to disconnected villages.*

*A country discovered!
Land of granite and steel gales.*

Unconscious womb.

People

One of the main things zines do is bring together people who share similar interests, lifestyles and values — or *something*. It can be as specific a group as "athletic lesbians with a political consciousness" or Rastafarians; other times it can be as broad as "anyone who needs a little self-esteem pick-me-up" — which might be most of us.

THE LETTER EXCHANGE
$8 from Steve Sikora, Box 6218, Albany, CA 94706

There's an entire world of letter writers out there bent on keeping the sometimes neglected art of letter writing alive; this is where they meet. Each quarterly issue of LEX (as it is fondly known) has scores of listings from people who want to write to others about just about any subject under the sun. They also offer an invaluable letter forwarding service so that privacy is protected. The hundreds of listings include topics as diverse as *Star Trek*, philosophy, and punk rock. This is the best way to find dozens of interesting people around the world to write to — or let to them find you.

DREAD TIMES
$1 from Jimmy Dread, 4245-3FF Hehi Road, Lihue, HI 96766

"News for the Nazarite," this one is for Rastas everywhere. It is slowly unfolding some basic doctrinal knowledge, along with bits of suppressed African-American history and notes on contemporary Reggae music. It's pretty wide-ranging in its exploration of Rastafarianism and related topics and offer grassroots religion at its finest.

The 1983 release of an upbeat single "Buffalo Soldier" by Bob Marley and the Wailers showed a sliver of history forgotten by the white-washed history books we were educated from.
Who were the buffalo soldiers Bob wailed about in that song? They were in fact members of the 9th, 10th, 24th, and 25th Infantry regiments of the post Civil War army. These soldiers were privates and noncommissioned officers of African descent. And although they were officially supposed to be fighting against the Cheyenne, Comanche, Kiowa, Apache, Ute, and Sioux Native Indians, these Africans were the only members of the occupational force the Indians would talk with concerning their differences with the U.S. government. The Indians dubbed 14 of the key Africans "Buffalo Soldiers."

The Letter Exchange

A Directory of Correspondence

THE COMPLEAT MOTHER
$12/yr from Jody McLaughlin, Box 209, Minot, ND 58702

"The Magazine of Pregnancy, Birth and Breastfeeding," this one is for mothers who want to raise their kids their way instead of at the beck and call of the medical establishment. They provide much support and many resources, concentrating on firsthand success stories and mother-to-mother advice. Features include extended breastfeeding, home birth, cloth diapers (even before that was trendy!), midwifery and many more alternatives they are open to. This is a visual manifestation of a large support network of women and men working together for healthier and happier babies.

Universe #1:
I'm healthy, wealthy and wise

Universe #2:
I'm totally psychic and can read auras

Universe #3:
I'm an idiot and I can't do anything right. I fail at everything

Universe #4:
I am really from outer space, and I'm headed home

Universe #5:
Whatever my mind can believe, I can achieve

Universe #6:
I am so in tune with my own Higher Power that I am in a constant state of bliss and ecstasy. God/Goddess loves me all the time

Universe #7:
I'm a regular guy. I work. I go home. I watch tv. I go to sleep. I wake up again. I'm normal

Universe #8:
I create my own reality out of my beliefs, thoughts and feelings. I can de-create anything I really dislike.

Shopping for Universes

It has been said that all universes are available, and the choice is made by us, consciously OR not-consciously. If we aren't aware of choosing universes, then our habits and patterns choose our universe for us.

Posi-affirmations:

I am consciously choosing a universe that contains what I most want.

I am in charge of which universe I live in.

I can travel between many universes.

If I don't like any universe, I can remove myself from it, as long as most of my 'parts' agree!

CORPUS CHRISTI MARINER NEWS
$1 from David C. Holiman, PO Box 1960, Corpus, TX 78403

A newsletter for Merchant Marine folks in the Corpus Christi area, mostly of retirement age or thereabouts. Editor David Holiman keeps track of members and ex-members, talks about various sea lift operations, offers news and notes from mariners along the Texas Gulf Coast on matters social, medical, and job-related, or adds his own witty flavor to subjects like "military cuisine." Basically this is what the folks on the waterfront are up to, whether it be retirement or shipping out anew.

Longshoreman Gilbert Mers was born in 1908. He graduated from highschool...and moved to Corpus Christi in 1929. Gilbert operated a fruit stand at Charlie's Bait House on North Water Street (now Surfside) just north of the OLD BRIDGE. Next to the Bait House was the original hiring hall of ILA LOCAL 1224. In July of '29 Gilbert quit the fruit stand and started working on the ships. By October he was admitted to the Local, and by 1932 he was the President of the Local. In 1935 Mers led a successful strike on the Corpus waterfront which resulted in a new contract and which got the attention of the west coast maritime unions, then called the Maritime Federation of the Pacific Coast. An agent of the M.F.P.C. talked Gilbert into leaving

Corpus to organize a similar federation of Gulf Coast unions, or rather a confederation of the "rank & file" of the ISU and the ILA. The officer unions quickly identified with the idea, and the M.F. of the Gulf Coast was created in March 1936.

THE POSITIVE TIMES
$4 from Jerry Posner, Box 244, West Stockbridge, MA 01266-0244

Ever want to create your own reality, preferably a happier and healthier one? Well, you're not alone, and the folks here will help you metaprogram yourself towards that goal. With serious and humorous essays, cosmic billboards and short blips, they convey a feeling of happiness and fun for the future. It's a zine of affirmations and positive thinking — a no-holds-barred attack on those negative monsters we carry around with us. Crammed full of positive messages, from bumper stickers to transactional analysis, Jerry gives us self-esteem enhancing memos with a healthy laugh and a glint in his eye.

You are infinitely more cosmic than you think you are. Your thoughts define your reality. You judge yourself. You can easily improve the quality of your thoughts, thus improving your entire life. You don't have to judge. You are loved more than you realize. You are noticed by infinite intelligence. You are cared for. You are.

FULL-TIME DADS
$4 from PO Box 120773, St. Paul, MN 55112-0773

A journal for fathers who are primary caregivers, whether through custody as a result of divorce or death, or as an arrangement within the family. These are men who consider taking care of their kids their main responsibility in life and they write about the grievances and joys of fatherhood — and the anger at the prejudice of the American public for not recognizing their contributions. There's lots of support and encouragement here, plus book reviews and resources for other information and always articles about the ongoing changes in American culture that make this a viable lifestyle.

THE DUPLEX PLANET
$2 from David Greenberger, PO Box 1230, Saratoga Springs, NY 12866

A long-running zine of questions and answers of the elderly, whom David has known in various senior centers and nursing homes. The result is a combination of wit and knowledge, along with the occasional complete nonsense, and it is quite friendly. He asks leading questions like "Tell me an outrageous lie" or "What's more important, romance or food?" or "Where would you erect a statue of yourself?" and records the responses from his sources, who generally answer with charm and grace. He intersperses his questions with photos of these participants and on the whole creates a wonderful forum of conversation for some people who don't get to have any.

WHAT'S "PIZZAZZ"?
LEO GERMINO: Nothing to eat is it? Is it a song?
ED ROGERS: Something to eat, is that what it is?
LEO: That's too hard. Some of us haven't gone that far in high school.
ED: Pizzazz — what does it mean?
LEO: Is that a country?
D.B.G.: No.
LEO: What is it, really, tell us the truth — both of us are baffled. Do you know yourself what it is?
D.B.G.: No.
LEO: (LAUGHS) You might have to look in the dictionary and it might take you quite a while. Maybe that's the name of a country in South America or Europe. What do you think, you think it's in Mexico?
ABE SURGECOFF: It might be dirty.
ED: I never heard of it, pizzazz. I don't know what it means. What does it mean?
ABE: It means part excretion.
ED: I never heard, I don't know what it means.
D.B.G.: John, what does "pizzazz" mean?
JOHN FALLON: I don't know — "how are ya"?
D.B.G.: No.
JOHN: I don't know what it means then.
ERNIE BROOKINGS: Is that human nature, bizarre?

GIRL JOCK
$3 from Rox-a-tronic, 2060 3rd St., Berkeley, CA94710

A magazine designed by and for "athletic lesbians with a political consciousness" is by far the most fun you'll have raising your own consciousness. These women are for real; they laugh at themselves as easily as they laugh at others — which they do a whole helluva lot. Locker room memoirs, a Lesbian Lexicon, Long-Haired Lesbians and the stigma they face, self-help best sellers for the 90s ("Tell Your Inner Child To Shut Up"),the glories of watching football and how to keep your girlfriend interested, and on and on. Roxxie and pals fill their zine with terrific comics and a healthy attitude revealing the less serious side to being an athletic lesbian in the latter 20th century. Humor will always be the cure for fear.

This certificate hereby entitles you to: **Express all of your deepest and truest feelings ALWAYS** by order of all that is good and real.

THE "MADE EASY" SERIES FOR THE MODERN LESBIAN

Love, Sex & Relationships

People write about what interests them — and what interests more of us than the eternal subject of love and all its ramifications? Add to this the fact that it's much simpler to be safe in zines, where the publisher can control the circulation, than in public, and you get a wonderful medley of publications, addressing every possible permutation of interpersonal relations. Everything from sex roles to sex play gets considered quite seriously in this part of the zine universe, where people can be themselves without fear.

LOVING MORE
$4 from PEP, PO Box 6306, Captain Cook, HI 96704-6306

The zine of Polyfidelitious Educational Productions, a support group for those who prefer a lifestyle of closed group marriage. There are a lot of people out there working on the frontiers of changing definitions of family and community, but mostly they stay out of the public eye. PEP is courageous enough to stand up and say "Hey, we're different, and we're OK!" And so they are, not to mention inspirational to anyone else contemplating becoming part of a life outside of the norm.

POLYFIDELITY: A specific form of equalitarian group marriage including more than 2 spouses; A group in which all partners are primary to all other partners as demonstrated by actions such as sharing a strong emotional bond, home space & resources, and making important life decisions together equally; As a marriage, sexual relationships exist between all partners in line with their sexual preference (i.e., in a heterosexual group every man and every woman would be lovers, in a lesbian group all the women would be lovers with each other woman, etc.); sexual fidelity is to the group; and all partners share an intent of a lifelong commitment together.

FRIGHTEN THE HORSES
$5 from Mark Pritchard, 41 Sutter St. #1108, San Francisco, CA 94104

Proudly proclaiming itself "a document of the sexual revolution," **FTH** takes sexual writing into pastures where few dare to venture. Though their core is exploration of modern sexuality in fact and fiction, they have run stories featuring child sex and photos of a dramatized rape/play scene, both to disapproving letters from some of their audience. Along the way the writers here explore the many ways in which people can develop their sexual identities, and the forces which are suppressing some of them in today's society. Fearlessly exciting writing.

For me, being queer is to "bisexual" as "gay" is to "homosexual." It has power because I'm demystifying and reclaiming a word that's been used against me. It unites me with gays and lesbians, to whom I've always felt kinship (more than to straights), and it includes people of every sexual underclass — homos, bi's, transvestites, transgenders, and that huge area called Other — so that I feel like I belong to a huge, varied group. Queer issues are primarily about visibility and the fight against bashing — queers who don't assimilate are easily recognized targets — but also include abortion rights, domestic partners rights and free expression struggles. And because we're marginalized by the "gay" community as well as the straight world, our fight also has to do with challenging roles written by assimilated lesbians and gays.

GARY MONSTER MAGAZINE
$3 from Gary Monster, 311 Palmerston Blvd. Bsmt., Toronto, Ontario, CANADA, M6G 2N5

It's hard to know what to make of **GMM**. Gary puts it together from scraps of the popular media — sometimes whole news stories, sometimes just pictures of strippers — peppered with his own idiosyncratic commentary. Sexual themes, often revolving around homosexuality or celebrities, pop up continually but are never explained. An enigma from the back of someone's brain.

J.D.s
$3 (no checks) from Bruce La Bruce, PO Box 1110, Adelaide St. Stn., Toronto, Ontario, CANADA, M5C 2K5

This was the first, and is still one of the best, of the "homopunk" zines, directed at young gay punk rockers. They've got a very distinctive sense of style, including outrageous campiness (no closets here!), leather, tattoos, skateboards, motorcycling, and more. Plenty of hot fiction, drawings of young butch women in love, photos of young men in compromising positions and punk attitude show up here. Bruce is also the man behind the fabulously successful underground homopunk movie *No Skin Off My Ass.*

ON OUR BACKS
$5.95 from 562 Castro St., San Francisco, CA 94114

"Entertainment for the Adventurous Lesbian," this zine has been a real success story, now up to a relatively hefty circulation with slick covers and lovely photography. They carry all manner of material for lesbians interested in sex: stories, an advice column, photo spreads, articles and opinion pieces. Trying to have something for everyone in the community, they sometimes offend a few, but their commitment to an authentically lesbian sexuality remains strong.

BIMBOX
$5 from Johnny Noxzema, 282 Parliament St. #68, Toronto, Ontario, CANADA M5A 3A4

The folks behind **Bimbox** are outrageously gay and delightfully inventive — which may explain the trouble that one of their issues had with the US Customs Service, being seized despite its cute little pop-up bodily organs. Never fear, they found alternate ways to get it

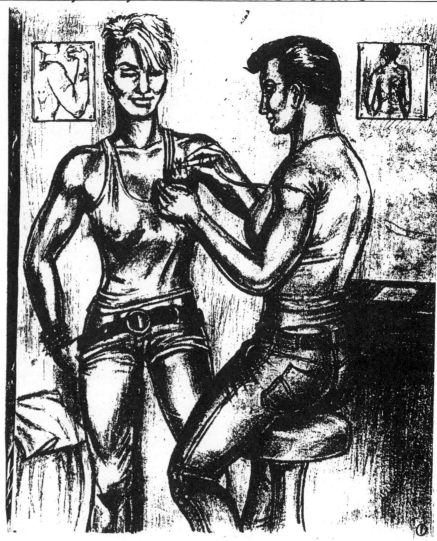

in, and your subscription dollar is safe here — though your morality may not be. They fight back against rampant homophobia by putting forth an attitude of outright heterophobia, and have been pleased to pass along literature from the Society for the Complete Annihilation of Breeders with their mailings. Young, angry and wild.

CHIRON RISING
$5 from PO Box 2589, Victorville, CA 92393

Subtly subtitled "Entertainment for Mature Men and Admirers," **CR** carries drawings, photos, and stories for those older men who are interested in their same sex — or for younger men interested in the older men. In a society where even senior sex isn't spoken of often, this is double courageous, and they've had a lot of trouble getting distributed. Despite this they've been around for almost 50 issues, providing an essential service to their readership and helping lonely men get in touch with one another.

RFD
$5.50 from PO Box 68, Liberty, TN 37095

This "Country Journal for Gay Men Everywhere" has developed quite a following for its mix of homosexuality and the great backwoods. They've been very active in networking together rural gay men who might otherwise have trouble finding kindred souls, and publish a mix of fiction and articles which resonate with a quieter, simpler life. They've also been active in exploring the Radical Faerie movement of gay men going beyond the stereotypes of masculinity which dominated some of the initial homosexual visibility in this country.

At gatherings, Radical Faeries call back
the little Radical Faeries each had been,
with love and gratitude to him for laying
claim to so many good things and
holding the line against being made a
"man" of by the well-meaning and
sometimes not so well-meaning people
of his early life, and bid him to come
where the fairies are ready with open
arms to receive him as the fairy prince
he has always known himself to be.
Faeries at gatherings therefore become
the small boys they once were, charming
and delightful, venturesome and fun-
filled, with arms over shoulders and
around waists communing ceaselessly in
endless enjoyment and recognition of
one another. Gatherings are held in
remote places of great natural beauty
and many of the Faeries love to be
nude. Hence the atmosphere of a
gathering is a sustained erotic high
Faerie sex, like the voices of Faeries, is
confident, wide-ranging, and free-
flowing.

CROSSTALK
$24/yr from Kymberleigh Richards, PO Box 944, Woodland Hills, CA 91365

"The Transgendered Community's Newsletter," this is a support zine for transvestites, transsexuals, crossdressers and others who are trying in one way or another
to change or broaden their gender iden-
tity. They carry a lot of news shorts on the
problems and triumphs such people
have had in society, as well as practical
advice on everything from finding shoes
to applying makeup.

WORKING GIRL
$1 from PO Box 11981, Berkeley, CA 94701

There are actually quite a few zines and
magazines out there for women in the
sex industry — not just prostitutes, but
peep-show dancers, strippers, mas-
seuses, escorts, phone sex workers, and
so on. This is one of the newest, and it still
has a raw zine feel, as if there is not much
separating Katy and the reader. She
writes bluntly and honestly of her experiences, emphasizing what it's like on the
other side of the transaction, leaving the
legal issues to others.

*I work in a "Fantasy Booth" where I put
on "private shows". The customer puts in
five dollars for every three minutes that
he gets to talk to me and watch me
through a glass window. There is a
phone set up for conversation, and a
computerized slot takes the money to
meter the time. A pretty slick set-up,
really.*
*Now, since I get to keep one half of what
I bring in, it is to my benefit to coax the
man into staying awhile, or to tip me for
"special shows" (dildos, anal, domination, etc.). Obviously a man will stay
longer if he's involved in the show — if he
masturbates. Also, I just feel more
comfortable is he masturbates, it's more
of a mutual thing. If he just sits and
watches me, I sort of feel like a dog
performing tricks.*

FEMINA
$5 & SASE from Ms. C. Deering, PO Box 1873, Haverhill, MA 01831

This is "The Voice of Feminine Authority,"
a no-frills zine for dominant women looking for hints on how to go about their
profession better. They're not into B/D or
S/M play-acting, but rather domination
as a life form, in which the Domina is
actually the one guiding the relationship rather than (as in much S/M) the
supposed submissive partner. In addition to essays and advice, they carry a
selection of personal ads.

*Physical and psychological domination
are both necessary in the proper
handling of submissives. I believe the
mind is the most important tool of
training. Anyone can be physically
beaten down, but the mind can remain
free. This can be seen in examples of
hostages and victims of political torture.
It takes much more effort to "break" the
mind than the body. Again, sessions are
hard to judge as a form of training. A
good Domina who does sessions to
survive, will also assign homework, tasks
to be completed before the next session,
essays, research, etc. She may give the
slave audio cassettes to play in Her
absence or require him to make periodic
phone calls with a set ritual to perform
for Her over the phone. The point is, She
cares about his/her progress as a slave
and devotes some of Her own time. This
is an exception, rather than the rule for
most session Mistresses.*

dead men
don't rape.
SisterSerpents

Travel

Your local bookstore has shelves full of travel books for every conceivable vacation — but what if you wanted someone's real life experiences on the backroads of Negril? Or information on the best walking tours of Brooklyn?

OUT WEST
$2.50 from Chuck Woodbury, 10522 Brunswick Road, Grass Valley, CA 95945

This charming number has gained lots of exposure recently and we still think it's one of the friendliest publications around. It's "The Newspaper That Roams," written by Chuck Woodbury who takes off in his home/office RV and travels the American West in search of interesting characters, sights, sounds and bizarre occurences to write about.

Fortunately, the western states provide endless grist for his mill in the form of Logger Brugers, chipmunks, roadside attractions, and some of the most unique people you'll find anywhere. An active readership and a flair for humorous writing make this a good place to set awhile and wish you were Chuck.

THE COOL TRAVELER NEWSLETTER
$3 from PO Box 11975, Philadelphia, PA 19145

A travel newsletter for real people who

TAXIS ETC.

Jamaican taxis are often not metered. **Always** ask the fare before getting into a taxi. Only taxis with red license plates are properly insured and licensed to carry passengers for hire. Fares may be split between riders. Taxis, while convenient, can be expensive: a ride from Montego Bay to Negril takes about an hour and costs about $60 U.S. <u>Law states that all fares should be paid in Jamaican currency.</u>

The van-sized "mini-bus" may be the best way to travel if you know where to catch it and do not mind changing vehicles now and then, or crowding. The ride mentioned above costs under $10 U.S. on a mini-bus.

want to have some fun. It's a collection of grassroots travel notes from real people who've been there—they don't try to be an exhaustive guidebook, but invite personal recollections that can help set the flavor of a place. Cast as a series of letters and stories, it takes you to Argentina or a Czech theater or Spain or Venice or a walking tour of Brooklyn or of Beijing, with fun descriptions and a feel for the place traveled to.

JAMAICA TRAVEL WISDOM
$2 from Tom Sinclair, PO Box 609476, Cleveland, OH 44109-0476

A newsletter for the person who wants to travel to the island of Jamaica, get off the beaten path and do it sensibly. Tom discusses price spreads, places to stay, things to do, and how to get rid of the ubiquitous hustlers, among other things. This is grassroots and fun, with plenty of useful information to pass on, including alternative tourism and flavorful anecdotes from the editor and his readers.

Issue #14 • Spring, 1991 • $2.00

Ernie Pyle column debuts

The Newspaper That Roams

Out West

Roadside tourist traps explored! In search of Dime coffee

Newsroom cruises through Arizona, New Mexico. Mexican food binges en route...

HISTORIC ROUTE 66

Grand Canyon Explored

Out West visits Bagdad!

ROCK SHOP

CAFE

Reading this newspaper is the next best thing to taking your own road trip!

Spirituality

Religion and spirituality are contentious subjects, and can lead to innumerable schisms and differences of opinion — hence ideal for the zine world, where anyone can take their difference and turn it into a publication. For the most part these zines focus on the outrageous and non-mainstream religions, from the most gentle of neopagans to the nastiest of Satanists. Many of the groups and zines listed here may well be upset at being in one another's company, but they are all taking advantage of the power of zinedom to give expression to their beliefs.

ABRASAX
$5 from James M. Martin, PO Box 1219, Corpus Christi, TX 78403-1219.

A quarterly of magick and related topics published by the members of the Ordo Templi Baphe-Metis, otherwise known as the Order of the Knights of Baphomet or the Temple Order of the Baptism of Wisdom (modern magickians are fond of this sort of language). They discuss such esoterica as rituals for achieving magickal goals, but also come down to earth with lots of humor and look at things like the connections of Kenneth Anger's films to the Great Work. Many of the references here will be rather confusing to those not familiar with Crowley and his successors, but in their field they rank at or near the top.

On September 29, 1989, Berkeley police raided the Oakland, California headquarters of the Caliphate Ordo Templi Orientis, armed with a search warrant listing the objects of search as "drugs, paraphernalia involved in drug sales and use, and records of drug dealers," according to the Thelema Lodge newsletter. It does not take much in the way of imagination to understand the mental state of the resident of the lodge's Merkabah House when he excused himself from an Hermetics class and opened the door to a knock, only to see 17 police officers with drawn weapons. Many objects of sacred value, including athames and swords, were confiscated, and several persons were arrested on various trumped-up charges. And this, in a nation with a Bill of Rights! Lest anyone think that the raid was

justified by the hysteria attendant to the epidemic of crack cocaine (the cops' excuse), O.'.T.'.O.'. spokesman Bill Heidrick reported in the newsletter that once the arrestees got to the Berkeley Jail, their guards called them "devil worshippers." The search-and-arrest warrant had alleged that something called a "black baptism" had occurred on Merkabah House grounds (a groundless accusation no doubt leveled by a madman). Only a very small quantity of drugs were found — and no crack. Not only did the police confiscate the Magickal weapons as "illegal," they apparently pilfered rent and temple furbishment funds totalling almost $900.00.
The height of absurdity came when police confiscated a snapshot of an "infant white male child w/black cross across front of body" — which just happened to be someone's personal photo of a baby in a car seat, strapped in for safety!

THE BLACK FLAME
$3 from Peter H. Gilmore, PO Box 499, Radio City Sta., New York, NY 10101-0499

While "orthodox Satanism" may sound like an oxymoron to some people, it does indeed exist, and this zine is one of its leading exponents. Their orthodoxy is that of Anton Szandor LaVey, founder of the modern Church of Satan, and they require their writers to be familiar with the principles he espoused. However, **The Black Flame** is anything but an exercise in tedious self-reference, branching out to look at the use of Satanism as a practical philosophy for surviving a cold, uncaring world. They are also an excellent source for info on the various squabbles and feuds within the occult world, though as always one should be cautious of depending too much on one source in these matters.

The true Satanist will deal with people as individuals, eschewing collectivist doctrines such as racism. Satanists do not simply tolerate the freaks and misfits of society, they seek them out to gain wisdom from their fellow lone wolves. We are truly Wolfen, howling in the night songs of noir melancholy. But sometimes we choose to run in packs. We might even try to shake up the complacency of those who thoughtlessly embrace consensual-reality, by demonstrating that there is far more in Hell and on Earth than could ever be dreamt of in their philosophies.
And sometimes we find those feral children, wolflings who are abandoned because their alien natures are rejected by others, who reject them. They have yet to comprehend their uniqueness, and we embrace these fellow children of the night, lighting their way along the Left-Hand Path with the Black Flame. What wonders we have to show you, who would cast off your mantle of self righteousness to enfold yourself in the cloak of Luciferian understanding.

CHRISTIAN*NEW AGE QUARTERLY: A Bridge Supporting Dialogue
$3.50 from Catherine Groves, PO Box 276, Clifton, NJ 07011-0276

While there are fundamentalists on both sides of the divide who view any dialogue (never mind any synthesis) between Christians and New Agers as dangerous or impossible, there are other voices exploring the rich possibilities of this particular spiritual interface. Under Catherine's gentle guidance the writers here consider the similarities and differences in the two world views, seeking to explore and explain and empathize rather than to overwhelm or dogmatize. From intercessory prayer to the delightful history of Saint Jehosaphat (the Buddha translated to Christian hagiography) there's plenty to read and meditate on here.

COMPOST NEWSLETTER
$2 from Valerie Walker (earmark "for CNL" on check/no cash, please), 729 5th Ave., San Francisco, CA 94118.

CNL is one of my favorite neopagan zines, exploring the world of alternative religions with humor, grace, intelligence and computers. They believe in innovation as well as tradition, and articles on spellcasting for a job in the computer industry rub elbows with looks back at the Greek myths. Regular columns present recipes with a spiritual bent and pretension-puncturing looks at some of

the kooks out there in the pagan community and elsewhere. A very successful synthesis of ancient traditions and modern sensibilities, from people with a lot of great ideas.

SEX: As a popular pagan person, I find this subject popping up wherever I go, especially when I go "skyclad" (our quaint euphemism for "Buck Naked". By the way, I've noticed that certain Big Name Pagans (BiNPs) prefer being skyclad simply because they're too lazy to dress up in fancy robes.) While I enjoy the freedom of walking like an animal, I find that I must constantly remind some "Perfect Love and Perfect Trust" people that, while my petals may be glistening in the morning dew, I do NOT pollinate with every blessed bee that comes along. Talk to ME, not my beauteous breasts. It detracts from your cool pagan image when you start drooling.

CULTWATCH RESPONSE
$2 from PO Box 1842, Colorado Springs, CO 80901

These people are pagans doing outreach in one particular circle: law enforcement. Specifically, the writers here (some of whom are pagan law enforcement officers themselves) are doing their best to counteract outrageous smears and hysteria on the part of some religious fundamentalists by supplying documented and well-researched articles on what various pagans believe and do. A welcome counterbalance to the spate of stories on Satanic child abuse and the like, which even if it existed would have nothing to do with today's pagan community.

DARK LILY
$4 cash from Magdalene Graham, BCM/Box 3406, London WC1N 3XX, ENGLAND.

An occult zine which unabashedly follows the "left-hand path" — what was traditionally called black magic, though that term doesn't seem to be much in use any more. It's written under the influence of a mysterious and anonymous Master, who gives instruction and exercises to those who wish to listen. Building a stronger self is perhaps the central message of modern left-hand occult teachings, and it's amply expanded on here.

MASTER: I know what is waiting in the wings to replace abolished tradition.
PUPIL: Why can't you tell me?
MASTER: You will understand that when you are ready to know. I cannot describe to you things that you cannot comprehend; I know you cannot comprehend them because, if you could, you would not need me to explain them to you. To tell you what those things are would be like someone who has reached the top of a mountain describing the view to someone who is only halfway up. However detailed the description, it would be nothing like seeing it for yourself.

RELIGIOUS FREEDOM ALERT
$1 from 5400 Eisenhower Ave., Alexandria, VA 22312.

The newsletter of the Coalition for Religious Freedom, a multidenominational group of religious people who are interested in a wide exercise of religious freedom as guaranteed by the Constitution. They are a valuable source of information on clashes between church and state, usually from the point of view of a church being attacked, whether it is the IRS against the Scientologists or the Amish battling for their right to have no safety reflectors on their buggies. An especially good place to keep up with deprogramming and home schooling struggles.

We should not hesitate to meet the atheists and Humanists in open forum on equal terms. If my religion is not good enough that I can powerfully share the message of the Gospel under the anointing of the Holy Spirit, then I sorely need to draw closer to God! (II Chronicles 7:14)
Let us seek and pray for a court decision or a constitutional amendment making it clear that the "free exercise" of our religious rights in the public schools and our unabridged "freedom of speech" are beyond question!
The prospect of one religion interfering with the free exercise of another clearly prompted the First Amendment. Each individual can constitutionally claim protection to share his moral values on

an equal basis with all others, regardless of religious overtones.

ASYNJUR
$2.50 from Cheryl Newton, PO Box 567, Granville, OH 43023

A serious journal for those interested in the old Norse religions. Unlike some groups promoting such symbolism, the writers here are trying hard to recreate the strong parts of that faith without wallowing in modern racist reinterpretations. They're strongest in retelling old tales, along with the lore of calendars and runes.

THE BAHLASTI PAPERS
$2 from PO Box 15038, New Orleans, LA 70115

The newsletter of Kali Lodge of the Ordo Templi Orientis, a bunch of ceremonial magicians engaged in serious study without necessarily being humorless. Indeed,

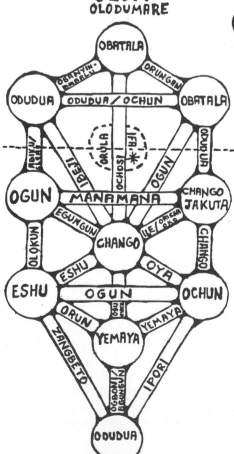

puns and stories and fantastic tales play an important part in their teaching, mixing here with the most unusual esoteric correspondences and symbolic prose. There must be a neat local group behind this paper outpost.

SOCIETE
$6 from Technicians of the Sacred, 1317 N. San Fernando Blvd. Ste. 310, Burbank, CA 91504

A zine for those with a serious interest in Neo-African religions — Voudon (more commonly called voodoo), Santeria, Macumba, and more, including such esoterica as Thelemic Voodoo and a

variety of other syncretic systems. There are lots of in-depth articles here, describing and exploring a variety of religions from the Caribbean, New Orleans, and elsewhere. A fascinating wealth of information waiting to be tapped.

THE SPIRITUAL REVOLUTIONARY
$3 from Kyle & Luna Griffith, PO Box 60327, Palo Alto, CA 94306-0327.

TSR comes from something like the far fringes of the world...though to the people who read it, it's got the ring of authentic truth. Kyle Griffith started channeling material one day, and before he was done he had a whole book called WAR IN HEAVEN, laying out a new view of the spiritual world as a battle between the Theocrats (bad guys) and Invisible College (good guys), with most live people as dupes and pawns. Every-

The Graeae lamenting the theft by Perseus of their dentures and only contact lens

thing from world history to rock music lyrics *fits in* perfectly. It all works as a total explanation for everything, and enough people think so to fuel this newsletter as a forum for further discussion of just what the heck is going on behind the scenes. Sexual liberation, the repression of the arts, earthquake prediction and how to become a Spiritual Revolutionary yourself are a few of the things you'll find in this wild romp.

Spiritual Revolutionaries are people who take an extremely radical approach to forming personal opinions about spiritual subjects. We have to be willing to learn exactly what our personal experiences with every aspect of spirituality are trying to teach us. We must have the courage to question all authoritative opinions about the nature of spiritual reality: our own pre-existing ones and those that accompany the information we obtain by reading occult and religious literature or hearing other people describe their spiritual practices and beliefs. We must be willing to sort through large amounts of false and unimportant information to find a few scraps of valuable knowledge. And above all, we must make the effort to think creatively about spirituality. We must actively learn spiritual knowledge as one actively learns a foreign language or other complex intellectual skill, rather than passively accepting elements of doctrine from outside sources.

In our opinion the key to making an active and creative quest for spiritual knowledge is to function actively and creatively in every aspect of life. The two of us frequently talk about our own lives and the lives of people around us in terms of "living as an artist."

THANATEROS
$6 from PO Box 89143, Atlanta, GA 30312

"A Journal of Trans-Traditional Metaphysics & Comparative Religion." These people have started with a fairly standard Crowleyan magickal base and mixed in lots of modern ideas, notably those surrounding the whole notion of Chaos, whether it be mathematical, physical, or psychological. The result is something like an academic journal with a wild subject matter and a devious sense of humor. Whether it is a new Gnostic version of the Tarot or an explanation of how quantum mechanics fits in with Qabala, the connections here are intriguing.

MEZLIM
$6 from PO Box 19566, Cincinnati, OH 45219

This "Independent Journal for the Working Magus" is another resource for the modern post-Crowleyan magician. Sex magick and uses of the Cthulhu mythos are among their strongest concerns. The material here is very professional, well-done and organized, but it orbits the further fringes of the mystical world.

TRIDENT
$5 from Embassy of S.A.T.A.N., PO Box 666, Whitehall, PA 18052

A Satanist zine which stands apart from most other Satanists as well as more conventional religious zines. Magus Yaj Nomolos, who runs the embassy, holds that Satanists should be purely secular,

rather than emulating religious orders turned inside out. He conducts an open forum here with a great deal of wit, making merciless fun of all those who disagree with him, and promoting his own brand of success and independent thought.

The so-called 'Satanic Religion' happens to be the clever invention of Western religious philosophies, designed to be embraced by dangerous non-conformists so they can be kept under surveillance as well as within the net of exploitation. That's why modern Satanists, claiming to be anti-religion, blindly go on conducting themselves by religious standards of measure. It is no surprise that this phenomena is typically proselytized by the social dropout,

commanding the attention and adoration of society's outcasts. Religious orders invite misanthropism, the hermit and lone wolf, the sinister rebel endorsing chaos, to provide the very forces of demonic evil with which they force and terrorize their flocks into line. Obviously, this brand of satanism is the most visible.

INTUITIVE EXPLORATIONS
$2 from Gloria Reiser, PO Box 561, Quincy, IL 62306-0561

A generally "New Age" zine with a variety of interests: Channelling, astrology, astral projection, training exercises for the enlightened soul, and even "spiritual cookery." A smorgasbord of beliefs and ideas for those dissatisfied with more conventional old age religions.

CES NEWSLETTER
$12/year from PO Box 7091, Burbank, CA 91510-7091

This one is for members of the Church of the Eternal Source, a neopagan group with a difference — they are making a serious effort to recover and practice the religion of ancient Egypt. One can argue about their authenticity but not about their commitment, as they are doing a very solid job of staying committed. Inspirational in its dedication.

GNOSIS
$5 from PO Box 14217, San Francisco, CA 94114-0217

A slick magazine of the "Western Inner Traditions," edited by Jay Kinney, who has a long small-and-underground-press history. **Gnosis** is about things like alchemy and Kaballah and the Rosicrucians and Gurdjieff — all the wonderful strange ways of viewing the world that lurk in our cultural background. The writers here draw on a wide variety of beliefs and viewpoints to present a selection of esoteric teachings and scholarly interpretations for the reader to consider. Even the ads are full of hidden messages for the knowledgeable student.

The hallmark, I suppose, of all the Gurdjieff groups is secretiveness. They do not want to be known by the curious. Their members strive to live their lives in such a way that those around them will probably never know of their participation in the Work. When asked directly, they may deny they know anything of Gurdjieff at all. In part, this attitude can be traced directly to the instructions Gurdjieff gave to his original groups: that they must not write down anything of his System, and that they must not talk about the work they were doing to those outside the group. And while the events of the last fifty or sixty years have unleashed a flood of once-secret esoteric teachings and previously unknown religious practices into a vast and growing spiritual marketplace, these attitudes have stubbornly stuck to much of the Work.

GREEN EGG
$5 from PO Box 1542, Ukiah, CA 95482

The Church of All Worlds started out as a fictional creation in Robert Heinlein's **Stranger in a Strange Land** — but then some people got interested and now, decades later, the CAW is a thriving

neopagan group. They celebrate the God-dess within us all, love and laugh, and keep track of current trends within the pagan community better than anyone else. They're a good source of news and reviews as well as inspirational and educational writing for anyone interested in a life-positive religion. Unlike some neo-pagan groups, the CAW is national, with a network of "nests" across the country actively looking for new members.

The greatest threat to Paganism's survival is not the hostile non-Pagan forces that actively oppose the Craft and Paganism, but the in-fighting and toxic gossip mongering that happens within the movement. These practices sapped energy from the movement and led to fragmentation in the early 1970s and this dysfunctional pattern seems to be intensifying again now that more Pagan and Wiccan churches are taking shape. May we learn from the past and find better ways to work through conflicts in the present and future.

NEW MOON RISING
$3 from Mystic Moon, 8818 Troy St., Spring Valley, CA 91977

A "Journal of Magick and Wicca," this one ties together many diverse parts of the occult community. It's rare to find a nature religion orientation, astrology, channeling, Tarot and ceremonial magick (so spelled by those who work in the serious traditions to distinguish it from stage magic) in the same publication, but they're all here. The emphasis is on useful information for students rather than on finding the One True Way.

Beltaíne

Movies & Television

Mainstream entertainment magazines offer their readers exactly what they want: mainstream entertainment. But what do the cult followers of splatter movies, offbeat television and hard-to-find oddities of cinematic history do? That's right: they produce their own fanzines in countless numbers and infinite categories and specializations. If someone's favorite television show was "Lancelot Link," chances are pretty good that a fanzine devoted to it would find an audience.

BLUE LIGHTS
Contact Vicki Werkley, 16563 Ellen Springs Dr., Lower Lake, CA 95457

For almost every television show there is a diehard contingent who worships its subject and will fight tooth and nail for its resurrection after its untimely demise. This is the newsletter from Spotlight Starman — one of the more active fan clubs around dedicated to the show about a sweet-natured visitor from beyond the stars who

assumes human form and gets into scrapes because he doesn't understand about money and cops and stuff (sort of like the New Testament). A virtual APA for "Starman"-fans with occasional excursions into simpatico shows such as "Quantum Leap" and "Beauty and the Beast." In addition to continued campaigns to put the series back on the air, they've also passed on all sorts of into about the episodes that were filmed (with special attention to some favorites, such as "The Wedding"), they hold conventions, publish new "Starman" ideas and generally have a lot of fun. They're

also sort of cause-oriented, with articles plugging plans to save the space station, or discussions of copyright law as it applies to exchanging videotapes. We found the issue focusing on pizza an inspired one, as it is perhaps the most widely recognized Starman (and earthling) food.

COFFEE AND DONUTS
$1 from PO Box 6920, Alexandria, VA 22306

A zine for fans of the now-vanished "Twin Peaks" TV show. Actually, it's one of many, but it's the only one we saw and the editors have published other zines in addition to this labor of love. Who knows what their future installments will offer what with the show's cancellation, but undoubtedly they will hang around, hope for reruns and agitate for an un-cancellation. There's plenty of TP trivia here, what the actors are up to (in the present and the past — some issues have comprehensive filmographies of the entire cast), articles on how the show fares (fared?) in the UK and lots of fodder on show creator David Lynch. ABC lawyers got a hold of all TP fanzines some time ago and forced name changes. Since then **Coffee and Donuts** improved considerably, with a new format and less drooling. First issues contained some silliness like a phony 900-number where you could call and talk to Lucy (the show's adorable police station receptionist) and recipes for those glorious pies and even a Chutes 'N Ladders type board game. For $2.50 they'll send you their "Best Of" collection from the first seven issues. A bargain for the pop culture archivist.

"Peregrines"   by Sandra L. Smith

Scott, did you know that the signals from all the TV shows ever aired are still traveling through the universe?

Oh, gross. Space pollution!

Not if they show our first season again!

Several critics have yelled about the use of violence in Twin Peaks (as well as other Lynch projects). Compared to other TV shows/movies the violence is minimal. It's more disturbing, because Lynch doesn't sugar-coat it, and his directing style puts you right in the center of things. Lynch does get away with more than most directors do, why? He understands that the people who sit

down and censor tv/movies are generally concerned with specifics, not subject matter.

FILM THREAT
$3.50 plus postage from 9171 Wilshire Blvd. Ste 300, Beverly Hills, CA 90210

This one successfully made the transition from homegrown zine to commercial commodity (I recently found it at my local downtown newsstand sitting next to **Vanity Fair** and **GQ**!) but still belongs to the zine universe, mainly because editor Chris Gore "arrived" with his integrity intact. In fact, we applaud him. **FT** is still one of the best (and most outrageous) of the zines devoted to weird movies and "The Business." Lots of low-culture media, and no-holds-barred reviews of underground and mainstream

videos and features make this an adventure to read. Crazed Christmas films, interviews with such names as Henry Lee Lucas (the subject of HENRY: PORTRAIT OF A SERIAL KILLER) (he thinks the movie stinks), Clive Barker and Traci Lords (and the ever-popular "Famous Extras" column), lots of hate mail (Gore refuses to publish love mail). In the past they've printed reviews of such hot video items as the one about the Go-Gos (the one they'd probably rather you not know about) and revisionist opinions on folks like Spike Lee and David Lynch. More recently they did almost an entire issue devoted to child stars with a comprehensive time line depicting the births, actions and ultimately violent or untimely deaths of most of them (included at the end was an open letter to Macaulay Culkin pleading with him to stay in school).

SCAREAPHANALIA
60 ¢ from Michael Gingold, PO Box 489, Murray Hill Station, New York, NY 10156-0489

A clockwork regular horror movie zine that goes in for longer reviews and is interested in things other than gore. Editor Michael Gingold has a distinctive review style which is commendable — he is fair without slobbering or disparaging anyone for cinematic crimes. Reviews for the discriminating viewer — titles have included NOTHING BUT TROUBLE, THE VANISHING, SLEEPING WITH THE ENEMY, MEET THE HOLLOHEADS — along with interviews with people like Frank Henenlotter (the man who brought us BRAIN DAMAGE and BASKET CASE) and director Steve Barnett. Recently Gingold celebrated his 100th issue anniversary and treated us to a Top 20 horror film list, top 10 non-genre titles and the top 50 individual performances — and just when you think you have it all, Michael includes the complete SCAREAPHANALIA index, an alphabetical listing of every film every mentioned in the zine. He also plugs other movie zines and sometimes even sits in on their issues as guest reviewer. Who says it's gotta be high culture to survive?

NAKED!SCREAMING!TERROR!
$1 from David Todarello, MPO Box 67, Oberlin, OH 44074-0067

This one's for all the things that were too gory or sleazy or just plain bad for the editors' other publications. A horror zine that strikes out over new ground on its infrequent excursions into the world. They review things like BLOOD CASTLE and THE AMAZING TRANSPLANT with amazing dexterity and then go on to devote entire issues to things like Asian horror films, with dozens of weird and wild movies that you could probably spend months tracking down. One issue has a 70s theme, spotlighting movies made during that much-maligned decade — including THE BEAST IN THE CELLAR, RAW MEAT and DEATH GAME. Don't read it alone or at night.

NAAPM NEWSLETTER
$10/yr from 2735 Benvenue #3, Berkeley, CA 94705

This quarterly publication is the newsletter of the National Association for the Advancement of Perry Mason, and once you know that, there isn't a whole lot else we can tell you. It's a long-running zine for the Masonite (of which there are many, trust us!) that's always interested in exploring aspects of Perry's career and its presentation to the public. They also interview lots of folks connected with the show (old and new) — including story editors, producers, PM authors and semi-regulars on the show. A fan club in the traditional mode, although it never neglects Erle Stanley Gardner's other written works. Issues concentrate on subjects as diverse as previous Perrys (namely those 30s detective flicks which boasted at least 4 different Perrys and Dellas), filmographies, investigations into Perry and Della's relationships. Issues always contain ads for Masonia old and new, classifieds, a pen pal service and cable TV listings for the show.

THAT'S EXPLOITATION!
$3 from Gene Freese, 6426 Durango Dr., Ft. Wayne, IN 46815

Film reviews and commentary devoted to exploitation movies and their infamous stars. Gene obviously loves this genre and is never condescending in his assessments of fringe media culture. We end up finding out more about these movies than we would from, say, less impassioned sources. There are reviews of ultra-B flicks like CHAINED HEAT, ANGELS HARD AS THEY COME, and career profiles of the most familiar faces in the cinema. Grizzly Adams star Dan Haggerty, Don Stroud, William Smith, Charles Napier and the evil B-man Wings Hauser (who could forget his wretched character in A SOLDIER'S STORY??) Gene also gets in filmographies for a number of B-movie leading femmes, including Linnea Quigley and Elizabeth Kaiten. It's about time someone paid attention to this troupe of actors.

STICKY CARPET DIGEST
$1.25 from T. Deja, 38-27 147th St., Flushing, NY 11354

A fun and freewheeling horror/sf movie zine, with assorted closeups on other parts of pop culture. The reviewing style is honest and doesn't splutter with outright adoration — and usually allows for dissent (they very often have open debates between staffers and guest reviewers). Movies for the masses, with plenty of side-tracking for such adventures as "Great Moments in Over-Acting," a look at some Carradine Brothers stinko movies, movies about science that goes too far, horror movies and what we can learn from them, a serialized article on Elvis' movie career, blaxpoitation pictures, and one special "All Mike" issue with movies featuring Michael York, Michael Caine, Mike Hammer and other reasonably famous Mikes. There's also a bit of music reviewing and chats with bands like Too Much Joy (the band who got arrested for playing Two Live Crew covers in the same place the Crew got busted) and the Jack Rubies. A good mix of mainstream and utter esoterica.

Friends of the Gang Debs include:

John Huston, Jeffery Kennedy, and Cher

"Marge has been bitten by a beaver"

LIGHT, LIVELY JOLLY TIME TEENAGE GANG DEBS

INFRA-MAN (1975; Prism Video) This film is better than sex. The ultimate Brain Burner, Infra-Man is guaranteed to turn every thinking cell in your body into phosphorescent sludge. It's THAT good. The Princess Dragonmom is invading the surface-world, and the finest Chinese cardboard technology is used to turn dowdy Raiman (Li Hsui-Hsien) into Infra-Man, a kung-fu super-hero who chops his way through a wild assortment of mutants, including She-Demon, Plant Guy (these names are, of course, made up; they don't have names in the film), Fright Wig Guy — he does a little dance before blasting Infra-Man with his horns, Fat Spider Guy, Plumbing Supply Guy — he has a wrench and a drill bit instead of hands, and the ever-dreaded Spring-Action Bowling Ball Twins! This film is like watching an extended Burt Reynolds fight scene. You know the kind, where people fight and all of a sudden someone jumps in front of the camera and say "Arugula Milkshake," or some such nonsense. There's no plot or logic to get in the way of rubbersuits pounding each other into egg foo yung. Without a doubt, Infra-Man is the greatest achievement in Hong Kong movie-making history. You owe it to yourself to see Infra-Man. — Sergio Taubman

THEY WON'T STAY DEAD
$1.50 from Brian Johnson, 11 Werner Rd., Greenville, PA 16125

A zine of sleazy movies and other bits of trash culture. Low-budget coverage of strange and cheesy movies and associated madness. Reviews range from the mild SATAN'S CHEERLEADERS to the hardcore grossout DEATH SCENES (with FUNNY CAR SUMMER, CANNIBAL HOLOCAUST and HEATHERS making appearances, too). They've also got a bit of other culture including performance art and cultural artifacts like the classic Aurora plastic monster and the Revell "Visible Head" model. What makes this movie zine stand out is that it dares to be disapproving of some things in the B-movie world and that the editors stick to the stuff they appreciate. A friendly little zine of film and video and modern life that would rather do a few things at length than a lot of brief stuff. Worth the price of admission.

TEENAGE GANG DEBS
$2 from Erin Smith, 5812 Midhill St., Bethesda, MD 20817

A fanzine that reads like a "Nik-at-

Nite" commercial and covers a lot of the same ground. It's a tribute of sorts to television culture and does a great job of bringing back all those Saturday nights in the 70s for us latter-day baby boomers. Past issues have included a two-page spread of appreciation for Patty Duke, a two-part interview with Stanley Livingston ("Chip" from My Three Sons), a closeup look at Hanna-Barbera, several appearances of Bea Arthur ("Maude"), not to mention an awesome reverence for The Brady Bunch (the lost Brady cousin, a cover featuring Bobby, and an in-depth look at Jan's character). There's also some reminiscing for the artifacts of yesteryear, including Viewmaster and other paraphernalia. This is not silly fluff — this is actual and fun-lovingly faithful coverage of a time too many of us want to forget. A true labor of love.

GRINDHOUSE
$1 from J. Adler, PO Box 1370, Murray Hill Station, New York, NY 10156

This film zine would be a handwriting expert's field day — let's just say that the ranting and printing here does not lead one to suspect the editors of being completely balanced. They review all manner of exploitation and gore, right down to snuff flicks, from the environs of the sleaziest movie houses in New York City. Features reviews of sleaze porn, soft porn and plain old low budget film, all revolving around the theme of bloody horror. Each review is descriptive of the overall action and cross referenced for actors appearing in each (quite a lot of work for a zine!) They pan TEXAS CHAINSAW MASSACRE III and praise CLASS OF 1999, so that gives you a little insight as to where they are coming from. They also take a look at BLONDE EMMANUELLE, SPACE AVENGER, and THE UNBORN. Comes out irregularly, but they say those four issues will get to you sooner or later. It's a little psychotic looking, but don't let that put you off — it's definitely an original.

FROSTBITE FALLS FAR-FLUNG FLIER!
$10/4 issues from PO Box 39, Macedonia, OH 44056

A zine of "Rocky and Bullwinkle" and the rest of the Jay Ward stable of cartoon characters, probably the only one of its kind, and one of the only places (besides Ward's son) you'll find this much Wardaphilia in one place. Issues sometimes have special themes, such as the one entirely devoted to Dudley Do-Right (with dialogue quotes, a list of episodes, etc.), but mostly they represent a potpourri of the classic animated show. Plenty of R&B trivia, quizzes, a complete list of "Fractured Fairy Tales," Hoppity Hopper, Sherman & Peabody and anything else they may find. One issue has a look at "Fractured Flickers," Ward's reworking of silent movies. The editor tracks all manner of media mentions as well, so don't be surprised to find this mention in one of his lovingly constructed issues.

AUTOPSY
$1 plus Age Statement from Chris Doolan, 89 Pangeza St., Stafford Heights, Brisbane, QLD 4053, AUSTRALIA

The one-man zine of hardcore everything, although Chris' chief love is obviously the lower reaches of video, obscure B-movies and horror/gore/sleaze cinema. The real challenge to doing a B-movie zine in Australia, of course, is finding things to watch that the censors have not sliced to ribbons. Did you know that "Last House on the Left" is STILL banned down under? But somehow he comes through, reviewing for us such gems as "The Newlydeads," "Necromancer," "Scream For Help," "Spermula," and even mentions a few to avoid, such as the latest from the director of "Nekromantik." There are also other things in life that Chris likes to write about, including some hardcore music, metal and the state of censorship in QLD (apparently there is plenty). Sometimes he'll even pay tribute to certain icons of the genre, such as horror star Coralina Cataldi Tassoni. He has definite tastes and doesn't give slack easily (you may find your favorite sleaze movies trashed unmercifully), but is fascinated by the underside of life and has little patience for such generic nonsense as the Elm Street films. Very respectable zine.

LIFESTYLES OF THE BODILY DISMEMBERED
$1 from Jason Stephenson, 1702 Burns Avenue, St. Paul MN 55106

This is a splatter zine, concentrating on films but getting into books as well. It goes for such gems as "120 Days of Sodom," "Hellraiser," and the Reanimator stuff, among others. Featured horror includes "Nekromantik," the band State of Mind, and the book version of "Silence of the Lambs." Their spicy lead stories usually set the tone for the rest of their reviews. Lots of space is spent on each review, enabling them to be treated with loving care.

MORE FUN THAN EATING A RAZOR BLADE!

Potpourri — III

Some zines tackle subjects that no one else dares to touch. In others, the editor's preoccupations combine two or more disparate fields into one medley. Any way you look at it, there is a lot of miscellaneous flotsam and jetsam in the zine world. Here are more of these odds and ends from the fringe.

KOOKS MAGAZINE
$5 from Donna Kossy, PO Box 953, Allston, MA 02134

There are a lot of people who don't quite seem to have both oars in the water (and some of them seem uncertain where the river is in the first place). The most interesting of these bring a sublime innocence to their efforts to analyze and comprehend the universe that classes them as Kooks and makes them the subject matter of this zine. Donna has been tracking and corresponding with the Kooks for years, coming up with a mixed bag of religious crusaders, radio mind-control, manifestoes stapled to telephone poles and obscure privately-published rants. She makes a strong effort to meet these people on their own terms, presenting their theories and ideas for any reader with an interest in expanding their own mind, and occasionally coming up with contributions to a taxonomy of kookdom.

39=YHVH ECHOD-ONE GOD
I, ALONE, TEACH THAT GOD BROUGHT NY METS TO VICTORY 13 YEARS AFTER 26th YOM KIPPUR (YOM KIPPUR WAR 73 at 39th YOM KIPPUR OF ISRAEL. (SIGNING HIS NAME INTO NY METS: & INTO BASEBALL & INTO WORLD HISTORY SO WHILE I WATCH GAME, AND RECORD ALL THE SIGNS OF GOD'S CREATION, AS I ALONE TEACH, I HOLD THAT PUBLICATION IN MY HANDS— AND WHEN GIANTS WIN BY SCORING 39 POINTS & SIGNING GOD'S NAME & IDEA OF 9-10- THE DOUBLE CLOCKWORK MAN LIVES IN AND 1776-1777 & 9 cycles 47-48 & 10

DISTURBING DREAMS AND DRIED BLOOD
$1 from Kevin Hibshman, 43 Front St., Lititz, PA 17543

This is a mixed zine, part literary, part music. It features original poems and short stories as well as reviews of new music, with the balance sloshing back and forth from issue to issue. There's also the occasional opinion piece and original art. The bulk of the zine is printed by hand, giving it a friendly, personal look which nicely complements the personal, direct orientation of most of their poets.

I'm getting pretty damned tired of this yuppie establishment world today. How come you never see a long hair on a shampoo or soap commercial? Doesn't the everyday white collar advertising exec think metal people have any concept of personal hygeine? As a matter of fact, they happen to be one of the most cleanliness conscious groups of people I know, or care to associate with. In fact, they probably help the shampoo moguls put gas in their damn BMWs! Ever see a rock star with a less than dazzling smile? No, that's right. They don't have

bad breath, receding gums, or ring around the collar either. I'm also sick and tired of them being categorized as Satan worshipping vermin.

DUMPSTER TIMES
$2 from W.S. Duke, PO Box 80044, Akron, OH 44308

All sorts of interests find their home in this zine — thirty years ago, "counterculture" would have been an apt description, but nowadays no one quite knows what that means. There are pieces on guerrilla art and theater, original poems and short stories and playlets, and reviews of music by punks and major groups alike. A spirit of fun and anarchy imbues the writing, though the politics are usually implied rather than explicit.

Boredom takes all forms, but the most common is embodied in people. How do you set up defense against such a brutal attack? One that comes from all directions? One that comes at all times of the day? Some, but by no means all, suggestions for what to do when you suspect someone is trying to bore you, are listed below:
1. Act insane — scream, flail arms, drool, etc. until said boredom goes away. If you don't need to act, so much the better.
2. Imagine a painful death for the borer. In most cases, it won't actually work out that the demise will come to the person, but we can try.
3. Wildly insult the person. (But take care — be sure not to insult anything the person says, or you can be sure they will continue.)
4. Walk away — this one is obvious.
5. "Destroy What Bores You On Sight" (wisdom courtesy the Feederz).

OTTERWISE
$1 from PO Box 1374, Portland, ME 04104

As animal rights becomes a more popular cause it's no surprise that animal rights zines are showing up. This is one, aimed at the 8-13 age group, a niche none of the mainstream animal rights groups seems to be hitting. With a mix of

MASCULINE   FEMININE   NEUTER

short, easy-to-read articles, drawings, photos and activities, they try to awaken a respect for animals in children. Animal testing, vegetarian recipes, fur coats and just the sheer variety of the animal kingdom are all found here.

NO POETRY
$2 from Julee-Peezlee, PO Box 4763, Boulder, CO 80306

Julee puts out a weird mix of mail art and social commentary. Her activities extend far beyond this zine into mailing such things as a set of nine brightly hand-painted plaster skulls, or tiny minicomics, or earrings made out of toy guns. **No Poetry** tends to contain a mix of images to shock and images to make you think, opposing sexism on one page and being cheerfully blasphemous on the next. Hard-hitting but sometimes baffling.

GAUNTLET
$8.95 from 309 Powell Rd., Springfield, PA 19064

Small press people tend to be real close to the issues of censorship, recognizing that many social and financial pressures act as *de facto* censorship even in the absence of repressive laws. **Gauntlet** is an annual which covers all the issues they can find along these lines, "Exploring the Limits of Free Expression" as the subtitle has it. The writers here look at banned books, movie ratings and the battles to get a good one, classroom repression, Customs seizures (the first issue of this zine was banned in Canada) and more. In addition to the news, they reprint images and stories which have offended people, from conservatives to the PC crowd, daring the reader to test their own free speech quotient. A very

strong zine, and a must read for anyone who's not aware of all the pressures on the independent media in America today.

In 1985, the ninth grade honors English class at the Prospect Park high school was issued a beginning college-level textbook, called Story: Fictions Past and Present. *One section of the 1,071-page book contained short stories, many written by well-known modern American authors, such as Bernard Malamud, James Baldwin, and Ralph Ellison. Pretty heady stuff for 14 and 15 year-olds, maybe, but that's what honors programs are for; to challenge students who want to excel. But the students never got a chance to be challenged by those writers; their works were torn from the textbook. In all Michael Coyle, the English teacher, told his students to rip 15 short stories out of the book and throw them in the trash.*

SMILE
$2 from PO Box 3502, Madison, WI 53704

Actually, there are many zines named **Smile**, all done by people named Karen Eliot, drawing on a tradition of reusing these seminal names which originated in Britain in the mid-80s. This is one of the chewier American variants, full of deep analysis of the social situation from the point of view of those who are quite horrified by it. Drawing in the Situationist tradition and drawing on other artistic insights, the writers here argue for greater personal freedom and a reversal of the course of modern civilization. Various issues have celebrated different aspects of a continuous revolution including enhanced sensuality, nomadic culture, free child rearing and art as everyday life.

Inspirational though rather difficult to read in places thanks to thickets of intellectual vocabulary.

Schiz-Flux challenges the intellectuals that do papers for university professors and whoever else is interested to do research on alternatives to capitalist production and social relations. Plans for the creation of liberated zones and wedges of green areas that expand over concentrated sources of capital. What land and areas would be suitable for the making of international junctions; for nomadic desiring cultural architects and people into alternative culture and politics. How to get rid of the state war machine economy. Exchange relations, the dead end disease of capitalism. The world war force networks and their fascist allies and their means to oppress and exploit weaker nations. How to set up an area with the basic crucial minimum needs with the least amount of work done for the needs of survival. Maximize individual freedom and be connected with the world networks of people doing the same thing. How to set up junction points for facilitating nomadic internationalism. What kind of symbiotic relationship could possibly exist by integrating the city and the countryside in terms of culture and social relations and providing the basic necessities to live. What could be done with the material structures that exist now

THE UNINTELLIGENCER
$1 cash from J.C. Coleman, PO Box 3194, Bellingham, WA 98227

One might think of Coleman as something of a mutated Andy Rooney. His zine consists of short essays, most cynical, about life in the modern world and what's wrong with it. But there are occasional flights of fancy in which, for example, the sexual habits of anthropomorphic tuna figure heavily, leading one to wonder just which modern world he is inhabiting. Crusty and puzzling by turns, **The Unintelligencer** will probably offend most people even as it gets them thinking.

My answering machine answers my telephone every time, without exception, Whether I am home or not, whether I want to talk to someone or not, if someone wants to talk to me she will talk to the machine first. Those who are not willing to talk to the machine will not talk to me.
If I am able, I listen to the person taping a message, and if I want to speak with that person at the time I will do so. If I do not, I may elect to return his call later, write, visit or do nothing at all.
Some people dislike answering machines, and outright refuse to leave a message. But I feel that my telephone is mine, and so my rules will apply. And if they find it rude that I knowingly elect not to pick up the receiver when it is activated, then that is their own problem.
Another reason I have the machine answer the phone is telemarketers. Telemarketers peeve me. Fortunately, most are trained to hang up on answering machines and so I no longer have to deal with them. But there are a few organizations which will leave messages on machines; and, as with wrong numbers, they are ignored.
Wrong numbers add a little amusement and curiosity to answering machines, though. Some of them are pretty odd. I got a message for Katherine from Maraie at Obidia Salon asking to call her her appointment. Oh well, I guess Kathy'll get the news a little too late

to change the way people relate to each other in them or would this project be impossible. Would the skyscrapers and other buildings that maintain the concentration of power have to be leveled. What kind of structures could be integrated into the environment without dominating the surrounding human, plant and animal population. To fit into the existing wild areas without destroying them. How to give back to nature instead of raping it.

DUMARS REVIEWS
$2 from Denise Dumars, PO Box 810, Hawthorne, CA 90251

This is a specialized review zine — it specializes in whatever catches Denise's eye. This includes a lot of dark fantasy, horror, and poetry, anything having to do with free speech or libraries, and a potpourri of hip culture. She goes well beyond the written word, reviewing movies, TV shows, restaurants, spicy food, and occult supply stores as well. Bits of poetry and opinion are sprinkled in as leavening to the intelligent opinions here.

Dateline 12-8-90 Your Tax Dollars In Action
Recent news reports have revealed that officers from the Lynwood Sheriff's Station have been up to some unusual tactics in fighting the gang situation. A number of them have been calling themselves by a gang name, "The Vikings" and have been seen giving hand signals to each other and even placing graffiti alongside gang graffiti to let gangs know they are being watched. This bizarre behavior was endorsed by L.A. County Sheriff Sherman Block. Gee, maybe we should buy them colors.

SALON
$5 from Pat Hartman, 305 W. Magnolia #386, Fort Collins, CO 80521

"A Journal of Aesthetics" which explores many topics in the world of the arts, from censorship to criticism to fashion to creativity. A variety of artists and writers converge here to dissect and explore their universe, with a great deal of depth and wit, leaving each issue full of opinions and views to devour. In a bid to be an art-object itself, each issue is numbered and signed by as many of the ——— —d writers as Pat can round up ——— s.

The Edwardians and Victorians ascribed great powers to literature. Memoirs, letters and journals of those periods in history are full of references to relatives in delicate health, not allowed to read anything inflammatory. The poet Swinburne was advised by his doctor not to read Byron. Virginia Woolf, when recovering from her mental breakdowns, was forbidden both reading and writing. People still set great store by the written word.

Concerned parents vigilantly watch and challenge many books assigned in schools. They worry that their children will be exposed to such concepts as reincarnation, suicide, disrespect for authority, secular humanism, the fallibility of parents.....These people will tell you that Hitler was a disciple of New Age

thought.

Concerned parents, like all censors, believe that getting rid of a few books will cure whatever they perceive as being wrong with the world. We're not talking about unenlightened rednecks in backwater communities. In Jefferson City, Colorado, **A Day No Pigs Would Die** *was challenged as unsuitable for children.*

It's ironic that book-banning is still so popular, in an age when children (and adults) are far more influenced by TV, radio, video games and even magazines. The urge to ban books stems from an urge so quaint as to amount to superstition: the belief that books matter; the belief that books mean something. And by believing it is so, the censors make it so.

PILLS-A-GO-GO
$1 from PO Box 1432, Bloomington, IN 47402

The "Journal of Pills" produces an attractive newsletter with all the latest medical and legal news revolving around those cute little medicines you can slip in your mouth. They track Prozac lawsuits, promising new pills, the ins and outs of the pill industry, the marketing factors behind pill design, and more. Amusing and with the occasional nugget of vital information.

The latest drug to hit the street scene is a veterinary sedative/anesthetic called Ketamine. Obtained in liquid form and reduced to a powder, dealers charge about $20 a dose for the stuff, calling it "Special K". *They say Special K causes pleasant disorientation and hallucinations for several hours. The DEA is now thinking up ways to tighten up controls over it.*

WHAT HAD GONE

Splatter, Death & Other Good News

Everybody's got their own demons to face. The ones who probably sleep best at night are the ones who face them daily. The folks who produce these zines probably sleep the soundest of all — and delight in giving the rest of us nightmares.

FESTERING BRAINSORE
$1 plus Age Statement from PO Box 82, Buffalo, NY 14212

This unassuming little zine starts off with splatter movies and other cinematic marvels but then heads off into much sleazier territory. It's primarily devoted to being gross and wins top honors for sending shudders down our spines. Infant suicide, necrophilia, ghoulish art, murder, you name it. One page will offer an interview with Kitten Natividad while somewhere else you'll find advice on writing to mass murderers. If you were searching for something to bring the gorge rising to the back of your throat, look no further.

WEEKLY WORLD NOOSE
$1.50 from 333B N. Park, Tucson, AZ 85719

If suicide attempts are cries for help, what are zines about suicide? Morbidly funny, in this case. This little zine celebrates the fine art of suicide, seeing it as a rational, and even aesthetic, response to a predictable and miserable life. Mostly it's about all the good reasons for killing oneself, though they also get into such side issues as what your pets will do after you're gone, great sports suicides, copycat suicides in Italy and the like. Nasty stuff, and the sort of thing that most mothers would not want their impressionable darlings to read. One wonders how long it will be in operation; will the editor follow his own prescription for dealing with the world?

The contradictions inherent in society's opposition to suicide are blatant. On the one hand, we are told that the suicide achiever is a victim who needs help -- whether he wants it or not. On the other, we are informed that he is a criminal, because suicide is illegal.

Since it is not possible for a person to be simultaneously the perpretrator of a crime and its victim, this view on the subject is obviously insupportable. Under the weight of its own absurdities and hypocrises, it creaks like an old toilet seat beneath the bulk of a prosperous business man. This creaking is evidence of faulty logic.

Now let us examine, by way of contrast, the crisp, coherent reasoning of those who advocate suicide: Pain and suffering can only exist iin living things. A person who has killed himself is no longer a living thing; therefore people who kill themselves cannot experience pain and suffering. Because people who don't experience pain and suffering are happier than those who do, it follows that suicide increases the amount of happiness in the world.

Have a happy day.

BOILED ANGEL
$3 from PO Box 5254, Largo, FL 34649-5254

A compendium of bizarre comics and gross stories, all designed to turn your stomach. It's got vulgar pictures, nasty language, graphic stories of torture, plenty of blasphemy — and that's the tame stuff. Then there's gore, sexism, necrophilia, cannibalism, Satanism, mutilation, festering wounds and distorted bodies. Then again, if you look hard enough, you'll find some pretty good reasons for maintaining the First Amendment — which the editor knows from first hand experience isn't all that easy to do sometimes.

Thanos

Part 3:
Resources

G E T T I N G
S T A R T E D

By this point, perhaps you're convinced that small-scale publishing is the thing for you, and you need a few hints on how to get started. If so, great! The pages ahead should hold a lot of useful information to get you started on the road to zine success.

On the other hand, maybe you still don't see the point and wonder why people would spend all their spare time and money doing something that, in the great majority of cases, will bring them nothing but mail to answer and bills to pay. The reasons break down pretty neatly into three classes: Fun, Fame and Fortune.

Fun (and its corollary, Friends) is an almost-certain outcome of self-publishing. There's very little to match the feeling of pride that comes from watching your creation go out in the mail, just like a "real" magazine. The hard work is worth it, just for the pleasure of seeing the finished product. Along with this fun comes contact with people across the country and around the world.

Fame is a bit more unlikely. If you start small — and we think you should — maybe only ten or fifty or a hundred people will read your first effort. If you keep at it for a couple of years, you might get up to a thousand or two. Let's face it, even 2,000 happy readers are not going to get you the Nobel Prize for literature — or a mention in the *New York Post* (although the *Village Voice* or *Rolling Stone* is not out of the question) But in some areas of the zine field, there are less grandiose awards. Science fiction has the Hugo and FAAN awards. Poets have a number of competitions open to them (although as far as I can tell many of these competitions exist only to separate the budding poet from an entry fee). But newcomers don't win the Hugo award. To aspire to that level of fame you probably have to know exactly what you're doing right from the start, and concentrate on getting your zine into the hands of the People Who Count, pumping up your circulation to reach more potential award voters, and so on. That's not my idea of fun.

But perseverance and hard work will bring you a bit of "fame" in limited circles. Just about everyone who publishes poetry probably recognizes Merritt Clifton's name, thanks to his long-running review-zine *Samisdat*. Many punk rockers would be able to tell you that *Flipside* is published by Al, or *MRR* by Tim Yohannon. After nine years of writing reviews I seem to be turning into an authority on the underground and alternative press. I've done interviews for newspaper and radio and television, been invited to write articles for other magazines, and given a few lectures. I don't expect to make the front cover of *Time* at this rate, but it's satisfying to be recognized for your work.

Fortune is nearly impossible. There are fanzines out there that support their editors — though not in style — but the vast majority lose money. If you can do your photocopying at the office and get your stamps from your father, you can reduce expenses. But you're not going to get rich.

But who cares? I'm firmly convinced that fanzines are for fun, not for profit. (I'm not as rigid about this as the hardcore SF fans, who refuse to even recognize anything you have to pay for as a"real" fanzine.) Zine publishing keeps us off the streets, helps us meet new friends, and brings us hundreds of interesting things to read, and for all that it's a dirt cheap thrill.

Despite my devotion to zines, I have one very serious word of warning to budding publishers: Time. You won't have any left if you get seriously involved in putting out a zine. I have missed deadlines on term papers, taken incompletes in graduate school courses, and done my Christmas shopping on December 24th, all because of the time that *Factsheet Five* soaked up from my everyday schedule. The temptation to do just a bit better, to write just one more page, to send out just ten more sample copies, is irresistable — even after you've already spent countless hours collating and folding and stapling. Friends and family won't understand your addiction. And trust me, you will be addicted. All you can do is try to keep it under control by repeating the mantra, "It's only a hobby."

By now this book should have made clear the fact that the zine world is vast and rich. The question is: where do YOU fit in? Don't be scared off by the number of other small publishers out there. With a little luck and perseverance, you can find a market niche and fill it well.

The folks from Light Living Library (publishers of *Message Post*) have a few suggestions about picking a zine topic in their pamphlet "How Do You Do a How to Do." The two most important are "Tap your experience" and "Be specialized." By doing so, you should be able to find a topic that will attract readers while allowing you to have fun.

Tap Your Experience. If you're a punker, stick to music (that's probably what you planned anyhow, right?). If you've developed a lot of cheap home workshop methods, there are people waiting to hear about those. If you're active in the local alternative politics scene, maybe you can pass on tips to others. Trying to publish a zine on surfing from the Black Hills of South Dakota is probably a bad idea.

Of course, you don't want to carry this rule to extremes and feel inhibited from using a zine to give you the experience you want. We all have our own senses of humor and some experience with laughing, so humor magazines are open to us all — and the same could be true for literary or poetry zines. Committing yourself to a subject by publishing a zine can be educational and help you develop your expertise.

Be Specialized. No matter how good your music zine is, if you try to compete head-on with *Rolling Stone* the first week you're dead meat. A conservative political zine shouldn't try to emulate *National Review* immediately. It's OK to have goals, but you've got to work up to them. A way to start is to learn to do one special thing better than anyone else and expand from there.

The easiest way to specialize is by geography. There are hundreds of punk music zines out there, but if you're the first one in Left Flank, Minnesota, you're all set (assuming there are any bands or clubs in your area!). While *Factsheet Five* covers fanzines as exhaustively as it can, no one (as far as we know) is reviewing zines published outside the US. If you can combine a strong subject with a regional emphasis, you can develop a regional audience.

You can also specialize by subject. If there are too many music zines in your city already, focus in tighter. Is there room for one discussing industrial music? How about ska? Similarly, you can compete with *Mother Earth* by concentrating on hydroelectric power, or mixed-row gardening.

You can also specialize by trying to capture the attention of a particular audience. A punk zine directed to lesbians and concentrating on music by womyn might be a hit — provided that you're not a male bricklayer from the Bronx. If you want to appeal to a Norwegian community, a zine about Norwegian genealogy could develop an audience.

The important thing to remember about specialization is not to carry it too far, not to paint yourself into a corner from which there's no escape. A zine for Maltese drummers in southern New Hampshire probably isn't going to make it, no matter how scintillating your writing. You have to have an audience to get started, and just as importantly, you have to have room to grow.

Ready now? Got your subject all picked out? Great. Let's talk about getting it down on paper.

P R O D U C T I O N

Now that you've got a zine, it's time to consider the nitty-gritty details of production. Most people think of printing when they think of publishing, but there are a lot of other things that must be done before you can make copies of your immortal words.

For starters, the words have to be written. This may sound simple, but it's the most important thing if you want to publish a successful fanzine. People want writing that is easy to read. Even if they can't spell themselves, they'll be upset by misspelled words. Even if they can't write anything more creative than a grocery list, they'll notice a bad style. So the aspiring writer should draft and correct, draft and correct again, until she's got the best she can write. With enough practice, you can get away with a single draft, particularly if you're working on a computer and can correct mistakes as you go. But the only substitute for experience is painstaking care. After your first million words or so, your style may be well-established, but before that it deserves some attention.

Even tougher than getting your own writing under control can be editing others' writing. Many people write their own fanzines cover to cover. Others of us aren't so lucky, and rely on outside writers or columnists to do some of the work. There are two hard parts to working with other writers: finding them and taming them.

The easiest way to find writers is to get something out on the market and let them find you. If you're prepared to pay for work, get yourself listed in the *International Directory of Small Presses and Little Magazines* and writers will beat a path to your door, presenting you with some of the worst writing you've ever seen. Remember, if you get unsolicited material that you don't like or can't use, there's nothing wrong with returning it — or trashing it, if there's no return postage included. If, like most of us, you're looking for writers who will work for free, you'll have to trust the grapevine. Get your zine reviewed and ask the reviewer to mention that you need writers. Ask your friends. Badger your relatives. It's amazing how many people nurse a secret desire to write.

Taming writers depends on making sure the terms of your relationship are very clear before they do any work for you. Make sure they understand the terms of payment (if any), or how many free copies of the finished work they'll be getting. Be sure they know their deadline. We like to send reminder postcards to our columnists about two weeks before deadline if their columns aren't in yet. You have to agree on the topic or guidelines — surprises can be nasty, especially if they come in at the last minute when it's too late to find a replacement. And writers should understand that "to edit" is an active verb. You need to have final say over content and length — so be sure they know that. If they're going to be heartbroken or go stark raving mad if you touch a single word of their deathless prose — you're better off without them. Believe me.

Once you have all the material for the first issue of your zine, and all your writers have coughed up their articles (on time? unlikely but possible), the

The Elements of Style
by William Strunk, Jr. and E.B. White
MacMillan, 1959

The Chicago Manual of Style
University of Chicago Press

You wouldn't try to repair a car without some instruction; why, then, do so many people assume that writing is a natural skill? If you've never had any training, it's worth looking at a few books to avoid common pitfalls. *The Elements of Style* (more commonly known as "Strunk & White") is the classic in the field, a slim volume that is widely available in paperback, and worth an annual review by any writer.

If you plan to submit your work to other publications, or just want to know the standard way of dealing with everything from bibliographic citations to when to include the standard abbreviations for shillings and pence in a sum of English money, *The Chicago Manual* is the authority to refer to first, although its near-$40 price may encourage you to visit it at your local library.

The Alternative Publisher's Handbook: A How To Manage An Alternative Periodical
by Joseph Scott Lane

$7 from Tunnel Publishing, PO Box 4083, Terre Haute, IN 47804-4083

Over the years there have been a number of booklets and pamphlets on the subject of running your own zine or underground newspaper. Published in 1991, this is one of the few that is still in print. Joe Lane focuses on the techniques and trials of putting out a small-town tabloid paper, with an emphasis on the financial realities of trying to make a living off the endeavor. (The reality is that it is darned hard to avoid losing your shirt). The best parts are his stories from the trenches of actual independent tabloids. Fred Woodworth (editor of *The Match*) contributes a chapter on distribution with some good ideas, though it's flawed by his cantankerous views on certain subjects.

next job is to create a master copy. These are the actual pages which the final zine will be printed from. Some zines are handwritten cover-to-cover, and some of these are even pretty legible. But most of us don't have a printing or handwriting style that lends itself to comfortable reading, and must resort to some sort of technology. (This may not be true in the punk fanzine world, where illegibility sometimes seems to be prized. And a zine made up completely of drawing would be an exception.)

The cheapest way to get everything looking good is to type it all. Even if you have to buy a used manual typewriter (getting rare, by the way) and learn to hunt-and-peck from scratch, it's worth it for the finished product (if you are a beginning typist you'd better allow a *lot* of time for your first issue!). If you can afford it, a newer typewriter (maybe even something self-correcting) is better. Some points to consider:

• How does it feel to type on? You're going to be spending a lot of time at the keyboard, so pay attention and get one you like.

• What type of ribbon does it use? Carbon film ribbons produce much better looking zines than nylon or cotton. The Smith-Coronamatic (R) cartridge system is incredibly convenient, allowing quick corrections by swapping ribbons. You might go for a used classic self-corrector type like the IBM Selectric II. On the other hand, you can buy a lot of correction fluid for the price of one of these machines.

• How hard does it type? You'll probably want at least a carbon copy of all your work (one would be better if it had adjustable impact so you can make multiple copies). If you're using ditto or mimeo printing the ability to type hard is even more essential — take some masters along and test as you shop.

• How many typefaces can you get? If you get a daisy-wheel or golf-ball typer, you can change typefaces without buying a new type-writer, and give your zine some design variety.

Go out and look at everything, and then buy whatever you like best and can afford. It's possible to spend thousands of dollars on an electric typewriter that has a computerized memory, spelling checker and who knows what else (though if you have that much money, you should probably be looking at computer systems instead), but for most fanzines, a portable electric model can be found for under $200 if you take your time and shop the sales. Used typewriters can be much cheaper than this, but are often in horrible condition — and repair shops typically charge a minimum of $35 to do anything. If money is tight, check the classifieds, flea markets, word-of-mouth and garage sales. Always dicker and remember: once you buy it, you're stuck with it.

The next step up, if you can afford it, is to buy yourself a computer. Word processing is much more efficient for most people than typing, primarily because it is much easier to correct errors on-screen than on-paper. We wouldn't have even attempted this book without a computer to work on. A good word processing program will allow you to justify your text, count the words you have written, or move text from one file to another — this last can be used to insert a standard subscription notice in each issue, for example. Depending on what type of system you get, a computer can also maintain your mailing list, keep track of your fanzine's budget, print form letters, give you games to play when you should be writing instead, and do many other things.

The computer market changes so fast that it would be senseless to try to tell you what model to purchase. In general, the longer you can wait and the more money you can spend, the better deal you can get. The only way to know how good a deal is is to shop around. Here are a few things for the ziner to keep in mind:

• What kind of printer can you get? Letter-quality printers produce type that is impossible to distinguish from typewriters, but do they not handle graphics. Dot-matrix printers can reproduce computer graphics but the text is low-quality and may not copy well. A compromise is the "near letter quality" dot-matrix printer, which can produce very good text, particularly if the original is to be reduced. Beware: many printers will not work for ditto or mimeo masters. If this is what you intend to use it for, be sure to test it before buying. These days, the laser printer has set the new standard, allowing the publisher to mix text and graphics on the same page, but at considerably more expense than other types of printer.

• What operating system does the computer use? Check your friends' systems and buy something compatible with them if you can. You will benefit from their knowledge and program base. These days the choice for most people is between IBM-compatible and Apple MacIntosh systems. A fullblown desktop publishing system will cost about the same for either type, and there is plenty of software available for both. People will hotly argue the advantages of one or the other, but we've never been convinced that there is anything more than personal taste involved.

• What type of mass storage device is available? A 'hard disk' would be nice to hold everything, but the average fanzine will fit on a 'floppy disk' with only slight inconvenience, an example of which may be the cost of floppies or making sure they are all properly labeled so there is less chance of copying over your zine's contents.

Some people will tell you that it is difficult to get used to working on a computer, while others will tell you that it is the greatest thing since sliced bread. The only way to find out is to try it for yourself. If you're not familiar with computers, try to get some time to play with one before buying. Good dealers don't object to customers playing around (although it might be out of line to try to produce an entire zine in their office). If you can, get your friends to show you the ropes and try their machines, or find a computer at a college or library. Used computers are almost without exception obsolete and not worth spending money on. But exceptions to this rule exist, especially for those technically-minded enough to keep an obsolete machine running.

The Fantastically, Fundamentally Functional Guide to Fandom for Fanzine Readers & Contributors

The Fantastically, Fundamentally Functional Guide to Fandom for Fanzine Editors & Publishers

Respectively $3 and $8 from Susan M. Garrett, 14B Terrace Ct., Toms River, NJ 08753

A pair of resource zines aimed at media fans (those who are most interested in Star Trek, Star Wars, Doctor Who or other mass-media SF and fantasy shows) in particular, with sections useful to those ordering other SF zines, or even zines in general. Media fandom can be fairly odd (letters of inquiry before ordering are recommended, for example) but the basics of getting and submitting to zines are the same all over. *The Guide for Readers & Contributors* includes a glossary of terms, notes on adzines, how to order by mail, "The fanzine bill of rights," record-keeping for writers, and more.

The Guide for Editors & Publishers covers (again with an eye towards media fandom) everything from soliciting work to dealing with printers to selling your final zine. Some of the problems are unique to the genre (like bootlegging — most of us would be *happy* if someone sold copies of our zines) and on a few points I distrust the advice, especially her discussion of being a small business, but on the whole this is an excellent set for the beginning publisher (in media fandom or any other area).

Desktop Communications
$24/6 issues from 530 Fifth Ave.,
New York, NY 10036

Personal Publishing
$24/12 issues from 191 S. Gary Ave.,
Carol Stream, IL 60188

Publish
$39.90/12 issues from PO Box 55400,
Boulder, CO 80322

There are a lot of magazines about "desktop publishing" — the production of magazines entirely on computer screen, without the traditional muss and fuss and rubber cement fumes. If you can scrape up the time and money to get into this field, you'll want to subscribe to a few to keep up with the latest developments in this fast-paced and confusing field. *Publish* is the best of the bunch, but the others are worth a look.

If you want to get even more high-tech, you can have the words for your zine "typeset." Typesetting is the way "real" books and magazines have traditionally been produced, and is much more flexible than typewriters or home computers (although home computers are catching up rapidly). You can either take your manuscript to a printer and have him typeset it, or do it yourself. Buying a typesetting machine is beyond consideration for most fanzine publishers (we're talking thousands of dollars for the cheapest models) but there are a number of places now that can take transmission of text from computers via phone modem and generate set type. This requires you to have a home computer (or access to one), but it also gives you complete control over your format. In larger cities you can also take computer disks in to places that will run your words off on a laser printer for around a buck a page. If well done, this can be nearly indistinguishable from traditional typesetting. I used this process on *Factsheet Five*'s first venture into the chapbook field and was quite happy with the results. One thing to note: if you use typesetting you'll pay each time you write something and have it set, instead of paying once for a typewriter or computer (plus paper and ribbons, which are of negligible cost compared to typesetting).

Most people like to spruce up their text with some illustrations. If you can draw, you're all set — just do your own "illos." Most of us aren't so lucky, but fortunately there are a couple of alternatives. The first is to use "clip-art" — images now in the public domain that have been re- published from old sources specifically for this purpose. Clip art has the disadvantage of resembling the ads in telephone books — the art style is at least 30 years behind the times in most cases. But some people can make it work for them. Dover Books carries a wide range of clip art (some of which is not old-fashioned), though their prices may be a bit on the high side. You can buy clip-art books at a good stationery or art-supply store.

The other alternative is to find a real live artist, or several of them. Artists have to be treated with care, just like writers, although my experience has been that they are less fussy (perhaps because they have fewer outlets for their work). Again you must make sure you communicate clearly from the outset. Let the artist know what size work you need — are you going to reduce things prior to printing or not. It's important that they know what printing method you're going to use and what media they should use — for example, most offset printing won't pick up blue lines, in art or anywhere else. Can you shoot half-tones or do you need line art? In addition to a copy of the final work, many artists want their originals back. If this is the case with your artists, honor the request. Good artists that will work for the wages we pay (that is, for free) are hard to find, and should be treated well. Don't lose their artwork! If you treat them well, other artists will appear and offer you their stuff, and you're off and running.

Now that you've got your text and artwork in good shape you've got to get it down on the page. It's time to consider layout. (Actually, you should consider layout while you're working on the contents, but it's easier to write about it sequentially.) Let's talk about tools first, then principles.

To some extent the tools you'll need are specific to the printing process you choose. For now let's assume that you're using photocopying or offset printing to reproduce your work. (Ditto and mimeo considerations will be discussed later. Full-color work is well beyond my scope. If you can afford full-color work, chances are that you can afford to have someone else do all the scutwork that we more impecunious publishers have to tackle ourselves anyhow.)

What you basically need is some way to attach little pieces of paper to big ones. The little ones are the sections of text (handlettered, typed, printed or typeset) and artwork. The big ones are the finished pages which are going to be reproduced. Most simply, the little ones can be attached with small rolled up pieces of tape, applied to the *back* of the originals (tape on the front will show up when printing). Most of us, though, use rubber cement, a gooey substance which dries without wrinkling paper. Buy yourself one small jar — the kind with a brush in the cap. After you have the jar, it's much cheaper to buy rubber cement and rubber cement thinner in large cans and refill the small applicator jar. Or you can get a pastepot if you can find one. This is like the little jar, but the brush stem is adjustable which allows you to avoid dripping rubber cement all over the place. Professionals avoid most of the mess of rubber cement entirely using a waxer for their layouts. A waxer is an electric device that gives you a constant supply of melted wax with a roller — wherever you want you simply wax the back of your original and press it down. The big advantage of wax is that you can take a piece back off and move it around a lot. With rubber cement, once it's in place it's there. "Real" publishers use fancy desktop waxers costing hundreds of dollars. But hand models starting around $50 to $100 can do an adequate job for the small zine. If you ever get a chance to use a waxer, you'll never move back to rubber cement.

Other useful tools include a blue pencil, a transparent plastic ruler, an X-acto knife, scissors, and typing correction tape for covering errors (the adhesive kind that comes in narrow strips). Make sure that your pencil is "non-repro" blue/invisible to the camera — if you can't find one that says that, go for a "sky blue." You can also spend money on an eraser designed to pick up rubber cement. However, if you just pour out a glob of rubber cement on your desk and let it harden, it will do just as well and not cost as much.

At a stationer or drafting supply house you can pick up a lot of other useful stuff — as much as you can afford. One thing to get when you're starting out is a few sheets of "transfer letters." These are sheets of plastic with headline-size lettering on the back, which you can transfer to your copy by rubbing the front with a small stick or ballpoint-pen cap. Buy one test sheet of any brand you are not familiar with to check the quality before making any substantial investment — some of the cheaper brands simply do not work properly. I've always liked C-THRU myself. You can also find uses for a few rolls of edging tape (transparent tape with lines or devices such as arrows or dots printed on them) — these make nifty borders if you like that sort of thing.

It's important to remember that the camera (which shoots your master copy to make the film that makes the plate that your work will be printed from) sees a bit differently from you, and that your reader will see whatever the camera sees. The camera sees in black and white only, not color. Blue pencil is invisible to it, while red is indistinguishable from black. We don't use any other color on our stuff —it's too much of a gamble as to

Earth Care Paper Inc.
PO Box 7070
Madison, WI 53707
608-277-2900

Fidelity Products Co.
5601 International Pkwy.
PO Box 155
Minneapolis, MN 55440-0155
800-328-3034

Quill
PO Box 4700
Lincolnshire, IL 60197-4700
708-634-4800

There are lots of places out there that will sell you office supplies by mail and put you on their mailing list if you ask. It's worth getting some catalogs and shopping around for price. (Also check your local "office warehouse" store, if you have one). Earth Care has an excellent selection of recycled paper products, while Fidelity is strong on fancy (and expensive) graphics arts tools. Quill has the best all-around selection and good quantity pricing.

how it will turn out. Another thing the camera will see is smudges and fingerprints — which will darken and print out on the plates in ugly black. So be careful around your master copy. Excess rubber cement can be removed with the rubber cement pickup — that glob of dried rubber cement you made. Small mistakes can be taped over with typewriter correction tape. "White-out"correction fluid has an unfortunate tendency to smudge things and build up into little white peaks that leave shadows on the final copy, so we don't use it often. If you need it, though, it can be a lifesaver. There are special versions of correction fluid designed for use on copies and on ink. These are much less prone than the basic typewriter version to making nasty blotches.

Before you start doing the layout of your master copy you should think about it. You want to design a page that's pleasing to the eye. Don't clutter it up with too much stuff, and make sure what's there is easy to follow. (One classic mistake is to continue lines of text on both sides of a drawing, as if the reader's eye could keep hopping over the picture). There are lots of graphic design books that will guide you in the layout process. Unfortunately it seems to be a difficult talent to learn, but keep at it. Hiring a commercial designer is far too expensive for the fanzine publisher. If you have a friend with design skills, it's worth buying her pizza and beer or offering other suitable bribes or trades, especially if you can't seem to pick up the layout knack yourself.

The first step in layout is to plan what goes on which page (assuming you're printing more than a single page). If you don't do this, I can guarantee a lot of frustration when you have to rip things off the page that didn't quite fit and glue them down somewhere else. Start by making up a "dummy book" of your fanzine (this is particularly important if you're using folded pages). Take small sheets of paper (8 1/2 x 11 sheets cut into quarters will do) and collate, fold and staple them. Go through and number the pages, then take apart the sheets and you can tell what goes on the back of what. For example, in one of *Factsheet Five's* formats, pages 16 and 47 went on one side of a large sheet, and pages 17 and 46 on the other.

The next step is to "dummy up" the individual pages. Make a rough sketch of each page, showing which articles are going where, what headlines are to be lettered in, where advertisements and artwork go, and so on. One way to make this process easier is to buy a bunch of acetate page protectors, put a single sheet of blank paper in each one, and do your dummies with grease pencil on the front. This allows you to make easy changes. Once you've prepared dummies of all the pages, you're ready to go on to the actual layout and pasteup.

The idea is to get all the type and art for each page (in two-page sets) glued down in the right place on one sheet, ready to be photographed and printed. Many big printing houses will do the layout and pasteup work for their customers — you bring them the dummy and all the text and art and they put it in place. But it costs you. We underground types can't afford this, and the cheap printers we deal with won't do it anyhow. You want to bring them "camera-ready" pages. To prepare each camera-ready master page, begin with a sheet of paper the exact size of the finished two-page spread. If you prefer, and if your printer will understand, you can work on a larger sheet, with a blue-pencil outline indicating the borders of the actual pages. If you do this, put a small black arrow outside the boundary, one pointing in at each of the four corners, which indicates to the plate-maker where the border is. Now, using your non-photo blue pencil lightly block in the layout you've planned, indicating where text, art and headlines go. Don't worry about being neat — none of this will show up in the end. It's only meant to guide you. Using your ruler, draw in the locations of any folds or borders. Make sure to leave margins if you plan to staple your zine.

Now you're ready to start laying down the actual type and art. Take the first piece to go on this page and cut it out of whatever larger sheet it's on. Get as close to the letters or drawing as you can so you won't end up with overlaps. Round off the corners — sharp corners have a tendency to stick up and make shadows. Now put this clipped-out section face down on a sheet of scrap paper and coat it evenly with rubber cement (or wax it, if you're lucky enough to own a waxer). Only a light coat is needed, so wipe the brush before applying the cement. Then take the cement-coated piece and position it on your master page. You don't have to get it exactly perfect the first time, since you can move it around a little while the rubber cement is drying. Theoretically you can even peel pieces up after the rubber cement is dry and reposition them. In actuality, this results in curled, shredded, smudged and destroyed originals and a nasty temper. Better to do it carefully the first time. Check for straightness with your ruler or T-square. When it's in the right place, press the piece down firmly, smoothing from the center to the edges to prevent wrinkles and bumps. Take up any excess rubber cement immediately with a tissue, or wait for it to dry and use a pickup. Be careful! Wet rubber cement attracts finger-prints and burns them almost indelibly into the paper.

Once all the pieces are in place you can put in headlines. If you're a gambler you can use transfer letters and apply them directly onto your final page. I prefer to create the headlines separately, then glue them down as with the text. When all the headlines are down , and you've waited for all the cement to dry (and removed the excess), it's time to do borders, if you're using them. You can use border tape, or do what I did in my poverty-stricken days, — use a fine red pen (remember, red looks black to the camera) and the ruler. (This is where a transparent ruler comes in handy, since you can put it over the copy and still see where you want the line to go). A red pen is also handy for filling in holes in transfer letters or making minor corrections to art or text.

Now you just have to repeat this process on every page. When you've done them all, go back once more with a rubber cement pickup and clean up any remaining smudges. Then place the whole pile reverently into a clean file folder.

You're all done. Great! Now you're ready to have it printed.

P R I N T I N G

Fanzines could not have existed in the Middle Ages when trained monks were the only way to copy something. Fortunately modern technology has made things a good deal easier. Indeed, the current zine boom is in large part attributable to the invention of the photocopier, the personal computer, and other technologies which have removed the necessity of expensive craftsmanship. In this section I'll describe the printing options available from the simplest and oldest to the most high-tech.

The earliest zines were produced on the letterpress — Gutenberg's invention, which involves using movable metal type to set up each page, inking the type, and impressing it directly on to paper. Nowadays a letterpress is most likely to be used for limited edition art, lithographs and engravings, but it would be classy for someone to do, say, a punk fanzine via letterpress.

Science fiction fen ("fen" is the plural of "fan" in the SF world) started their fanzine boom with the hectograph. A hectograph is basically a pan of gelatin. One prepares a specially-inked master sheet and lays it down on the gelatin so that the ink soaks in to the gelatin layer. Then individual sheets of paper are smoothed on to the gelatin until they pick up the ink. From time to time I see a hectograph kit in a large stationery store, but from what I've heard about the time and tedium required in this process, I'm not anxious to try it. However, if your great-uncle Fred stashed one in the attic, dig it out — you might like it and at least it would be free.

Another relic of early SF fandom is the carbon-paper zine. People just crammed carbon sets into their typewriters and produced all the copies directly — just like the samizdat in pre-Yeltsin days — but as this limits you to a circulation of at most twenty, it's not a very attractive option, especially in these days of super-cheap photocopying.

Then there's the spirit duplicator, or "ditto machine" as it is more commonly known (Ditto is actually a Bell and Howell trademark, but they haven't been exactly vigorous about protecting it in recent years). You've all seen ditto at school — it's that purple stuff that smells funny. The process starts with the preparation of a master sheet. A ditto master consists of three parts — a white front sheet, a tissue interleaf, and a purple (usually) backing sheet. To use one, take out the tissue paper and type or draw directly on the front sheet. The back of this sheet will pick up ink from the backing sheet, and it's this ink image (which is of course reversed) that is used to print the final material. (If you forget to take out the tissue sheet, the ink will end up there instead of on the front sheet. If you absolutely have to, you can then use this tissue to print from, but it will wear out and tear quickly).

A ditto machine vaguely resembles a real press. All types have some way of attaching a can of ditto fluid, or a reservoir to fill. Ditto fluid is basically denatured alcohol, and in a pinch regular rubbing alcohol can be used, though it will cost you a lot more. (Fannish lore maintains that some ditto zines have even been printed using vodka as a solvent.) Whether by hand

THE SAMISDAT METHOD
by Merritt Clifton
$10 from Pretzel Press, 111
Washington St. #1, Troy, NY 12180.

Merritt has been publishing his own fanzine Samisdat for years on a variety of used offset presses, and has made doing more with less into an art. This book distills his knowledge of how to buy, run and repair a press into easy lessons for newcomers. He's also got advice from other underground printers — there's a whole network of folks running Multiliths and AB Dick offset presses out there. Includes ideas on cut-rate mimeography, cheap sources of supply, and even tells you when to pour beer into your press.

Printers Hot Line
$2.25 from 1003 Central Ave., PO
Box 1052, Fort Dodge, IA 50501.

"The Nation's Largest Marketplace for Buying and Selling Printing Equipment, Supplies and Services" is the proud masthead here. Mostly they are a source for used presses the size of your garage and costing ten times as much, but there are a few things in here for the small publisher. They do carry ads for small offset presses, and bring out a bit of news from the desktop world as well.

crank or electrically, the printing drum is turned round and round, paper goes in one end, and copies come out the other. In between sheets, the master is lightly re-coated with solvent, and the paper then presses against it to pick up a little of the dissolved ink.

Ditto is a fairly cheap process (you can get a used machine for $50; paper is $5 or less a ream, masters about 8 for a buck, and fluid $7 a gallon) and there are still those of us who use it today. After a little practice it's easy to master. The basic thing to watch is the fluid flow — too much fluid and you get a runny mess rather than a good copy, too little and it's too dim to read. There is usually a lever or dial for controlling this sort of thing. One major disadvantage of the process is that all art and type must be put directly on the master. Typing on the master is not hard, but you also have to get your artists to draw there. One way to handle this is to mail masters to your artists with the spot you want the illustration in marked. Leave the tissue paper in when you mark the master — this will keep your guidelines from showing up on the master — but make sure your artist knows to take out the tissue before drawing. You can get masters in several colors (red, blue and green are the most common, but I've seen yellow, brown and black as well) and these can be slipped behind the front sheet at the right time to create a single multi-colored front sheet.

There is a process called Thermofax that takes camera-ready copy (just as you would make for offset or xerox) and supposedly makes it into a ditto master, but it generally doesn't work worth a damn and you can't afford the machine anyhow. Of course, if you have access to a Thermofax thanks to academic or corporate connections, you might choose to try to master this beast despite my opinion.

The major disadvantage of the ditto process is that one can only print a limited number of copies, since the ink is part of the master. Once it's gone, you're through. Many people say that 100 copies is the upper limit for ditto, but this isn't true. I've done runs of up to 500 copies in a pinch. The secret is to get a lot of ink on the master and then use it sparingly. Use purple masters only (for some reason they are inked most heavily) and an electric typewriter with the copy control set to the maximum. If you keep the fluid flow light, masters made this way will give you hundreds of readable (though dim) copies on white paper. For a larger circulation, one must examine other printing methods.

The next step up in complexity, but still one that can be done at home, is the mimeograph. You've surely seen mimeographed things: relatively crisp black print, often with a ghost impression caused by stacking sheets with slowly-drying ink together. The classic church bulletin is a mimeograph production. The basic process is again fairly simple: One "cuts" a master from a wax-covered stencil. Typing or drawing on this stencil pushes the wax aside, revealing the porous paper beneath. The master is then placed on the mimeograph, which forces ink through the areas that are not covered with wax. Turn the crank or push the button and the paper is run past the now-inky stencil.

A variety of types of mimeographs are available on the second-hand market, from various manufacturers. The way to get one is to hunt around until you find what seems to be a bargain. If at all possible, see the machine in action before buying it — otherwise you may discover just how complex mimeo innards are and how expensive repair service is. If you're lucky enough to find two junk mimeos of the same model you may be able to recombine pieces to make one working machine — but only if you're a pretty good mechanic. There are new ones available, but I personally have never been willing to spend the money.

Since the ink is supplied from tubes, the number of copies from a mimeograph master is nearly unlimited — it make take hundreds of thousands of copies before the master will fall apart if it's treated well. On the other hand, the separate ink can be something of a curse — it is said that the only way to avoid getting it on your clothes is to mimeograph in the nude. Mechanic's cream hand soap (it smells of ammonia) will take it off your body. But I don't know of anything that will take mimeo ink off of your clothing. I wear old clothes myself. Most mimeo inks are also slow to dry — this leads to ghost copies of one page leaving images on the ones above and below while the copies are stacked. To combat this, you can run the machine slower, buy more expensive fast-drying inks, or "slipsheet": insert a piece of card stock between copies as they come off the machine. Real mimeo fanatics run sheets through the machine one at a time and set them out to dry individually.

As with the ditto process, art and typing must be combined directly on a single master. However, for mimeography there is a process known as electrostencilling which transfers camera-ready copy to a stencil. Wonder of wonders, it works fairly well, although large black areas tend to print abysmally even if the stencil looks good. Of course, an electrostencilling machine is fearsomely expensive (to me, "fearsomely expensive" means anything that costs more than my '71 VW Bug) and not often found on the used market. Perhaps you can find one available for your use at a school or other organization, or buy one in concert with other publishers. If you're fortunate enough to have access to one, put as much art as possible on one sheet of paper, making sure that the blacks are crisp and there are no smudges. Then run it through the machine to make a single stencil master with all your art. This can be sliced into pieces and the individual illos inserted into your production stencil with stencil cement — do this *after* typing everything else onto the master, as electrostencils are rather fragile.

The ditto machine and the mimeograph pretty much marked the limit of technology for zine publishing for many years. Then came the photocopier explosion — and, shortly thereafter, the fanzine explosion. True, long before the photocopier a few brave or resourceful (or well-heeled) souls used offset to produce beautiful zines. Nowadays it's easiest to start with commercial photocopying days and work your way up to offset if you're successful.

We're all familiar with the photocopy process and pretty much take it for granted. It's amazing the access we all have to this printing technology and hard to imagine life without it. Now anyone can buy a home copier new, for under $600 — or lease a commercial machine for around $60 a month. Or you can haunt the used markets and maybe pick up a bargain. Older copiers are being refurbished by their manufacturers and sold cheaply. If you're going to buy your own copier, one thing to consider in addition to the paper cost, is the cost of the supplies it uses. Service is also ruinously

Terminology for the World of Lithography
$18 from PPC Publications, 356 South Ave., Whitman, MA 02382

If you can convince this prepress firm that you represent potential business, maybe they'll send you this. It's a glossary of terms you might want to know when talking to your printer, assuming you're doing relatively complex things. Logo-type, Misomex, Antique Finish and Vacuum Frame are among the terms they define.

Printer's Ink
On request from Thomson-Shore,
7300 W. Joy Rd., PO Box 305,
Dexter, MI 48130-0305
313-426-3939

Thomson-Shore is a short-run book-printing house; they specialize in books with press runs of 5000 or fewer copies. We've used them a couple of times, and they do a reliable and timely job. They'll give price quotes over the phone for book projects. **Printer's Ink** is a quarterly newsletter for their customers, talking about the way they do business — another good place to improve your printing savvy. Bluelines, trim sizes, and bindery types are much less of a mystery to me after a few years of reading **Printer's Ink**.

expensive, starting, in my area, at $50 an hour with a one-hour minimum, plus parts. Make sure you understand what your true costs will be before you buy. Also, most very small desk copiers are only capable of, say, 30 copies a minute, if that. At that rate it would take something like two and a half hours of nonstop copying to print 200 copies of a 40 page zine. Stay away from older machines requiring two-step processes or funky coated papers; supplies and service for them are vanishing fast.

For most people, the simplest way to get things photocopied is to use a commercial shop. This market is one in which it definitely pays to shop around. The first thing to look at, particularly if your job is relatively small, is self-service machines. These can cost less than 3 cents a copy in larger cities. Unfortunately, many of them are there solely to draw you into the shop, and produce truly crummy copies. If you're intending to go the self-serve route, make sure you test out the machine well in advance of the time that you actually need it.

Most people producing a zine will be better off at a commercial shop. Prices can range from under 4 cents a side (overnight, bulk rate, big city) to 15 cents or more (boondocks). Double-sided copying, demands for immediate service as opposed to overnight, and bound originals can run up the cost, as can using special papers or demanding anything complex .

Master copy for the photocopy process is prepared the same as for offset — the camera is just as unforgiving and the master must be just as clean. Before you leave your job at the shop, ask to see a sample copy if you've any doubt as to what it will look like — many big places will give you a sample for free, and advise you on any apparent problems. When you order a job, make sure you specify everything: paper, number of copies, single- or double-sided, whether to collate, and any other special instructions. You can complain if they do it wrong, but only if you can prove you told them to do it right. I've had overnight photocopy places put page 2 on the back of page 17 and then complain that I never told them the pages were numbered. Spell it out! Don't expect them to see the obvious. It also pays to count your copies when you pick up the job, particularly if the price is the lowest in town. Some shops routinely short large jobs by 5-10% of the total copies ordered.

The color photocopy process offers some interesting options. It takes substantially longer and costs substantially more than black and white work (single-copy prices are around 50 cents and up), but (miracle of miracles) it can indeed produce full-color copies. (Remember: there's no such thing as "invisible blue" pencil for the color photocopy machine!). They tend to be a bit shiny and are on relatively heavy paper. I wouldn't put out a whole zine this way, but the color can have a striking effect on a cover. One way to limit the cost to around 15 cents per zine is to use 1/4 of a single 8 1/2 x 11 sheet as an inset on each cover. Of course it means you must do hand assembly of the cover on each and every copy you send out — which is fine for a small press run, but formidable for a 1000-copy zine.

Some people are choosing another route for zine production: they simply prepare the material on their computer, and have their printer print out as many copies as they want to send out. If you already own the equipment it may be your cheapest route to getting something ready to mail. But I don't think a whole lot of this approach myself, especially since most practitioners of the method are still using dot matrix printers. The copies tend to be poor quality since the continual printing eats up ribbons in a hurry, and the paper is usually flimsy. And think about how long and how noisy the printing process will be before you start. Laser-printed originals are more feasible, since per-copy costs are almost as low as with photocopying. But if you can afford a laser printer you can probably afford to have the work photocopied.

And then there is offset printing — which was used to make this book, and which most large zines use. In offset printing, a "plate" is made photographically from the original master copy (this is why it's called "camera-ready copy"). The plate is then attached to an offset press, where it goes through a water bath that wets down all the areas that aren't supposed to print. Then it goes through an ink bath, and the ink sticks to the parts that aren't wet. Then the inked plate is pressed against a rubber cylinder, leaving a reverse-inked copy of itself. A sheet of paper is pressed against the rubber cylinder, and, *voila*, a copy emerges. The whole process happens at high speed, and is amazing to watch; if you get the chance, take a close and careful look at the press while it's running your job. The original offset presses were huge affairs (and some still are — this same basic process prints newspapers), but over the years they have shrunk. It still takes thousands of dollars to buy the whole setup new. Only a few dedicated ziners ever get their own, but they get good results for their money — and their time and sweat. If you want to do your own offset printing, get a copy of Merritt Clifton's book, *The Samisdat Method*, which combines the knowledge of a number of outlaw printers.

Offset technology is cheap enough that lots of entrepreneurs get into the business — hence the rise of the "instant-printing house." Instant printers often combine a photocopy operation with a small offset operation. You can use the same master to get estimates for each, and decide which method to use at the last possible moment. Generally, offset pricing starts off with a certain price per plate ($2.50 at the place I used) and adds a price per page that is less than the cost of photocopying (one and a half cents for me). If you are going to print enough copies, the per-page printing cost will absorb the cost of the plate, and the job is more economical with offset than photocopy — providing any other costs, such as folding, collating, or stapling are also taken into account. Some of this finishing work costs extra with offset, so make sure you get firm quotes for the entire job both ways if the price is close. Apart from the cost, there really isn't that much difference between good photocopy and offset these days, except that offset can turn out large jobs faster, and serve as a bit of a status symbol for some people.

Beyond small offset presses lie various pieces of machinery of interest to the person who is trying to turn a fanzine into a magazine. At some point offset on large newsprint sheets ("web offset") becomes more economical than regular offset. The web press is a bigger piece of equipment, capable of printing multiple pages at one time. This puts some constraints on the editor — for example, one can more cheaply print eight pages than four pages — but it means less handling of paper and lower costs per page. On the other hand there are higher setup costs. So while it may take hundreds or thousands of dollars to start up a newsprint zine, once you get going copies will cost only a tenth of a cent or so per page. Once again, if you're

D. Armstrong
2000M Governors Circle
Houston, TX 77092-9976
713-688-1441

BookCrafters
PO Box 370
613 E. Industrial Dr.
Chelsea, MI 48118
313-475-9145

BookMasters, Inc.
638 Jefferson St.
PO Box 159
Ashland, OH 44805
800-537-6727
419-289-6051

Marrakech Express
500 Anclote Rd.
Tarpon Springs, FL 34689-6701
813-942-2218

The Printing Factory
PO Box 277
Neconset, NY 11767
516-361-9394

A couple more short-run mail-order printing houses. If you've got a book project in the works, it's worth shopping around and comparing price quotes.

going to go with web offset, make sure to get price quotes from several printers . Even in the same city, prices can vary substantially. There are also mail order companies specializing in short run offset jobs, which are a worthwhile alternative if you live in an area where costs are high.

B I N D E R Y

Printing the pages is not the end of making a fanzine by any means (unless, of course, you intend to post single sheets on telephone poles and be done with it). Next comes finishing work: trimming, collating, folding and stapling — more formally known as bindery (even though most of us never actually bind anything into a book).

You shouldn't have to worry about trimming unless the circumstances are exceptional — the finished sheet from the press will be the size you want, presuming you wanted a standard letter or legal size. If you want a smaller piece of paper, though, it will probably cost you extra, as this means extra hand work by the printer trimming the sheets down. Unfortunately there isn't an easy way to do this at home. For very small press runs you can use a pair of scissors, but the fascination of this quickly pales. If you only need to cut one sheet into two identical smaller sheets, you might be able to use a paper cutter at your school or office — but if you have a large print run, it's going to take a long time. Even the office paper cutter probably won't cut more than a few sheets at once — professional printers use a "guillotine" type machine that cuts straight down instead of at an angle, and can go through a lot of paper quickly. These machines are hard to find and expensive to purchase. My advice is to stick with standard paper sizes and avoid trimming whenever possible.

Collating (putting one copy of each page into a complete set — the finished fanzine) is some of the worst grunt work in the world as far as printers are concerned, and consequently can be very expensive. The newest copiers will automatically collate their output, which means you can usually get collated sets at no extra charge when you're using photocopy. Offset presses, though, don't do this, so someone has to put the sheets together. And of course if you're using ditto or mimeo printing, you're stuck with the job.

My advice is to do it yourself, even if someone else is doing the printing. It's not all that tough and you can save a hell of a lot of money. For a zine of six or eight sheets you can collate from stacks laid out in line , in order, on a table, picking up one copy from each stack and piling up the complete sets off to the side. A better idea is to use collating racks, which hold the sheets up at an angle to allow you to quickly grab one of each. An experienced collator using a rack can collate thousands of sheets an hour with little effort, and watch MTV at the same time. If you can't find real collating racks, a cheap alternative is a metal correspondence rack. Bend the slots down at an angle and you're all set. Two of these next to each other with eight slots each will let you collate sixteen sheets.

One trick for collating is to make your fingers sticky — better yet get little rubber tips to wear over them, which are less messy.

Depending on your format — like if you want to put out a digest-sized zine (5 1/2 x 8 1/2) — you may need to fold every sheet. It can be expensive, so again you may end up doing it yourself. Everyone knows how to fold paper, but what you don't know yet is how to prevent your hands from turning red and raw in the process. One way is to find some kind of "folding bone," a wooden or plastic stick you can use instead of your fingers to crease the fold. Some people use pottery tools, but there's surely something in your house that will work for you. Some hardy souls use a strong fingernail. Others wear a cheap glove on one hand, or pad the exposed surfaces with band-aids. I find that the latter method works surprisingly well. Just remember to put on your protective padding *before* you feel the blisters.

Finally, whatever your format, you need to staple. Again, printers seem to feel that their stapling crew needs to be able to afford filet mignon. A regular office stapler is sufficient for some jobs, but there are two other varieties that you ought to know about. First there's the long-arm stapler, which uses long staples and allows you to apply a fantastic leverage to them. This machine can staple up to 100 sheets at a time without having any fall off the back end. But for folded zines, the solution is the saddle stapler, which is designed so you insert your collated zine with its spine along the saddle, insert one staple neatly in the spine, slide it over a few inches and insert another. A long-arm stapler should cost you $35 or less, while a saddle stapler may run $80-$100. The investment is worth it. One caution: even though they look like they would, saddle staplers don't take the same staples as office staplers. Buy the right staples and you'll save a lot of time on clearing jams. There are also electric staplers and electric saddle staplers that don't require the use of muscles, but in my experience they jam about every third staple, so I don't use them.

If, like most of us, you take the do-it-yourself approach to bindery, you'll find that the work increases with the success of your zine. *Factsheet Five*, for example, started as 25 copies of two sheets, stapled together in one corner. By the time it was a thousand copies of 16 sheets, folded over and saddle-stapled, the bindery work had gone from about ten minutes to 25 hours. Somewhere in that evolution things got to be pretty boring for one person working alone. The traditional solution is a "collating party." This simply consists of inviting your friends over and making them help with the work. (It's one way to find out just how much your friends will put up with!) For the modest expense of beer and pizza, plus free copies of the zine to those who helped, you can get things done a lot more quickly, and have people to talk to during this most boring of fanzine jobs.

If your operation gets big enough, the hard labor drops off dramatically, because with a large-sheet offset process, like the web press, the printer pretty much has to do the bindery work for you as a part of the price. The publisher just picks up finished, folded, stapled copies, ready to mail.

M A I L I N G

Now that your magnum opiate is ready, the next step is to get copies to your thousands of eagerly waiting customers. Some people — I call them posterists — handle this step very simply. Armed with thumbtacks, masking tape and a staplegun, they descend on the sleeping city with their single-sided words of wisdom. By dawn copies are attached to telephone poles, newspaper vending machines, and bulletin boards. I've heard of copies being tucked into church pamphlet boxes. Posterists tend to be either lunatics or revolutionaries; in either case, they're less concerned with a specific audience than with getting their words to the widest possible population of unsuspecting normals. But apparently some posterists don't get the feedback that they crave this way. I can think of three who have republished their works in book form. And there are at least that many who have run afoul of their local authorities for posting on "public" property.

For most of us the distribution process is a bit more complicated: we have to deal with the US Post Office or one of its competitors.

There are several options (all subject to change: check for current rates): The fastest and gentlest class of mail is First Class (called Priority Mail for packages over 12 ounces). More expensive classes of mail, such as Express Mail or Special Delivery, tend to be completely out of reach of zine publishers -- and are generally unnecessary. The charge for First Class is 29 cents plus 23 cents for each additional ounce, with the over-12 ounce rates starting out at $2.90 to anywhere in the country. If you can afford this, great. First Class mail gets beat up sometimes, and lost sometimes, but it's been my experience that this doesn't happen often. If you mail First Class, it is legal to include personal letters or scribbled notes in the zine, which is not true of the lesser classes of mail. Most ziners start out with First Class, if only because they don't know about the alternatives.

The second option is Second Class mail. Second class is intended for magazines, and requires you to publish yearly statements of mailing in which you break down your distribution scheme and list your owners. The big catch with second class mail is that it's for "legitimate" periodicals. You have to be sending out at least 200 copies at least twice a year, and half of everything you mail has to go to bona fide subscribers. The local postmaster is entitled to demand records from your bookkeeper to back this up, and if you can't satisfy him, you're out of luck. On the plus side, second class costs around as much as bulk rate (although the form to fill out is considerably more complex), is forwarded at no charge to the publisher, and gets treated fairly well while it's on its way. But most of us, who swap large numbers of our zines for other stuff, rather than having large subscriber bases, simply can't qualify. I have heard that some postmasters count arranged trades as subscriptions, so if you have your heart set on being second class, you can always propose it to yours. It didn't work in Albany; everything hinges on the local postmaster's interpretation of "requested copies."

Third Class mail is for flyers, circulars, books, and merchandise under 16

Mail Magazine
$24/yr from Gold Key Box 2425, Milford, PA 18337

This one is "The Journal of Communication Distribution." Much of it is directed at the big corporate mailroom manager, but there are tricks and tips for the smaller business mailer as well. They're very strong on keeping up with the Postal Service's plans and changes, and are often the first ones to correctly announce new rates. Barcoding and automation are occupying increasing amounts of their page space nowadays.

Mast
$15/yr from RB Publishing Company, 6400 Gisholt Dr. #208, Madison, WI 53713-4800.

A professional magazine "for mailing and shipping professionals." From it you can learn what mailroom managers across the company are making, find out about barcoding for faster delivery, and compare various overnight services. The ads occasionally feature scales, postage meters and other mailing aids within the financial reach of the moderately large publisher.

Domestic Mail Manual

International Mail Manual

Postal Bulletin
Respectively $36/year, $18/year, and $56/year from Superintendent of Documents, US Government Printing Office, 941 N. Capitol St. NE, Washington, DC 20402-9371

These are the official manuals for the postal system, and well worth subscribing to if you do a lot of mailing. The Manuals are the size of phone books, with all the applicable rules and rates for every class of mail. The Bulletin is a weekly, with the latest changes and updates as well as lots of internal postal memos.

Chiswick Trading, Inc.
33 Union Ave.
Sudbury, MA 01776-2246
800-225-8708

Consolidated Plastics Company
1864 Enterprise Pkwy.
Twinsburg, OH 44087
800-362-1000
212-425-3900

National Bag Company, Inc.
2233 Old Mill Rd.
Hudson, OH 44236
216-425-2600
800-247-6000

Uline Shipping Supply Specialists
950 Albrecht Dr.
PO Box 460
Lake Bluff, IL 60044
708-295-5510

These companies carry a variety of packaging and shipping supplies in their mail order catalogs, from corrugated cardboard cartons to shrink wrap to self-sealing reusable bubble-pack bags. Whether you want to ship a zine, a cassette tape, or toxic waste, they probably have something for you.

ounces. In other words, most zines can be mailed at this rate. It costs the same as First Class up to 5 ounces, but after that there are price breaks, so it's something to consider for large fanzines. For example, a ten-ounce zine would cost $2.36 First Class but only $1.44 Third Class. Third Class pieces under an ounce are also subject to the non-standard price surcharge, but I don't know why anyone would send something weighing under an ounce by this rate.

Fourth Class is in general a Parcel Post rate, but ziners can sometimes use the Special Fourth-Class Rate (also known as Book Rate). To qualify as a book your zine must be at least 8 pages long (blank pages don't count), contain no advertisements except for announcements of other books from the same publisher (most postal employees don't know this), and be permanently bound (staples are OK). Videotapes, records, and computer diskettes, among other things, may also be sent at this rate. The prices are good, starting at $1.05 for the first full pound and going up 43 cents for each additional pound to something like seven pounds. The drawback is that Book Rate material is likely to be drop-kicked across the mail-sorting facility, so be sure to wrap it well.

There's an even cheaper Library Rate that can be used only on materials sent to or from libraries — if you can get a librarian to mail your stuff at work, you can get away with murder on the postage. If you have any such contacts, I'm sure they know the story better than I do.

If even Third Class seems like a lot of money (and it will if your circulation reaches any appreciable figure) it's time to look into Bulk Mail. Most fanzines don't, I suspect because Bulk Mail involves planning and up-front costs that you have to stay in business to recover. There is a first-class presort rate, which saves you a few pennies, but it requires mailings of 500 or more pieces and is probably out of reach for most ziners. Third Class bulk, though, can be used any time you're sending out 200 or more pieces, be they fanzines or Christmas Cards (as long as there's no personal writing inside!). To use it, you first have to get a permit. This means going to the major postal facility in the area (call your local PO and ask them where to go), filling out forms, and putting up the front money. The fees go like this:

$75 application fee: this is one-time only, and it may not be charged if you're lucky. It depends on how well your local post office knows the ropes. I've batted one out of two on this.

$75 yearly fee: this must be payed every year in January (and also when you first sign up).

$75 permit imprint fee: this is one-time and isn't strictly necessary, but if you pay it you can stop licking stamps and just put one of those cute little bulk-mail notices on the envelope.

$150 or $225 may seem like a lot, but it isn't considering the price breaks. The basic rate for Bulk Mail is 19.8 cents for each piece up to 3.3 ounces (roughly 82 cents a pound for larger pieces). Let's say you're sending out 200 zines at three ounces each 4 times a year. First class, that would cost you $600 a year. Bulk mail, the first year would cost you $383, and the following years would be only $308 — a substantial savings, to say the least. And it gets better as your circulation and weight rise.

Of course, there are drawbacks. Bulk Mail has to be sorted by zip code, rubber-banded into packages, labelled and sacked by you before it goes to the post office. Although there are printed regulations covering all of this (right down to the number and placement of rubber bands), be prepared for your local postal workers to tell you something completely different — the post office is really a lot of little companies wearing the same uniform, not one big corporation. Humor the local guys — they're the ones you have to deal with. You have to deposit money to your bulk-mail account a few days in advance of the mailing itself to cover postage. And the mail itself gets treated like garbage by the postal workers, so you have more damaged and lost copies. This can be minimized by proper packaging: I had to start using heavier stock for the cover of *Factsheet Five*. Another way to minimize the handling is to check out where bulk mail in your area is sorted. All bulk mail in the Albany area, for example, goes through the Albany main post office. By having our bulk mailing account there rather than at the Rensselaer Post Office, we saved the zines one trip in a postal truck and at least a bit of rough handling. I think Bulk Mail is worth the hassles — especially if the alternative is to go out of business.

When you start mailing out of the country, the trade-off between price and speed becomes even more excruciating. Canada and Mexico aren't too bad; although you can't bulk mail to these countries, First and Third Class are only marginally higher than to the US. But Europe and countries farther afield can be murderous to mail to. First Class will run you 50 cents for every half ounce, but at least it will get there in a reasonable length of time. Sea Mail costs no more than First Class to the US would, but can take months (literally) to reach its destination. I suspect that we don't see more fanzines from foreign countries — and vice versa — simply because of the crushing postal costs. However, there is some light on the horizon in the form of remailing services, who offer special consolidation rates taking advantage of some of the volume discounts the USPS offers. When you start sending large numbers of zines out of the country, it's time to call one of them.

I can't emphasize enough the importance of keeping a good relationship with the folks behind the counter of your local post office. These are the people who can keep your zine from getting anywhere, or who can come up with a way for you to save money on the mailing — it depends on how you treat them. Get to know them by name, chat a bit, tell them what you're up to (this works best in small towns), ask for copies of the applicable rate charts so you know what you're talking about, and your mailings will go a lot smoother.

Mail preparation can be a tricky thing. The basic idea is to make sure your mail can survive the trip — one useful test is to fling it across the room, at the wall, as hard as you can. If the package bursts open, you didn't pack it well enough. (You think I'm joking? Go tour your nearest large mail-sorting facility. While you're there, contemplate the most sublime rubber stamp the USPS uses: "FOUND IN SUPPOSEDLY EMPTY EQUIP-MENT.") Basically the PO's only requirements for mail are that it not destroy their machines or be so oddball as to require hand-sorting. Thus

United Parcel Service
800-348-1008

UPS remains one of the most economical ways to move large quantities of zines around the USA. They are now competing in the express delivery arena as well, but the bulk of their business remains the standard 3-5 day delivery. They'll pick up at your home or business for a $5 charge per pickup, which beats the heck out of hauling dozens of cartons down to their dock. If you're shipping a lot at once, inquire about their high volume program, which lets you do the paperwork in advance yourself. UPS will also send you their latest rate charts just for a phone call.

Federal Express
800-238-5855

The folks at Federal Express are invariably pleasant on the phone an in person, and if you need a package delivered overnight in the USA they will take care of it. (Some other services will *promise* to take care of it and occasionally mess up). I feel secure when I commit my packages to them, and it's sometimes worth paying a premium price for that security.

packages must be rectangular, within certain weight limits and so on. This should pose no problem for the average fanzine publisher. One major question is whether or not to use an envelope on your zine. (A precautionary note: you *must* use envelopes on all mail leaving the country). On the one hand, it is cheaper to just fold your zine in half, staple or tape it shut, and write the address on the cover. On the other hand, zines in envelopes tend to arrive in better shape, and the recipient doesn't have to shred her fingernails removing staples. But the cost of envelopes can be prohibitive. If you're going to use envelopes, check into buying them by the box — or by the case. You'll be surprised at how much money you can save. Another thing to look into as your circulation rises is self-sealing envelopes, which can save your tongue or your sponge a lot of effort.

There are some alternatives to the post office, though not that many. UPS, while legally prohibited from carrying First Class matter, can be an economical alternative for large (around a pound) fanzines, as compared to First Class mail. But UPS can't deliver to PO Boxes or some other addresses, and this will pose a large problem for the typical fanzine. The only thing I use UPS for is shipping bundles of zines off to distributors — it's fairly quick and a lot cheaper than First Class mail for ten-pound parcels.

With all classes of mail, and all carriers, you must pay attention to the weight of what you're sending. A postal scale is almost a must if you're not going to be using the same number of sheets of the same paper stock each issue. Even if you use a small home scale it would be prudent to check a sample copy at your local post office on their scale; this can help save costly mistakes like having the whole stack come back to you marked "Insufficient Postage." If this happens, you'll be sorry, since the stamps you applied will be cancelled and won't count towards remailing. Also, be aware that there are surcharges for "non-standard pieces": that's anything less than an ounce which is over 11 1/2 inches long, 6 1/8 inches high, or 1/4 inch thick. This is good for an extra ten cents. It's also worth knowing that anything less than 1/4 inch thick that is not at least 3 1/2 by 5 inches is prohibited from the mails, as are most non-rectangular packages. Check your postmaster for details if you're worried.

PROMOTION AND FINANCING

In this section we'll deal with the twin questions of how to keep your baby alive and how to get it out to people. Many ziners fall down on the promotion and financing end of things, and even though they're providing a great service or putting together an entertaining project, no one knows about it or buys it. This is bad news for all concerned, both the uninformed public and the bankrupt ziner.

Advertising is the first thing to think about. For the ziner the most powerful advertising method is word of mouth, but s/he can help it along. The first thing to do is get your zine reviewed in other zines, the larger and more respected the better. (Even a bad review will draw some readers, and is thus better than no review at all). *Flipside* is a good place for music zines to start — *Factsheet Five* is good for anyone. What you're looking for is a place with a large readership and a commitment to publicizing other zines. *Whole Earth Review* and *Utne Reader* are among the larger magazines which review zines, but it can be very hard to get them interested in your publication, especially when you're just starting out.

The beginning ziner should also consider doing some advertising. I wouldn't pay for any — I don't think it's worth it — but many zines will trade advertising space: you run their ad, they run yours. Contact individual publishers for details. A good size is around 2" by 3". At the minimum, your ad *must* contain your name and address, price, ordering instructions, and a description of the zine written so as to interest people. It doesn't hurt to get your ads typeset and include some graphics even if your zine itself is mimeographed on newsprint. You don't have to write sleazy Madison Avenue ad copy, just something that will catch the eye of those you're aiming the zine at.

Another thing to think about is subscriptions and "the usual." By selling subscriptions you commit yourself to publishing a certain number of issues (even though the subscriber doesn't have much legal recourse and a lot of zines have folded and walked away with the money) and you increase your paperwork. But you also increase the number of sales of each copy that you can count on before you publish. "The usual" refers to the practice (which originated in science fiction fandom) of giving zines away in various trades, the most common being for another fanzine, for contributions of money, for material to publish, or for letters of comment on the previous issue. If you are willing to swap for other zines, you'll find a lot of publishers willing — but you'll have to cover the costs of printing and mailing those copies somehow. You might get thousands of dollars worth of zines in every month, but you can't buy groceries with zines and it will be decades before a major library is interested in accepting your collection so that you can take a tax writeoff.

Before you can think about subscriptions, you have to set a single-copy price. This can be a difficult task. If you set the price of your zine high enough to cover printing and postage, even with no margin for your time or for profit, you'll very likely price yourself out of the market. This is because you're competing with other zines that have higher press runs, more readers, and lower unit costs — and with publishers who don't care whether they lose money or not. They can afford to sell for a buck apiece — you are almost forced to go along, or no one will pay for yours. In some cases, of course, it *is* possible to recover costs — for example, if you're getting your printing for free or if your audience can't find your information anywhere else. (Some very specialized zines do well with cover prices as high as $7 or more, though I haven't seen any in the double digits yet). But such situations are rare. Prices for other zines on the market range from about 10 cents to $10, and I'm sure the former sell a lot faster than the latter. For moderately sized zines with decent printing, $1 to $3 is the usual range.

I think the best bet is to consider what your price should be to recover costs — *all* costs — and then pick an even amount not too much less than that as your cover price. In figuring costs, be sure to factor in free copies. For example, if you spend 72 cents printing each copy and 52 cents mailing, then 400 copies will cost you $496, or $1.24 each. But if 150 of these copies go out for free, to reviewers or trades, then you must recover $1.98 from each of the other issues to break even. In this case I might choose to set my cost at $1.75 or $2.00, depending on how many pages I was publishing and what the other zines in the market were charging.

Having picked a price, you have to consider a discount structure for samples, subscriptions and other cut-rate copies. Traditionally a sample copy costs less than the full cover price, so that people can see what you're doing cheaply. The theory is that they'll like it and subscribe and you'll make your money back. For years I sold sample copies of *Factsheet Five* for $1 — a substantial loss, particularly when the cover price got up to $3.50 (and *that* didn't even cover costs). But I just didn't get that many subscriptions out of the deal, and finally said the heck with it. We started selling samples for the full cover price. (We still lost money on samples, because they went out first class rather than bulk rate, but the loss wasn't as bad). Another thing to realize is that any sort of sample discount offer will haunt you for years. We still get the occasional $1 check for a sample, from someone who's been reading three-year old zines, and all we can do is honor it.

Another thing I used to do was offer discounts for payment in stamps. Small amounts of cash, and particularly small checks, can be a hassle to deal with. In order to encourage people to send stamps — which I can always use — I gave a slight (about 12%) discount for such payment. I finally discontinued this when I started thinking about second-class mail, where discounted subscriptions become a major record-keeping hassle. Many other ziners, particularly those whose banks are now charging a fee for excessive check-cashing, offer a cash discount and charge a higher price for payment by check. (A hint to those plagued by small checks made out to funny names: get yourself an automatic teller card and use it to deposit your checks. If there's no clerk to argue with, you can get a bank to take most anything. I endorse checks to *Factsheet Five* to indicate that I'm doing business under that name: "Factsheet Five, Michael A. Gunderloy d/b/a Factsheet Five" or "Factsheet Five, Michael A. Gunderloy, Publisher," depending on which of my banks I'm dealing with. Then I just toss them in the teller machine. It works.)

Finally, there is the question of subscription price. Real magazines give a substantial discount to people who subscribe to a lot of issues. My advice to fanzine publishers is to let people subscribe at a multiple of the cover price for a relatively small number of issues. For example, when *Factsheet Five* was $2 an issue we took subscriptions at $8 for 4 issues. This doesn't look like much of a deal — until you realize that the price of FF went steadily up, and subscribing protected subscribers against price increases for a year. People who subscribe really do end up saving money. I think most fanzines tend to rise in price as the editors get better and want to improve their content, size and format. So if you feel that you must offer a discount, keep it reasonable — that is, keep it to an amount you can afford to lose if everyone on your mailing list suddenly subscribed. And try to be up front about what happens if you fold. You can probably get away with not returning subscription money if you go out of business — but you'd better not try to get back into publishing later. People have long memories. Better to guarantee refunds, or to announce in advance when you'll be folding and stop taking subscriptions.

Of course, subscription money is meant to pay for future issues. But if you're like most other zine publishers, you'll use it to pay for current issues. (In fact, if you're like most of us, it'll end up intermixed with the money used to buy groceries and pay the rent). This is fine, but be sure to keep track of your position. If you sell a whole lot of heavily discounted subscriptions today, your next issue is financially secure — but the one after that may be a big problem.

Any fanzine should consider trading with other zines if the publisher can possibly afford it. Eventually you may have to get selective to get your trade costs under control, but putting out your own zine can be the cheapest way to get dozens or even hundreds of others in return — one of the biggest fringe benefits of publishing. When setting up trades, you should establish whether you're trading all-for-all or one-for-one. All-for-all (each sends the other every issue) is more common. In one-for-one trades a quarterly trading with a monthly, for example, would only receive four issues a year in return. With any trade, you'll have to be willing to trust the other publisher; unless you publish on identical schedules someone is bound to get ahead now and then.

We've already discussed contributors' copies; with most fanzines, the practice is to give one or two copies to everyone who contributed artwork or articles. In some cases copies are also given to those who have provided production assistance — for example, collating or sticking on mailing labels.

"Loc" is a SF fannish acronym for Letter Of Comment. It is a time-honored fannish practice that anyone with enough gumption to write a letter commenting on a fanzine should get a copy of the next issue. When this tradition grew up, postage and printing costs were substantially lower, and there was less impetus to put things on a break-even or profitable basis (indeed, many traditional SF zines do not take subscriptions at all). In the modern world, if you open yourself up this way, you'll never get any subscriptions at all. In most zine circles, not giving away copies for letters won't bother anyone, but if you're trying to deal with SF fans, they'll be encouraged to think of your product as inferior (or even unclean) if you

State Retail Service Association
110 LaVista Dr.
Easley, SC 29642
803-855-8764

Anything you can do to make it easier for people to send you money will result in increased sales. Unfortunately mail-order companies find it almost impossible to interest a bank in giving them a credit card merchant account these days, thanks to increasing incidences of fraud. If you're ready to start taking MasterCard and Visa in payment for subscriptions, you should first contact every bank in your area to see if they will help you. If not, try calling SRSA, a company that specializes in helping small businesses get such accounts. You'll pay a slightly higher fee (which is why you should try dealing with banks directly first), but the increased business should more than make up for it.

don't. Still, if the choice is between bankruptcy or living on the wrong side of the tracks, I know which I'll take.

Whatever methods you finally settle on to allow people to receive your zine, you should make sure that they are listed prominently in the first page or two of the zine, along with with your subscription rates, if you take subscriptions, and your address. You can't get orders if people don't know how to find you. It also helps to put the single-copy price right on the cover, particularly if you're trying to sell copies via distributors or newsstands.

You can't afford to neglect your listkeeping either. Maintaining the mailing list on odd scraps of paper is a sure way to lose track of people and ruin your credibility — it only takes a few letters of complaint to other fanzines to make yours seem like a bad risk. At the absolute minimum I would suggest maintaining a card file of your mailing list. Each card should contain one subscriber, together with her mailing address, the date her subscription expires, some note of why you're sending it to this person, and any other useful info you can think of. At the far end of the mailing-list scale, computer owners should investigate the possibility of a mailing-list program. If you can't find one specifically tailored for mailing labels in your price range, think about using a database manager or even a text editor to keep track. Shareware programs such as PC-FILE or File Express can perform all the needed tasks. They allow one to insert, delete and edit names and to print out lists in various orders — alphabetical for the publisher and zip code for the post office, as well as special lists of, for example, all record companies in the mailing list. If you do computerize, check out adhesive mailing labels designed for computer printers — they'll save you a lot of work and only run about $10 per thousand in small lots, less if you buy five or ten thousand at a time. For 25,000 labels, I only paid $2 per thousand.

I wish I could tell you how to make sure your subscribers re-subscribe when their time runs out, but I haven't much of a clue on the subject. The most elementary thing to note is that you have to tell them: rubber-stamp TIME TO RENEW by the mailing label, or send them a black-bordered postcard halfway between their last issue and the next one. Even with this reminder, you'll probably lose more people than come back. But, everything you can do to make renewing easier for your subscribers will work out to your advantage. Sending out renewal forms with postpaid envelopes and taking credit cards are both excellent strategies that will pay off immediately for most zines.

As your zine grows you'll want to consider selling some copies through distributors. Distributor copies will make you less money, but since you can mail a bunch to one address there is some offsetting saving in postage. Typical arrangements are to allow a 60-40 split (that is, you take 60% of the cover price and the distributor takes 40%) on ten or more copies for consignment sale (that is, you don't get a penny until and unless they are sold). Make sure you settle a return policy with the distributor: how long do you want to allow for the copies to sell, on unsold copies do you want just covers or the whole issues back of unsold copies, and who pays the postage on returns? There aren't that many distributors willing to carry small-scale zines (you'll never get into Waldenbooks even if you do produce something better than *Soldier of Fortune*) but even selling fifty copies this way can vastly improve your bottom line. And people who pick up a few copies at the newsstand often turn into subscribers.

See Hear
59 East 7th St.
New York, NY 10003
212-982-6968
Catalog $2 in USA, $3 elsewhere

The only all-fanzine shop in the entire world, specializing in music zines.

EBSCO Sample Issue Program
Cecelia Pearson
PO Box 1943
Birmingham, AL 35201
205-991-1479

EBSCO is a major library subscription agent, helping libraries around the country keep their periodicals under control. Their representatives attend all the major librarians' conventions, and one thing their booth does is display sample issues of new periodicals. For $45 you can have your zine out where hundreds of librarians will see it, and you'll get a list back of the ones who have expressed interest in a sample copy. Write for a list of their current conference plans.

T   A   X   E   S

Now that you've earned all that money, your government is going to want a cut. *WE ARE NOT TAX ATTORNEYS.* We're not responsible for any misinterpretations below, on our part or yours, and you would be well advised to check with a professional in these matters to find out about your particular case. All we intend to do is outline a few areas you should look into.

Sales taxes can be trying for a small zine, especially the tax on your printing. Even that few percent can add up to a major sum. Many states have laws exempting a magazine from sales tax on its supplies on the grounds that the magazine itself is intended for resale. You may be liable for the tax yourself, in which case getting a resale number is hardly worth the bother. Or the permit may be too expensive to be worthwhile. But it's worth checking with the state Tax Board to see what the details are in your particular jurisdiction. In New York, as a publisher I'm exempt from sales tax, and getting a resale number just required filling out a few forms and waiting ten minutes. I have to file quarterly informational returns, but don't owe any tax. In Massachusetts, on the other hand, it's almost impossible to get an exemption unless you're widely sold on newsstands. Under Massachusetts law, magazines apparently have to be "widely available" in the state to qualify for an exemption.

Then of course there is the income tax. This is really only a problem if you're making money, as the Feds are hardly going to go after you for failing to take a deduction. By far the majority of fanzines are not mentioned on income taxes — instead, they're a part of the growing underground economy. In general this should be safe (but not legal!) — unless you get so big as to feel that you *must* file. Then you may have to explain how this huge business sprang up in the course of a single year. The alternative is to file as a small business every year. I believe in this case you can actually use business losses as a tax deduction, but you must show a profit at least two years out of five to show that this really is a business. The IRS puts out a Tax Guide for Small Businesses (Publication 334) which you ought to investigate if this more legal means of dealing with your profits appeals to you. My personal feeling is that you ought to bother with the income tax only if you think you'll be in the business for at least a decade and making money by the end of it. But it doesn't hurt to keep decent financial records now in case you decide later that you want to file. For example, if you do strike it rich suddenly, it might prove to your advantage to file amended returns for the earlier years showing a business loss — but you can only do that if you can prove it. Also remember that the more screwball your return, the more likely you are to be audited — and that goes double for Consitutionalist publishers.

As a final note, trading zines is a sticky point for taxes. It's awful close to barter, which as the IRS has been telling us for years, is taxable income. As far as I can determine, magazines sent for review are not taxable income — but I've never gotten a sure ruling on this.

Index